Карта на которой изображена... (map text)

Kругъ

ЧАСТЬ СѢВЕРНОЙ АМЕРИКИ

Охиоамхъ
Агунахъ
Лугулиханъ
Кызылмакъ
Готхабъ
Ченевуй
М. Доброй

Острова

Амеллянана
Путегмайъ
Пугуманъ
Айчирихъ
Амутанъ
Чивихъ
Игухъ
Лиснъ
Кулмать

Н Ъ

М. Немекамъ

М. Дугласъ
р. Бристоль

М. Еловой св Англинскихъ Картахъ

Сиутей
Афогнанъ

ЗАЛИВЪ БРИСТОЛЬ

Кукакъ
Есекполикъ
Сигпунакъ
Остр. Тунанакъ
Евхонешакъ

Большой
Плѣесъ

А. Акунъ
Акутанъ
Тагуланъ
Уналашка

Хуторъ вѣренъ гдѣ
живутъ руские люди

О. Монагю
Св. Иліи

Вьку Вильяма

М. Толстой
М. Тонкой

Островое
М. Крестовой Штурманъ
Здѣсь остался съ 19 чело-
Деменьевъ съ 1741 году

О Р Е

КАРТА
ШЕЛѢХОВА
СТРАНСТВОВАНІЯ

книги «Российского купца именитого
рвое странствование...», СПб., 1793.

Alaska History, No. 19

A VOYAGE TO AMERICA
1783-1786

Grigorii I. Shelikhov

Translated by Marina Ramsay
Edited, with an Introduction, by Richard A. Pierce

THE LIMESTONE PRESS
P.O. Box 1604
Kingston, Ontario, Canada K7L 5C8
1981

International Standard Book Number 0-919642-67-5

Printed and bound in Canada by: Brown & Martin Limited
                                  Kingston, Ontario

PREFACE

This book originated in 1958, with a letter received at the Center for Slavic Studies of the University of California, Berkeley. Hector Chevigny, author of the popular Alaskan historical works Lost Empire, on N.P. Rezanov, and Lord of Alaska, on A.A. Baranov, offered to turn over his notes and ideas to someone who might wish to carry on research which he had started. He had planned to write on yet a third notable of Russian America, Grigorii Shelikhov, until loss of sight forced him to lay the project aside. The letter was turned over to me; I was interested; we met, and an enjoyable and fruitful friendship followed. In frequent correspondence, and occasionally at the Chevigny apartment in Manhattan, we traded information and threshed out questions about all but forgotten people and events of early northwestern North America. This exchange so rekindled Hector's enthusiasm that he undertook another book, Russian America, 1741-1867, published shortly before his death in 1966. Termed "high level popularization" by one reviewer, his works have given thousands a carefully researched, eminently readable introduction to early Alaska. The present work, which owes its genesis to Hector Chevigny, is dedicated to his memory, in grateful appreciation for his council and the pleasure of his company.

Research on Shelikhov went slowly, with many interruptions, and much difficulty in finding source material. Preliminary versions of the introduction to this volume were read in 1974 before a gathering of the history faculty at the University of Moscow, and in 1976 at a meeting of the Alaska Historical Society, in Anchorage. Since then, more information has turned up. There seem still too many unanswered questions for a book-length biography, though Chevigny, with his gift for closing informational gaps with shrewd guesses and inference, could have handled it well in his own style. The fruits of the effort thus far are presented here with a translation of Shelikhov's own account of his principal achievement - his voyage and the founding - if one excludes Unalaska - of the first permanent Russian settlement in North America.

Indispensable to the study and evaluation of Shelikhov has been information accumulated over many years by the patient effort of others. In the 18th century, Muller, Staehlin, "J.L.S.", Pallas, and Coxe put together the history of the exploration of the Aleutian Islands, carried farther by V.N. Berkh in 1823. K.T. Khlebnikov, chief clerk at Sitka from 1818 to 1832, gathered a mass of information from the company records, and in 1835 published his biography of Baranov. P.A. Tikhmenev's history of the Russian-American Company was based mainly on documents, many of which were later destroyed. The American historian H.H. Bancroft gathered all that he could find that was pertinent to his History of Alaska (1886) including interviews with people

familiar with an era then less than twenty years gone. In
1907 some valuable material became available to American
scholars when the Siberian merchant G.V. Yudin sold his rich
collection to the Library of Congress. In 1913, generously
given access to the Russian archives, Professor Frank Golder
obtained a rich harvest of photostats. In the 1930's, the
Soviet historian S.B. Okun added much new information
through his book on the Russian-American Company, while in
Washington Dr. Tikhon Lavrishcheff translated material
from the Yudin and Golder collections for the unpublished
compilation "Documents Relative to American History."
Several documents from the latter appear in the appendix to
this volume. In the 1940's, Dr. A.I. Andreev published
two volumes of documents on early Alaska, concerned largely
with Shelikhov. In 1964, Dr. A.I. Efimov's atlas of early
maps of Siberia and the North Pacific appeared, in 1968,
Dr. R.V. Makarova's work on the exploration of the Aleutian
Islands and the development of the Russian fur trade, and
in 1971, Dr. B.P. Polevoi's cogent introduction and commen-
tary to a new edition of Shelikhov's book. Dr. A.I. Alekseev
has presented new material in several books on eastern
Siberia and the North Pacific. Dr. S.G. Fedorova's account
of the Russians in Alaska and California contains many
references to Shelikhov, and she and Dr. R.G. Liapunova have
made an outstanding contribution in the recently published
compilation of K.T. Khlebnikov's "Notes on America." Dr.
N.N. Bolkhovitinov has provided facts on Shelikhov in his
works on Russian-American relations.

Many others could be named. The late A.F. Dolgopolov
(Alexander Doll) kindly shared information gained in his
many years of study of Russian America. Dr. Lydia Black
read the manuscript and made valuable suggestions concerning
references to the anthropology and ethnohistory of the
Aleutian Islands.

Already based on the effort of many, this subject will
be taken farther, as new sources and new researchers appear.
For the investigation of Russian America has only begun.
Old, far off times; villains, builders and saints; several
rich and distinctive native cultures, and an intrusive,
distinctive European culture form a history which is a unique
and valuable adjunct to the "Great Land" of the present day.

Marina Ramsay did yeoman work in preparing the translation
Research and editing were aided by an Arts Research Grant
from Queen's University. Ross Hough and George Innes of
the Department of Geography did the map and the photography.
Linda Freeman did the typing.

Richard A. Pierce
Queen's University
Kingston, Canada

CONTENTS

v

ILLUSTRATIONS

G.I. Shelikhov. Engraving by V. Ivanov, 1795?

G.I. Shelikhov, bust and painting, origins unknown

G.I. Shelikhov, engraving by Smirnov, from P.A.Tikhmenev, 1861-1863.

Frontispiece, Shelikhov's Voyage..., 1791 edition.

Title page, Shelikhov's Voyage..., 1791 edition.

Three Saints Bay, Kadiak, 29 June 1790, by Luka Voronin.

Three Saints Bay, Kadiak, ca. 1881 (Bancroft Library).

Tomb of Shelikhov, Irkutsk, by James Gibson, 1968.

MAPS

Shelikhov's voyage, 1783-1786

Shelikhov's voyage, 1793 edition (endpaper)

Summary map, compiled under Shelikhov's guidance (from Andreev, 1948) (endpaper)

NOTE

The translation was made from the 1812 edition, with indication in brackets of variations from Shelikhov's original report of 1787, and the 1793 edition. Spelling generally follows the earliest version, but a few obvious typographical errors have been changed.

Transliteration follows the Library of Congress system, slightly modified. For consistency, Russian forms are used. Thus, Kad'iak instead of Kodiak, and Unalashka instead of Unalaska, and Aleksandr except where there is general western use, e.g., Emperor Alexander I. Ship names are in the Russian form except that of the Alaskan Mayflower, the Tri Sviatitelia, better known as the Three Saints.

vi

INTRODUCTION

Except for some attention paid Baranov and Rezanov, North American historians have almost ignored the outstanding figures of Russia's 120-year stay in the Western Hemisphere. Wrangell and Etholen, who were explorers, diplomats and administrators; Voznesenskii, a tireless collector in ethnography and natural science; Teben'kov, a ship commander, cartographer and administrator, and Klimovskii, Korsakovskii, Glazunov, Zagoskin, and Kashevarov who did pioneer work in mapping the Alaska coasts and interior--they, and many others, have long gone almost unnoticed in North American history.

Grigorii Ivanovich Shelikhov must also be placed among this group of notables relegated to obscurity. Shelikhov went far beyond his trading contemporaries to found the first permanent Russian settlement in the North and prepared the way for a trading monopoly which embraced the entire northwestern extremity of the continent from 1799 to 1867. If he had had his way, he would have spread Russian influence on both sides of the North Pacific. Yet, little in English has thus far appeared on his life.

Shelikhov has fared better at the hands of Soviet writers, who have honored his exploits in many scholarly and popular works. However, their portrayals make him a pillar of rectitude, stiff and stylized, and leave unanswered many questions about his life and activities. They have relied mainly on Shelikhov's own account of his voyage to America, published in 1791; on V. N. Berkh's history of discoveries in the Aleutians, published in 1823; on K. T. Khlebnikov's short biography which appeared in 1838; and on P. A. Tikhmenev's history of the Russian-American Company, published in 1861-1863. Some documents published in recent years help piece out the picture of the man and his times, but leave many questions. The answers to some of these may yet be found in Soviet archives, but meanwhile even reexamination of known sources can sometimes provide new insights and clues.

Shelikhov (his own spelling; others in the family spelled it Shelekhov) was born in the small southern Russian trading center of Ryl'sk, on the border of the Ukraine. One of the oldest towns in Russia, long a frontier outpost, Ryl'sk in the mid-18th century was still surrounded by walls and towers, built to ward off the Crimean Tartars. Except for a few stone or brick buildings the town was unimpressive. Most of the houses were of logs with thatched roofs, and tiny sash-windows. The huts of the poor had no chimneys. The streets were quagmires in spring and autumn, and dusty, rutted tracks in the summer.

1

Most of the inhabitants of Ryl'sk were engaged in trade. In the 1780's, out of 2,232 male inhabitants, 412 were classed as merchants, and 860 as petty traders. They purveyed hemp, silk, textiles, grain, wool, honey, wax, leather, cheese, and furs, as well as scythes and other agricultural tools imported from Austria.[1]

Shelikhov was born either in 1747, the date accepted by most writers,[2] or perhaps in 1748, the date in the epitaph on the monument over his grave at the former Znamenskii convent in Irkutsk. The epitaph was composed soon after his death, with the approval of family and close associates, and the stone erected five years later, so the inscription may be considered a document of some weight.[3]

The Shelekhovs were evidently a large family. Shelikhov himself says nothing of his ancestry in any of his known writings except that Peter the Great once bestowed silver cups (kovshi) on certain of his forebears.[4] Never one to shrink from prestige, he would probably have mentioned it if there had been anything else of note in his family background. The Soviet historian A. I. Alekseev cites a letter from Shelikhov mentioning "my father Ivan Afanas'evich Shelikhov", and has found the merchant Afonasii Shelekhov, presumably G. I. Shelikhov's grandfather, then 20 years of age, mentioned in the inspection data for Ryl'sk uezd for 1737.[5] These are corroborated by other sources. The diary of a Kursk landowner mentions for 29 January 1760 the marriage of a daughter of the Ryl'sk merchant Afanasii

(1) V. A. Prosetskii, Ryl'sk, Voronezh, 1966.

(2) A. I. Andreev, Russkie otkrytiia v Tikhom okeane i Severnoi Amerike v XVIII veke, Moscow, 1948, p. 40, cited here after as "Andreev (1948)", to distinguish it from the smaller 1944 edition, and from the translation of the latter by Carl Ginsburg, Russian discoveries in the Pacific and in North America in the Eighteenth and Nineteenth Century, Ann Arbor, 1952.

(3) See draft of the inscription in Library of Congress, Yudin Collection, Box 1, Folder 5, translated in Documents Relative to Alaskan History (typescript), cited here as D.R.A.H., v. 2, pp. 164-167. The text of the verse for the epitaph, calling Shelikhov a 'Russian Columbus', was first published in "Nadgrobie Ryl'skomu imianitomu grazhdinu Shelekhovu", Muza, February, 1796, p. 160. The entire epitaph was later published in Syn Otechestva, January, 1839, and in "Pamiatnik G. I. Shelekhova", Russkii Invalid, 1839:34, pp. 135-136.

(4) Andreev (1948), p. 207.

(5) A. I. Alekseev, "Kolumb Rossii", Voprosy Istorii, 1973:1, pp. 210-213.

Shelekhov.[6] Of 75 signers of an instruction (nakaz),
submitted in 1767 by the merchants of Ryl'sk to Catherine
II's Legislative Commission, outlining their complaints,
there is a representative of Afanasii Shelekhov, Potap the
son of Grigorii Shelekhov, Login and Ivan, the sons of Zakhar
Shelekhov, and Ivan Bol'shoi (Big Ivan), the son of Afanasii,
who is presumably G. I. Shelikhov's father.[7]

Some writers have stated that Shelikhov's father was
poor, but no evidence is given for this. In any case, in
1772, when he was about twenty-five, G. I. Shelikhov went
to the gubernia capital, Kursk. There he heard of several
Kursk merchants who had gone to Siberia, including Ivan
and Mikhail Golikov, and Semen and Aleksei Polevoi. Tales
of their successes probably caused young Shelikhov himself
to go to Siberia, to the major trading and administrative
center of Irkutsk.[8]

One Soviet writer, V. Iurkevich, has claimed that
Shelikhov went to Siberia to avoid military service, but he
gives no proof of this. Inasmuch as anyone going to Siberia
would have had to have a passport, to be presented in each
town, and a person subject to military service would have
been unable to get a passport, such a flight seems unlikely.
The eminent A. I. Andreev terms Iurkevich's statement
imaginary.[9] Probably, some of Shelikhov's family or
acquaintances had trading connections with Siberia and
the capable, ambitious young man could expect to be
welcomed there and be given a start on the road to fortune.

In any case, Shelikhov entered trade in Siberia in
1773[10] as a prikashchik, or agent, of Ivan Larionovich
Golikov (1729-1805), of Kursk, who had become a
merchant in Irkutsk gubernia.[11] In 1775, Shelikhov

(6) "Dnevnik Kurskogo pomeshchika I. P. Annenkova Kak
istoricheskii istochnik", Materialy po istoriiu SSSR, v. 5,
1957, pp. 661-883; see p. 770.

(7) "Nakaz ot zhitelei g. Ryl'ska", Istoricheskiia svedeniia
o Ekaterininskoi Komissii dlia sochineniia proekta Novogo
Ulozheniia, in Sbornik Imp. Russk. Ist. Obshch., ch. 13,
v. 144, 1914 (see pp. 393-403).

(8) B. P. Polevoi, ed., G. I. Shelikhov, Rossiiskogo
kuptsa..., (Khabarovsk, 1971), p. 19.

(9) B. Iurkevich, "Grigorii Shelikhov", Literaturnyi
almanakh (Kursk), 1940:2, pp. 230-269; A. I. Andreev (1948),
p. 41.

(10) Epitaph, op. cit.

(11) Russov, Nekrolog. Kurskii imenityi grazhdanin
Golikov", Minerva, 1806, ch. 6, pp. 10-12.

4

married.(12) His bride, Natal'ia Alekseevna, who, judging
by her letters, was an intelligent, forceful woman, became
his companion in his commercial ventures. Her family name
is unknown; it has been suggested that she may have been
the daughter or widow of some rich merchant, and thus an
initial source of Shelikhov's capital.(13)

    Shelikhov's earlier Siberian adventures can only be
conjectured. His duties probably led him from Irkutsk to
Kiakhta, center of a profitable trade with China, and in
1774 he first went to Iakutsk, over two thousand versts
northward down the Lena, and thence a thousand versts overland to Okhotsk. There, on the shores of the Eastern
(Pacific) Ocean, some of the merchants of Irkutsk were making
fortunes by backing expeditions sent forth to harvest the
fur wealth of the Aleutian and Kurile Islands.

    The activities of these merchants must have held special
interest for Shelikhov. Based at Irkutsk or Iakutsk, they
operated out of Okhotsk or from the ports of remote
Kamchatka, forming companies to send out vessels to obtain
sea otter skins. The vessels, primitive affairs thrown
together at Okhotsk, carried fifty to sixty promyshlenniks
(independent traders and hunters), who worked under a
contract with the owner of the boat, getting half of the
proceeds, divided equally among them. Their commanders,
termed "Russian Columbuses" by their contemporary M. V.
Lomonosov,(14) were as long on courage as they were short
on knowledge of navigation. The vessels were often out for
several years. Most of them would return, usually bearing
rich cargoes of furs, but usually with some crewmen missing,
and others exhausted by privation and disease. The men
drank up their share of the proceeds in the taverns of
Okhotsk, the merchants invested theirs in new ventures, or
made loans at usurious rates to others seeking capital. The
vessels were often sent out again as soon as they could be
refitted. Losses from damage or shipwreck hardly mattered;
one good success could make up for several years of losses.

    Established in 1716 for sea communication with Kamchatka,
Okhotsk was a poor excuse for a port; a line of log houses
and grog shops perched on a sandspit, menaced by flood tides

4

4
(12) Epitaph, op. cit.

(13) F. F. Veselago, Tridsat' pervoe prisuzhdeni uchrezh-
dennykh P. N. Demidovym nagrad. 25 maia 1862 goda, St. P.,
1862, p. 67; S. B. Okun', Rossiisko-Amerikanskaia kompaniia,
M.-L., 1939, p. 22.

(14) M. V. Lomonosov, Sochineniia (M., 1950-1959, 10 vols.),
v. 1, p. 150-151; v. 2, p. 83, cited in V. A. Perevalov,
Lomonosov i Arktika (Moscow, 1949), p. 53.

and locked in by ice from October until May. Yet, for two
centuries, for want of any other, the hamlet served as
Russia's main outlet to the Pacific and spawned expansionist
dreams. Its population, less than 2,000, looked toward
distant lands. In 1772, the Governor-General of Irkutsk
had included in lengthy instructions to Major M. K. Bem
(von Behm), newly appointed commandant of Kamchatka, an
admonition to encourage building of a vessel to trade in
the Kuriles and to investigate the possibility of trade with
the Japanese.[15] Lieutenant-Captain S. I. Zubov,
commandant of Okhotsk from 1774 to 1779, repeatedly proposed
to higher authorities the equipping of expeditions to secure
the Kuriles for Russia and to open trade with Japan.[16]
Some of the Russians forced to accompany the notorious
Count Beniovsky when he escaped from exile in Kamchatka in
1771 had returned to add their own tales to the growing
body of information on the wealth of Canton, Macao, and
other commercial centers of the Orient. Fur hunting
expeditions were making the Aleutian Islands fairly well
known. The island of Kodiak, larger than any of the
Aleutians, wooded, and with a milder climate, had been known
since 1761. There were proposals for the extension of
Russian activities to the North American mainland. As early
as 1766, the Okhotsk harbor commandant Colonel F. Kh.
Plenisner had written his chiefs that the American continent
as far south as California should be brought under Russian
sway. About a decade later, T. I. Shmalev, a successor to
Plenisner, proposed establishment of a colony in the Kuriles,
and sending three ships and 180 men to conquer Kodiak.[17]
As early as 1774, he and the Irkutsk merchant Pavel
Sergeevich Lebedev-Lastochkin bought for a song the hooker
Nikolai, and in 1775 obtained permission from the government
to send it to the Kuriles. The commander, the Siberian
nobleman Ivan Antipin, was told to subjugate the inhabitants
of the Kuriles and to try to make contact with the Japanese.
Instead, in 1777, word came to Kamchatka that the Nikolai

---

(15) R. V. Makarova, Russians on the Pacific, 1743-1799
(Kingston, Ont., 1975), pp. 87-88.

(16) A. Sgibnev, "Okhotskii port s 1699 po 1852 g. (istoricheskii ocherk)", Morskoi sbornik, 1869:11, pp. 57-58.
A. I. Alekseev, Okhotsk--kolybel' russkogo Tikhookeanskogo
flota (Khabarovsk, 1958), p. 86.

(17) V. K. Andrievich, Istoricheskii ocherk Sibiri (St. P.,
1887), v. 4, p. 57; Polnoe sobranie zakonov rossiiskoi
imperii, v. 18 (first series), #13,320, decree of 3 July 1779,
cited by Hans Pilder, Die Russisch-Amerikanische Handels-
Kompanie bis 1825 (Berlin, 1914), p. 4; A. I. Alekseev,
"Brat'ia Shmalevy, ikh zhizn' i deiatel'nost'", Letopis'
severa, 1962, v. 3, p. 103.

had been wrecked. Shelikhov and Lebedev sent a party by baidara from Bol'sheretsk to aid the survivors, and obtained the government brigantine Natal'ia to continue to the mission under navigator Petushkov, but for some reason Shelikhov at this point withdrew from the partnership. He got out just in time, for in January, 1780, after some encouraging contacts with the Japanese, the Natal'ia, under navigator Fedor Putintsev, with Dmitrii Shabalin as foreman and Iven Antipin as interpreter, was left high and dry on Urup Island by a tidal wave, a total loss.[18]

Shelikhov never dropped his interest in the Kuriles, but his main interest had shifted eastward. In 1776 he went to Kamchatka, where he and the merchant Luka Alin combined means to build a vessel, the Sv. Pavel, in Nizhnekamchatsk, and sent it to the Aleutians. In 1777, he persuaded his former employer Golikov, now prospering as holder of the liquor franchise for Tobol'sk and Irkutsk gubernias, to combine with him to build and send out the Sv. Andrei Pervozvannyi. The ship was wrecked but the cargo was rescued and sold at a profit.[19] In the same year he and the Moscow merchant Ivan Solov'ev and the Panov brothers of Tot'ma joined in equipping and dispatching the Varfolomei i Varnava (Bartholomew and Barnabas). About 1778, Shelikhov and the Kamchatka merchant Kozitsyn sent the boat Sv. Nikolai on the first of three voyages. In 1779, he and Golikov sent the Sv. Ioann Predtecha (literally John the Precursor, or Forerunner--St. John the Baptist) from Petropavlovsk. In 1780, Shelikhov built the Ioann Ryl'skii at Petropavlovsk with his own means and sent it out. In 1781, he and Lebedev-Lastochkin sent out the Sv. Georgii, and in the same year he and the merchant Alin again sent out the Sv. Pavel.[20] Thus, in eight years, Shelikhov participated to varying degrees in at least ten companies.

Profitable though these expeditions were, Shelikhov now asserted still greater returns could be obtained. The fur trade was declining, he stated. The visible decrease in furs, the hostility of the natives, and the violent conduct of the traders indicated that basic reforms were needed.

---

(18) Makarova, op. cit., pp. 87-92.

(19) K. T. Khlebnikov, op. cit., "Zhizneopisaniia G. I. Shelikhova", Syn Otechestva, 1838, v. 2, sec. 3, pp. 67-68; Berkh, A chronological history of the discovery of the Aleutian Islands (Kingston, Ont., 1974), pp. 56-57.

(20) Berkh, op. cit., p. 58 ff.

In his own accounts, Shelikhov says that he wanted to get away from the idea of having vessels of various companies on the coasts in sharp competition, or of having groups form, make their fur harvest, and then divide the proceeds and break up. He conceived the idea, he writes, of a single united company with a large capital which would form settlements, carry on the fur hunt systematically, study and exploit the other natural resources of these lands, and establish armed forces there to keep off foreign competition. He wanted to secure for his country the places occupied, to subjugate the inhabitants for Russia, to form settlements, and to seek still more distant lands.[21] He and Golikov decided to form such a company.

Or, at least, that is the account generally accepted. It would seem, however, that the origin of the idea of a Russian settlement in North America, aside from Shmalev's proposal, mentioned above, is a little more complex. On June 29, 1800, one Petr Kutyshkin, a commoner of Suzdal and an erstwhile associate of Golikov in the liquor franchise, petitioned the Emperor for redress. He stated that at Irkutsk in 1775 he observed how unprofitable the fur trade was becoming, and undertook an extensive study of how to improve the situation. He prepared a project for a single company, which would establish permanent posts in America. In 1779 he showed the project to Golikov. The latter decided to form such a company, and invited Kutyshkin to join as holder of 100 shares valued at 500 rubles each, evidently as compensation for his work. Kutyshkin also presented the same project to Prince Viazemskii, Procurator General of the Senate, but the latter held it for nine months without action. Meanwhile, Kutyshkin had to make a trip to Siberia on pressing business, so left St. Petersburg before any Senate decision on his project.

On arrival at Tobol'sk, Kutyshkin found Golikov preparing to go to St. Petersburg in 1781. "I informed him that my project had not yet been approved, and requested him to intercede for me at St. Petersburg. To that end I entrusted to him the copy of the project and other documents pertaining to it. Having received all of these, he obviously did not care to do anything about it; but instead he, his nephew Captain Golikov, and the merchant of Ryl'sk, Shelikhov, privately formed a company the same year, 1781, and bound each other with a contract without letting me know about it." Kutyshkin spent the next twenty years trying to obtain the compensation he felt was due him.[22]

---

(21) Report, Shelikhov to I. V. Iakobii, 19 April 1787, in Andreev (1948), p. 207.

(22) Petition, Petr Kutyshkin to Emperor, June 29, 1800, in Yudin Collection, Box 3, Folder 15, translated in D.R.A.H., v. 3, pp. 292-295.

Shelikhov, making no mention of this, writes simply that "I proposed, as a beginning, the establishment of a Russian colony in the newly discovered regions". He and Golikov journeyed to St. Petersburg in 1781, probably to obtain government sanction for their enterprise and permission to use government ships and supplies. On return, Shelikhov, Golikov, and the latter's nephew, Captain M. S. Golikov, set up a special "American, Northeastern, Northern, and Kurile Company", for a period of ten years. Although aimed mainly at exploiting the fur wealth of the American coast, the Company would establish permanent settlements on land annexed by Russia. It was capitalized for 70,000 rubles, to be used to build two or three ships, and to send them "to the land of Aliaksa, which is called America, to islands known and unknown, in order to trade in furs, to make explorations, and to arrange voluntary trade with the natives". In order that plans be better carried out, Shelikhov would personally command the expedition, make observations, and where suitable establish colonies and forts on the American coasts and islands. Their initial establishment would be on Kodiak.(23)

In Irkutsk, Shelikhov solicited from the government permission to build a number of ships suitable for sea voyages and obtained authorization to call upon government officials for assistance in case of need. He hired workmen, and after the usual difficult journey delivered them at Okhotsk together with needed materials, merchandise, and provisions. He was backed by an N. Demidov, one of the Ural mining magnates, who loaned him 50,000 rubles.(24) This was a large sum; it is not clear how Shelikhov had gained this important ally.

At the mouth of the river Urak, near Okhotsk, Shelikhov and the two Golikovs built three galiots, named, in the dismaying fashion of the day, as if to compensate by divine intercession for the shortcomings of the shipwrights and crews. Thus, they were the Tri Sviatitelia Vasilii Velikii, Grigorii Bogoslov, i Ioann Zlatoust (the Three Bishops-- commonly mistranslated as the Three Saints--Vasilii the Great, Grigorii the Theologian, and Ioann Chrisostom), otherwise known simply as the Tri Sviatitelia (Three Saints) or the Vasilii; the Sv. Simeon Bogoprimets i Anna Prorochitsa (Sts. Simeon the God-receiver and Anna the Prophetess); and the Sv. Arkhistratig Arkhangel Mikhal (the St. Archangel Michael).

---

(23) Andreev (1948), p. 208; P. A. Tikhmenev, A history of the Russian-American Company (Seattle, 1978), v. 1, p. 12.

(24) Okun' says this was N. N. Demidov, but the dates of Nikolai Nikitich Demidov were 1773-1828. It was probably his father, Nikita Akinfievich (1724-1789).

By late summer, 1783, Shelikhov was ready to embark on the greatest venture of his career. On board his vessels were 192 officers and men, including relatives Sidor Andreev Shelikhov and Vasilii Potap Shelikhov,(25) Shelikhov himself, his wife (his "faithful companion"), their two children,(26) and one of his partners, Captain Golikov. The presence of his family indicates a strong bond, and what he was prepared to risk.

All works on Shelikhov have mentioned that his wife was on the voyage, but his report of 1787 to I. V. Iakobii, Governor-General of Irkutsk, which formed the basis for his book, also mentions their two children (i dvumia det'mi). For some reason this was omitted from the book. Who were they? That curious, indispensable source of Russian biographical information, the Peterburgskii Nekropol' (Petersburg Necropolis), compiled from tombstone inscriptions in St. Petersburg cemeteries, indicates two daughters, Anna (February 15, 1780 - October 18, 1802), who married N. P. Rezanov; and Aleksandra (December 21, 1788 - January 1, 1816) who married G. G. Politkovskii, later a director of the Russian-American Company. But a letter written by Shelikhov in 1795 mentions a son, unnamed, and two daughters, Ekaterina and Avdot'ia. And a letter of October 24, 1797, from A. A. Baranov to I. A. Kuskov, informing him of Shelikhov's death, mentions three daughters, Anna, Katerina, and Avdot'ia, the latter to marry Mikhail Matfeich Buldakov, future chairman of the Board of Directors. So there were Anna, Aleksandra, Ekaterina and Avdot'ia. A list of early shareholders in the Russian-American Company also indicates a fifth daughter, Natal'ia Grigor'evna Meller-Zakomel'skaia, one of the largest shareholders, with 265 shares. The same list includes a Vasilii Grigor'evich Shelikhov, who by the patronymic is evidently the son, with 335 shares. Ivan Shelekhov, birth and death dates unknown, who served as director from 1799 to 1807, is sometimes stated to have been G. I. Shelikhov's son, but Tikhmenev refers to him as Ivan Andreevich (the son of Andrei), by which he was evidently a nephew or cousin. One may assume Anna to have been one of the two children who went to Kodiak, but the identity of the other, and indeed certainty as to the entire family, awaits further investigation.(27)

---

(25) Personnel book of the Three Saints, 1783-1786, Yudin Collection, Box 1, Folder 3, translated in D.R.A.H., v.3, pp. 157-160.

(26) Andreev (1948), p. 227.

(27) P.A. Tikhmenev, v. 1, p. 145; Grand Duke Nikolai Mikhailovich, Peterburgskii Nekropol' (St. P., 1912, 4 vols.). Letter, Baranov to Kuskov, 24 Oct. 1797, GBL, f. 204, sheet 7-8. A.A. Preobrazhenskii, "O sostave aktsionerov Rossiisko-Amerikanskoi Kompanii v nachale XIX v.", Istoricheskie zapiski, M., 1960, v. 67, pp. 286-298. B.P. Polevoi, introduction to G. I. Shelikhov, Rossiiskogo kuptsa..., (Khabarovsk, 1971), p. 124.

On August 16, the three vessels put to sea from the mouth of the Urak. The Three Saints, bearing Shelikhov and his family, was commanded by the experienced navigator, Gerasim Grigor'evichIzmailov, and the Mikhail by the sub-navigator Olesov. The commander of the Sv. Simeon is not known. He may have been Dmitrii Bocharov.

The small, clumsy vessels wallowed through the stormy Okhotsk Sea, and passed through the Kurile chain. On September 12, a strong wind came up, continuing for two days, during which the ships became separated. By previous arrangement they were to meet at Bering Island. The Three Saints and the Sv. Simeon met again two days later, and on September 24 reached Bering Island, where they prepared to winter, but the Mikhail, with 62 men aboard, failed to appear.

After a difficult winter on Bering Island, the Three Saints and the Sv. Simeon resumed their voyage in June, 1784. They skirted the Aleutians, lost and found each other, and on July 13 both arrived at Unalashka.

After satisfying their needs for fresh water and repairs, the two vessels put to sea again on July 22. Shelikhov thought it necessary to take along two Fox Island Aleuts as interpreters, and ten as workers. He calls them "volunteers". Martin Sauer, who was in the area with the Billings expedition a few years later, writes of the expedition giving transportation home in 1791 to "three natives [of Tanaga] and the neighbouring island of Kanaga, taken from hence in the year 1785 by Gregory Shelikoff, of whose behaviour in these islands we received very unfavourable accounts".[28]   Although we can assume from this and other reports that Shelikhov's own version of his activities must be viewed skeptically, Sauer's assertion does not agree with the facts. Shelikhov did not put in at the Western or Central Aleutians during either his east-ward voyage (1784) or his return voyage (1786). In 1785 he was at Kodiak. Sauer may have mistakenly attributed to Shelikhov reports of the depredations of other Russian fur hunters.

On August 3 the two vessels reached the island of Kykhtak, or as it became known, Kad'iak. The Koniag, the inhabitants of the island, had driven off previous visitors in 1761, 1776, and 1780, but now with 130 well-armed Russians and the ten Fox Islanders, Shelikhov intended to conquer this strong and independent people and to possess the island's wealth in furs.

---

(28)   Martin Sauer, An account of a geographical and astro-nomical expedition to the northern parts of Russia... (London, 1802), p. 223.

Anchoring in a harbor which he named Three Saints Bay, after his ship, Shelikhov writes that he sent men ashore in three baidaras to reconnoiter. The men in one of the baidaras managed to capture an islander and brought him back to the ship. Shelikhov received him, gave him presents, and sent him ashore. This first visitor remained forever faithful, says Shelikhov, and sometimes warned of attacks planned by his compatriots.

On August 5, three Koniags called in baidarkas. They were treated well, and during an eclipse of the sun, which occurred during their visit, were doubtless impressed by the visitor's unconcern over what was to them a disturbing phenomenon. This did take place, for Oppholzer's Canon of Solar Eclipses states that on August 16 [August 4, old style] an annular eclipse occurred in the area at about 1 p.m.(29)

So far, few natives had been seen, but on August 9, writes Shelikhov, another party sent out from the ships found, forty versts away, "a great number" gathered on a rocky spur. How many Koniags had thus come together to face invaders? Here there is a variant account, which is useful for comparison with Shelikhov's version. In 1787, one of his men, a surgeon's assistant named Miron Britiukov, submitted to Governor-General Iakobii a complaint alleging barbaric treatment of the Kad'iak natives by Shelikhov. Shelikhov naturally denied these allegations, and his warm supporter, Iakobii, dismissed them as baseless, but this hardly proves that the report was false. Britiukov says that all the natives fled from various villages, leaving their property. The Russians pursued them and caught two, who led them to the place where a great number had gathered.(30)

According to Shelikhov, when he learned of the gathering, he went to the place. He estimates their number at about 4,000, but this is an impossible figure. Lisianskii, who visited the region in 1804, says it was more likely about 400, and quotes the promyshlennik Sapozhnikov, who was present, as saying that the number was not more than 350.(31)

---

(29) Report, Shelikhov to I. V. Iakobii, May-November 1787, in Andreev (1948), p. 229; Theodor Ritter von Oppholzer, Canon der Finsternisse (Wien, 1887, reprinted in New York, 1962, as Canon of Solar Eclipses).

(30) Report, Miron Britiukov to I. V. Iakobii, November 2, 1788, in Golder Collection, Transcripts, Library of Congress, Box 3, Russian Archives of the State, Petrograd, VII, #2742, translated in D.R.A.H., v. 3, pp. 332-335.

(31) Iu. Lisianskii, A voyage round the world... (London, 1814), p. 180.

Shelikhov tried to persuade the natives to trade, but he continues, "the savages replied with a shower of arrows". On August 12, at midnight, he states, a great number attacked the Russian camp, with such fury that a smaller detachment might have been overrun. The battle lasted for a quarter of an hour. When the sun rose, neither killed nor wounded were to be seen, for all had been borne away in the night.

Britiukov, on the other hand, says that the sentries noticed the islanders approaching in the dark; they shot several times but did not kill any of them, and having no response from the enemy, disregarded the disturbance which, if thus, was hardly the "battle" claimed by Shelikhov.

Learning through one of the Fox Island Aleuts that the assembled Koniags awaited reinforcements, Shelikhov says he decided to chase them from their heights. Climbing the slopes, the Russians shot from their guns, but did little harm; the natives shot arrows. Shelikhov then brought up five 2-pound cannons. Terrified by the roar of these unknown weapons, and by the ruin of their weak fortifications, the islanders fled, leaving five wounded. Britiukov says: "...the armed band murdered about 500 of these heathen people. If we also count those who ran in fear to their baidarkas and, trying to escape, stampeded and drowned each other, the number will exceed 500". Gerasim Izmailov, questioned on June 25, 1790 by Billings, denied assertions that 150 to 200 natives were killed in the attack, but surmised that many in fear jumped from the cliffs into the water and into their boats and were drowned. "We found out about it when the sea cast their bodies on the beach. Six Russians were wounded in that fight".[32]

Shelikhov writes that he took up to a thousand prisoners, but then released more than half and took the remainder on the ship to the harbor. Of these prisoners he selected one elder (khaskak) to act as chief, supplied him with gifts, and gained his promise of assistance. Britiukov writes: "Many men and women were taken prisoner. By order of Mr. Shelikhov, the men were led to the tundra and speared. The remaining women and children, about 600 altogether, he took with him to the harbor, and kept them for three weeks". Izmailov partially corroborates this: "We took from 200 to 300 natives as prisoners of war. From this number Shelikhov ordered the selection of six to ten old men - I cannot recall the exact number; they were taken to the tundra and speared".

---

(32) Report, Miron Britiukov, op. cit.; testimony of Gerasim Izmailov, at Kad'iak, July 1, 1790, in Yudin Collection, Box 2, Folder 23, translated in D.R.A.H., v. 3, pp. 239-240.

Britiukov is borne out by Lisiansky, and there is yet another source. The Finnish naturalist, H. J. Holmberg, was in Russian America in the early 1850's, took down the tale of Arsenti Aminak, a very old Koniag in the village of Kaniagmiut. Aminak narrated the earlier visits of foreign ships, undoubtedly Russians, to Kodiak, and then told how another Russian ship arrived

> which in September headed for 'Staraia Gavan' (Three Saints Bay). The Russians had with them an old man from Unalaskha, named Kashpak, who in his youth had been taken as a slave from Kad'iak by the Fox-Aleuts, and who now served as an interpreter for the Russians. They demanded amanats (hostages) from our chiefs; we did not give them any. The island Sakhlidak had many settlements in those times, which, fearing retribution by the Russians because of their refusal, united into one settlement on the sea side of the island to be able to oppose them. Twice Kashpak was sent there with the following bargain: the chiefs should hand their children over as hostages, for the Russians wanted to raise them. Kashpak had many relatives among the inhabitants of this settlement; he implored them to willingly accept the demands of the Russians, since otherwise they would have to suffer the consequences. Kashpak was turned away on both occasions. The second time he was warned that if he appeared again with such demands he would be treated as an enemy. Thereupon Kashpak betrayed the until then unknown portage across the island to the Russians. The Russians went to the settlement and carried out a terrible bloodbath. Only a few men were able to flee to Aiakhtalik in baidarkas; 300 Koniags were shot by the Russians. This happened in April. When our people revisited the place in the summer the stench of the corpses lying on the shore polluted the air so badly that none could stay there, and since then the island has been uninhabited. After this every chief had to surrender his children as hostages; I was saved only by my father's begging and many sea-otter pelts.[33]

Shelikhov omits such unfavorable details of his conquest, and dwells instead on his efforts to win over the savages by more peaceful means. On one occasion he gathered many of the islanders to watch a demonstration of what gun·

(33) Heinrich Johan Holmberg, Ethnographische Skizzen über die Völker des Russischen Amerika, Erste Abtheilung, Acta Societatus Scientarum Fennicae, v. 4, 1856, Helsingfors, pp. 410-417.

powder could do.

> I had a hole bored in a huge rock, filled it
> with gunpowder, attached a musket lock, tied
> a long string to it which led under another
> rock for the protection of the one who was
> to manipulate it, and then, before a great
> number of peaceful Koniags, simultaneously
> with one musket shot, blew it to bits. The
> rumor spread everywhere about the amazing
> strength of our marksmen.

Besides such trickery, he distributed gifts, and
through interpreters conveyed to the natives "the bases
of the Christian Faith, the greatness of the church
service, the strength, mildness and mercy of the great
Monarch, the might and wealth of the Russian people, and
the clothes, food, way of life, and the trade of peoples
subject to Russia". According to Shelikhov, pictures,
mirrors, a Kulibin lamp (devised in 1779 by a Russian
inventor), books and writing were wonders for the natives
by which he won their esteem, trust and devotion. He
says the natives brought to him their children as hostages
and asked him to teach them to speak Russian and to read
books. From over 400 child hostages, he selected a number
of boys as interpreters, and taught some to read and write
Russian. He built a school for 25 boys. He tried

> to the best of my ability, to explain to them
> that...they would remain in ignorance until
> they became peace loving and copied our customs
> and mode of living. I showed them the utility
> and comfort of Russian houses, clothing and
> food preparation. They saw the labors of my
> workmen when they dug up the vegetable garden
> and sowed and planted seeds.

Most of this idyllic scene would appear a concoction.
Judging by the sketch of Three Saints Bay settlement made
by an artist with the Billings expedition in 1791, the
Russian settlement offered little to impress anyone. The
"Russian houses" were huts, little better than the dwellings
of the natives, the school was probably rudimentary, and
the planting of seeds, if it occurred, could hardly have
seemed more than a strange aberration of the newcomers.

Nor could the numbers of those subjugated have been
anywhere what Shelikhov claimed. By this combination of
force and persuasion he asserted that he had acquired for
Russia 50,000 new subjects, though all other estimates of
the population of Kodiak and the surrounding areas indicate
this to have been a wild exaggeration.[34]

---

(34) Petition, I. I. Golikov and G. I. Shelikhov to Empress,
February 1788, in Andreev (1948), p. 266.

But, although a foothold had been gained, the first winter, of 1784-1785, was a difficult one. Because of the lateness of the season and the hostility of the tribes, it was not possible to build adequate shelter. Many of the men got scurvy "from the damp sea air". Between January and April, 1785, the personnel book of the Three Saints reveals, out of 68 men listed, nine died of scurvy, one died of burns incurred while taking a steambath, and another died of "the French disease, contracted at Okhotsk". Entries after other names, "caught in thievery", "scoundrel", "thief and scoundrel", and "completely corrupt", further indicate the nature of the crew and the conditions under which all lived. The navigator Gerasim Izmailov is stated to have stolen from the company's goods over 30 gallons of alcohol, clothing, foodstuffs, and utensils, valued at 2,595 rubles. However, there are also entries which designate men who "showed valor", and were "trustworthy", "useful", and "good and industrious".[35]

Finally, spring came, and Shelikhov sent out parties to reconnoiter and obtain furs. Thus, on May 2, he sent 52 Russians, 11 Fox Island Aleuts, and 110 Koniags in four baidaras to Kenai Bay (Cook Inlet). This party returned in August with information about the inhabitants along the coast and in Kenai and Chugach Bays. Nowhere had they been attacked, and they brought back 20 hostages from various tribes.

The second winter, of 1785-1786, was passed with greater ease than the first one. There was better shelter and an improved food supply, but difficulties were accumulating. More men were needed to cope with hostile natives. Thus, at the beginning of December, 1785, two Russians, Stepan Kosmin Sekerin and Labanov, and a native interpreter, Efrem Shelikhov, together with the chief of Shuiakh Island who was held as a hostage, were sent to trade with the Kenais. On March 27, 1786, Shelikhov was informed that the chief of Shuiakh and his relatives had murdered the Russians and divided the Company's goods with the Afognak and Chiniak chiefs.[36] Britiukov states that in revenge for this, Shelikhov sent three baidaras of Russians and natives to Shuiakh and Afognak. Britiukov heard later that the party wiped out one village and the inhabitants of another had fled.

In addition, the expedition needed trade goods, yarn for fish nets, new kettles for cooking, and more men. Shelikhov therefore began laying plans to return to Okhotsk with the Three Saints to procure supplies and reinforcements.[37]

(35) Personnel Book of the Three Saints, op. cit., p. 157.

(36) Ibid.

(37) Andreev (1948), p. 180.

During all of this time nothing had been heard of the Mikhail, separated from the other vessels on putting to sea from Okhotsk in 1783. At last, on February 25, 1786, Shelikhov was informed by a letter from the leader of one of his hunting parties on the mainland that the Mikhail was at Unalashka. Skipper Olesov and his men had wintered on the Kurile Island of Shumshu and the next year, 1784, had arrived at Unalashka. There they wintered again, and the following spring, 1785, while leaving the harbor, had been driven by strong winds onto a rock, had lost a mast, and had had to return to the harbor to spend yet another winter. Shelikhov ordered a detachment to Unalashka to meet the Mikhail. They were to borrow whatever gear was needed for repairs from skippers of other trading companies in the area, dismiss the dilatory commander, and send him with any party returning to Okhotsk.

Preparing to leave Kad'iak in May, 1786, for the return voyage, Shelikhov entrusted the administration of the colony to a subordinate, K. A. Samoilov, leaving him lengthy instructions on how to rule his men and to treat the islanders. Samoilov was to establish posts on adjacent islands and on the mainland. The small number of men--as few as eleven--assigned to the various stations shows how little threat was posed by the natives by this time. Upon arrival of reinforcements from Okhotsk, additional stations should be established in the Kenai and Chugach countries and southward along the coast "toward California", to latitude 40°, with copper plates to be buried at various places to indicate Russian possession. Other trading firms were to be excluded from the occupied territory.(38)

On May 22, Shelikhov left Kad'iak on the galiot Three Saints, escorted, he writes, by the toions and elders of neighboring tribes. As they set out, they sighted the Mikhail finally heading in, more than three years overdue. Shelikhov stopped to discharge the commander, Olesov, on the spot, and ordered the vessel to join the Sv. Semen in the harbor at Afognak Island. From there, one ship was to explore the southern coast, while the other was to sail north toward Bering Strait, in search of new lands and islands. These measures taken, the Three Saints resumed her voyage.

In addition to a twelve-man crew, taken from among the promyshlenniks, and the Shelikhov family and other passengers, the Three Saints bore 40 natives--adults and children--some of whom had come "at their own wish", and others as "prisoners from various settlements". A third of these were to return by the next ship "after seeing the Fatherland and

---

(38) Instructions, G. I. Shelikhov to K. A. Samoilov, at Kad'iak, May 4, 1786, in Andreev (1948), pp. 185-199.

observing our domestic life", another third was to be sent
to the court of Catherine II, and the rest were to be taught
useful things in Siberia.

Many of the men were sick during the voyage, but some
of the islanders acted as sailors, thereby easing the burden
during the two months the ship was at sea. They reached
the Kurile Islands on July 30, and after being held back
several days by contrary winds, anchored at the mouth of
the Bol'shaia River off Kamchatka. Shelikhov at once rowed
ashore to buy fresh fish, but had no sooner done so than a
strong wind tore the Three Saints from her anchors and
carried her out to sea.

This was a calamity, for Shelikhov had hoped on
arrival at Okhotsk to send the Three Saints back to Kodiak
the same season with supplies and men to reinforce his
company there. No other vessel was likely to be available
at that season, and so he had no choice but to go to
Okhotsk overland. First, however, hearing that an English
trading vessel had called at Petropavlovsk harbor, he
hastened there to see this unusual visitor. Arriving at
Petropavlovsk on August 23, he there learned that the ship,
the Lark, belonged to the East India Company, and had come
from Bengal. Captain William Peters, in command, entertained Shelikhov liberally, and they arranged for the sale
of Peters' cargo.[39] Shelikhov bought 6,611 rubles worth
of goods, giving 1,000 in cash and a draft for payment of
the remainder in Moscow. He also gave the Englishman a
list of articles that they would need in the future,
providing the Empress would permit such trade. The Lark
sailed on September 3, Peters promising to bring another
assortment of goods. But he never returned; his ship was
wrecked in the Aleutians, with only two survivors.

Shelikhov writes that he left Petropavlovsk on September
4, and by way of Bol'sheretsk went to the fort at Tigil,
arriving October 2. He remained there for several weeks,
advising a representative at his company's trading post,[40]
and awaiting proper snow conditions. He left by dog team on
November 18. The route he followed was extremely difficult,
through territory uninhabited except for occasional villages
of Koriaks, apt to be hostile. He braved extreme cold,
bitter wind, and sometimes the dread purga, or blizzard,
saving himself only by burrowing in the snow for two, three
or even five days, unable to prepare water or food, having

---

(39) Agreement, G. I. Shelikhov and Captain William Peters,
at Kamchatka, August, 1786, in Andreev (1948), pp. 199-200.

(40) Instructions, G. I. Shelikhov to F. A. Vykhodtsev,
October 13, 1786, in Andreev (1948), pp. 200-204.

to eat snow to satisfy his thirst, and to eat sugar or gnaw
iukola (dried fish) for food.

Finally winning through, he arrived in Okhotsk on
January 27, 1787, four months after the safe arrival of the
Three Saints. Settling matters regarding the cargo, he
and his wife (and presumably their children, though they
are not mentioned) left Okhotsk by dog team on February 8.
They reached Iakutsk on March 11, and left the following day
for Irkutsk, arriving on April 6.

In Irkutsk, Shelikhov reported at once to Governor-
General Iakobii, submitting lengthy written accounts (one
of which became the basis for his book, as published in
1791), maps of the areas he had visited, and plans for a
great monopoly, to be under the Empress' protection. He
asked that the company be declared exempt from interference
by local officials, though declaring the partners would be
pleased if it were supervised by the Governor-General. In
case of delay of deliveries from Irkutsk to Okhotsk,
government warehouses in Okhotsk should be directed to
issue on credit ships stores and supplies from government
stocks. To hold existing forts and "to defend and protect
the people brought under the rule of Her Imperial Majesty",
he requested one hundred men trained in arms. Specialists
were needed, and two priests and a deacon to enlighten the
natives in the Orthodox Faith.

Reporting his encounter with the English on Kamchatka,
Shelikhov urged that further trade be permitted. When word
of the profits at Kamchatka got around, other traders would
flock there and then "that most remote region will blossom
into greatness and become world famous for its commerce and
the cultivation of its soil". In addition, "we may be able
in time to establish important and profitable trade relations
with adjacent territories, such as Japan, Korea, and the
ports of China and India". The Company should, in any case,
be given the right to trade with Japan, China, Korea, India,
the Philippine Islands, and with the Spaniards and the
Americans [Indians] in America. He requested permission for
the Company to establish its enterprises on any islands it
should discover and bring under the Russian scepter. He
climaxed his requests by asking a loan of 500,000 rubles for
twenty years, and the loan of one of the government ships
in the harbor at Okhotsk.(41)

Iakobii, whether from regard for the national interests
or for his own, fell in readily with Shelikhov's proposals.
Conveying them to the Empress, he pointed out the danger of
foreign encroachment and urged dispatch of a Russian

---

(41) Report, G. I. Shelikhov to I. V. Iakobii, April 19,
1787, in Andreev (1948), p. 212.

flotilla to the Pacific. He lauded Shelikhov's measures for
conversion and education of the natives, and his desire to
make further explorations. He knew how opposed the monarch
was to monopoly, he wrote, but the good works of the
Golikov-Shelikhov company demanded it, and aid was needed
for defense against the natives.(42)

Meanwhile, to replace Samoilov on Kad'iak, Shelikhov
made an agreement with the Greek shipper and trader, Evstrat
Delarov, with more than twenty years of experience in
Russian Far Eastern waters, to go from Okhotsk to Kad'iak in
May, 1787, on the Three Saints, under command of Izmailov.
Beside routine duties of management, Delarov was ordered
to take cattle, pigs, and goats from Okhotsk for breeding
purposes, and to try to sow grain and plant garden
produce. He was to further the search for all kinds of
metals, minerals and rarities, and in April or May of the
following year he was to proceed south on the Three Saints
as far as the 45th parallel, then continue along that
latitude in search of unknown islands to Kamchatka, where
he would unload furs and return to Kad'iak.(43)

In August, Shelikhov encountered John Ledyard, an
American who had sailed with Cook, and who was now hoping
to cross Siberia, get transportation to America, and then
cross it, thus going around the world. In a diary entry,
Ledyard wrote that Shelikhov told him there were 2,000
Russians on different parts of the coast of America--
clearly overstated in an effort to convince the foreigner
of the magnitude of the Russian effort--and offered him
passage to America on one of his vessels the following
summer.(44) An undated, unsigned memorandum, apparently
in Shelikhov's hand, and written at the same time, gives
the other side of the meeting, noting searching questions
by Ledyard as to the extent and date of founding of the
Russian settlements. To this the reply was given that the
Russian settlements had been established "long ago", that
trading operations extended well along the coast towards
California and into the interior, that all the people
there had been made Russian subjects, and that interference
of other nations in the area would not be tolerated.(45)

---

(42) Report, I. V. Iakobii to Empress, November 30, 1787,
in Andreev (1948), p. 259.

(43) Letter, G. I. Shelikhov to E. I. Delarov, August 30,
1789, in Andreev (1948), pp. 285-289.

(44) Stephen D. Watrous, ed., John Ledyard's journey through
Russia and Siberia, 1787-1788. The journal and selected
letters. (Madison, Wisc., 1966), pp. 44-45.

(45) Unsigned memorandum [by Shelikhov?], undated [ca.
August 1787?], Yudin Collection, Box 2, Folder 29, translated in D.R.A.H., v. 3, p. 250.

Shelikhov probably regarded Ledyard as a potential
threat to Russia's American colonies and fur trade, and
passed the word to Iakobii. In February, 1788, the
American was arrested in Iakutsk, returned to the capital
post haste, and on March 18 was expelled from the country.

But there were matters of broader import. About
December, 1787, Shelikhov, his wife, and Golikov left for
St. Petersburg to report to the government concerning his
voyage and plans, and to seek sanction for his requests.
The date of the journey is an approximation, based on the
need to wait for the best winter travel conditions, the
usual time of transit, and the presence of Shelikhov and
Golikov in the capital by February, 1788. That Natal'ia
Shelikhova accompanied her husband must be assumed from
biological evidence, for--if we accept the date given in
Peterburgskii Nekropol--she gave birth to their daughter
Aleksandra on December 21, 1788, so conception would have
been in about March of that year.

It must have seemed a favorable time to ask for
support. The government was interested in both the
Siberian and American coasts of the North Pacific. In July,
1785, the Empress had ordered the extensive expedition
under Captain Joseph Billings to be formed, and in 1787 she
ordered Captain G. I. Mulovskii to take four ships around
the world to the North Pacific. The Mulovskii expedition,
which would have been the first Russian round the world
voyage, had to be cancelled in 1788 because of the war with
Sweden, but the Billings expedition was active until 1792.

In February, 1788, Shelikhov and Golikov submitted a
petition to the Empress. In a highly favorable light they
reviewed Shelikhov's exploits in exploration, building
forts and establishing settlements, and in bringing 50,000
[sic] new subjects to the crown, in all of which "we had no
other object in mind except love of our country and zeal
for the public welfare". They described plans for further
explorations, and their intentions to move southward in
order to forestall any moves by foreigners. They proposed
to establish a small fort on the 21st or 22nd Kurile Island
for the purpose of trade relations with Asia and Japan.
For all of this they would need the aid previously outlined
to Iakobii, except that the sum needed from the government
was now scaled down to 200,000 rubles.[46]

At first all seemed to go well. The Permanent Council
(Nepremennyi sovet) examined Iakobii's report on Shelikhov's
activities and requests, and sent it to the Commission on

---

(46) Petition, I. I. Golikov and G. I. Shelikhov to
Empress, February, 1788, in Andreev (1948), p. 268.

Commerce.[47] That body recommended to the Empress that Shelikhov and Golikov be given the desired aid, along with medals, sabers, citations, and advancement in rank.[48]

But behind the scenes, Shelikhov's requests aroused indignation and vigorous opposition. "There has not been a report like this one...in twenty-five years", exclaimed Catherine's secretary, A. V. Khrapovitskii, in his diary, "they want a monopoly over the entire Pacific Ocean!"[49]

Catherine was of like opinion. "There has never been such a loan since the Senate gave out money and factories to willing people", she wrote on the report of the Commission on Commerce, probably referring to the lavish give-aways of Peter the Great's time. "Such a loan is like the proposition of the man who wanted to teach an elephant to speak during a thirty-year period. Asked why such a long period, he replied: 'Either the elephant will die, or I, or the one who gives me the money to teach the elephant!'"

The rights applied for, Catherine continued, were contrary to her rules against monopoly and exclusive trade. If Golikov and Shelikhov were given such rights it would unleash "a hundred-headed monster". Everybody else would want monopolies too, and there would be no end to it. Anyhow, most of the European trading companies had failed, and soon the English and Dutch would go the same way as the French. As for the request for a hundred soldiers, Russia was then at war with Turkey and Sweden and was faced by new international complications. Such a force was needed in Siberia--"A hundred men there are equivalent to a thousand here".[50]

In the end, all that Catherine approved were the least essential items recommended--the award of gold medals and silver sabers to Shelikhov and Golikov,[51] and a citation

---

(47) Protocol, Permanent Council on report (November 30, 1787) of Governor-General of Irkutsk, I. V. Iakobii, February 14, 1788, in Andreev (1948), p. 265.

(48) Protocol, Permanent Council, on report of Commission on Commerce, April 6, 1788, in Andreev (1948), p. 280, from Arkhiv Gosud. Sovet (St. P., 1869), v. 1:2, pp. 661-662.

(49) A. V. Khrapovitskii, Dnevnik...s 18 Ianvaria 1782 po 17 Sentiabria 1792 goda (M. 1901), p. 45.

(50) Empress Catherine's notations on Shelikhov's request, April-August, 1788, in Andreev (1948), pp. 281-282.

(51) Letter, September 4, 1788, Count A. A. Bezborodko to Procurator-General of Senate A. A. Viazemskii, reporting view of the Empress concerning report of Commission on Commerce, in Andreev (1948), pp. 283-284, which was in turn transmitted

lauding the achievements of both.[52]

Doubtless crushed by this outcome to his cherished plans, never afforded the chance to present his projects in person to the Empress,[53] given only a few tokens, Shelikhov had no choice but to return to Irkutsk.

His departure from the capital must have occurred none too soon. On November 2, Captain Joseph Billings, head of the government expedition to Eastern Siberia and the North Pacific, forwarded the complaint, previously mentioned, by the surgeon's assistant, Miron Britiukov, concerning Shelikhov's conduct toward the inhabitants of the islands of Kad'iak, Shuiakh and Afognak. Wrote Catherine's secretary, Khrapovitskii: "I recieved Billings' report and the description of Shelikhov's barbarism on the American islands. It has been ordered presented to the Senate, and it is clear how everyone tried to get Shelikhov a monopoly. He bought everyone, and if many more revelations are made, he will be in chains."[54]

The complaint was taken up by the State Council on March 29, 1789, but fortunately for Shelikhov a letter from Governor-General Iakobii labelled Britiukov a liar so that the matter was dropped.

Khrapovitskii's comment indicates that Shelikhov had spared no efforts in order to pull strings behind the scenes. It was probably during his stay in the capital that he made contacts which were to bring him his most valuable ally, young Platon Aleksandrovich Zubov (1767-1822),

to Golikov and Shelikhov in an ukaz of the Senate, September 28, 1788, in Andreev (1948), pp. 284-285.

(52) Citation text, October 11, 1788, in Tikhmenev, op. cit., v. 2, Documents (Kingston, Ont., 1979), p. 18.

(53) Tikhmenev, I, p. 19, states that Golikov was granted an audience with Catherine as she passed through Kursk, and gave her a map of Shelikhov's voyages and descriptions of the lands visited in America. See also A. Adamov, "Grigorii Ivanovich Shelikhov (1747-1795)", a biographical sketch at the end of his Shelikhov na Kad'iake. Povest' (Moscow, 1948), p. 113. However, the Empress' visit to Kursk occurred in June 1787, and the Kamer-fur'erskii tseremonial'nyi zhurnal (court calendar) does not mention Golikov among the persons presented to the Empress at that time. That in itself is not conclusive--a mere entrepreneur such as Golikov may not have merited inclusion among the august names on the court calendar--but in June, 1787, he is supposed to have been in Siberia.

(54) Khrapovitskii, op. cit., pp. 153-154.

soon to become the Empress' favorite. During Shelikhov's stay, however, Zubov was still a mere sergeant in the guards, and started his meteoric rise to the rank of count and prince only in the spring of 1789, after Shelikhov's departure. How Shelikhov and Zubov came together is unclear; it may have been through some family connection. During the 1780's, N. A. Zubov, the father of Platon, was the governor of Kursk gubernia. Or it may have been an association in Siberia, as through Captain-Lieutenant Savva Il'ich Zubov, the commandant of Okhotsk when Shelikhov arrived there in the 1770's, or the Irkutsk merchant Lavrentii Ivanovich Zubov, later one of the founders of the United American Company.

From Irkutsk, Shelikhov travelled to Okhotsk, in order to be there when the expected ship came in from America, and to see to sending one back. He found the town bustling with construction of two ships for the Billings expedition.

On July 26, the Three Saints, under command of Dmitrii Ivanovich Bocharov, arrived from America. The vessel anchored in the mouth of the Okhota under a strong east wind. Shelikhov immediately set hired hands and men loaned from the Billings expedition to the task of pulling the vessel into the mouth of the river, but the wind was too strong. In the evening the ship parted from her anchors, and was carried off by the storm. She was blown 400 versts, toward Udsk, then with a favorable change in the wind was able to return to Okhotsk, arriving on August 7. The cargo was then unloaded, and the men given their respective share of the furs and a long-needed rest.

On August 16, the veteran skipper Gavriil Loginovich Pribylov arrived with the Sv. Georgii, bearing a rich cargo of seal skins from new islands he had found in 1786. Shelikhov, who had a share in the venture (the main share belonged to Lebedev-Lastochkin) named the group the Zubov Islands in honor of his patron, but the name remained only in his own documents. Posterity was to know them under the name of their discoverer, Pribylov.

Shelikhov passed the winter of 1789-1790 in Irkutsk planning new efforts to obtain government aid. Governor-General Iakobii was removed, under accusations of corruption, and replaced by Ivan Alfer'evich Pil'. Repeating all of his old arguments, Shelikhov hastened to enlist the new man's support. He renewed his request for privileges, but said the request for a loan could be put aside temporarily.[55] Pil, as susceptible as Iakobii to Shelikhov's air castles, had approved the proposals and forwarded them to the Empress.[56]

(55) Okun', op. cit., p. 31.

(56) Report, I. A. Pil to Empress Catherine II, February 13, 1790, and two reports for February 14, 1790, and

It was also necessary to find a new manager for the
American colonies. Delarov was demanding to be replaced.
Shelikhov's eye had fallen on Alexander Andreevich Baranov,
a merchant from Kargopol who in 1780 had moved to Irkutsk,
where he prospered in the liquor trade, built a glass factory,
and in 1788 established a trading post in remote Chukotka,
on an arm of the Anadyr River. Twice Shelikhov offered him
the post on Kad'iak, but Baranov's prosperous and independent
business affairs had prompted him to decline. In 1789,
however, Baranov's undertakings in Irkutsk and Iakutsk took
a bad turn. In 1790 he arrived in Okhotsk in the hope of
saving his enterprise on the Anadyr, but while there he
received word that the Chukoti had destroyed his trading
post and looted his stores. Shelikhov was in Okhotsk and
again offered the position. This time Baranov felt compelled
to enter Shelikhov's service.(57)

Baranov and Shelikhov concluded a contract at Okhotsk
on August 10, 1790, and on August 18 the new manager sailed
on the Three Saints. Neither he nor Shelikhov could have
imagined that Baranov would guide the colonies for the
next 28 years. Their correspondence, carried on for the next
five years, until Shelikhov's death, adds to our knowledge of
both. Shelikhov is revealed as a kind of Russian Cecil Rhodes
with vast plans for shipbuilding, trade in distant parts
of the Pacific, discovery of new lands, seizure for Russia
of control over great areas of the Pacific Coast of North
America, exclusion of foreign traders, and new settlements,
always ready to demand the impossible of his subordinate.

Baranov is shown as a more pratical man, fully
cognizant of conditions on the spot, who yet, out of
unswerving loyalty, was willing to try to achieve the
impossible with the limited means afforded him, keeping up
the flow of furs secured by ruthless exploitation of his
own energies and of the labor of native workers and Russian
promyshlenniks. Hard fisted, hard drinking, hard bargaining,
he won the respect of the natives, his men, and foreign
skippers, and a renown which reached all the way to the
Imperial court in St. Petersburg. His selection was perhaps Shelikhov's greatest single achievement.

Successful in the field, undaunted by previous set-
backs, Shelikhov continued to seek government aid as a means
of expanding operations. Thus, he conducted some sort of

Memorandum on islands discovered by Golikov-Shelikhov
Company, February, 1790, in Andreev (1948), pp. 295-304,
305-315, 315-316, and 316-317, respectively.

(57) Ocherki istorii Chukotki s drevneishikh vremen do
nashikh dnei. Ed. by N. N. Dikov (Novosibirsk, 1974),
pp. 107-108.

negotiations for troops with Colonel Samuel Bentham, commander of a regiment in Siberia. The famous liberal Alexander Radishchev, then on his way to Siberian exile, wrote his friend and patron, A. R. Vorontsov, from Tobol'sk about May 8, 1791 that: "You may be assured, the 'princeling' Shelekhov has not demanded soldiers for nothing. I hear on good authority that Colonel Bentham has given him 100 men from his battalion with which to continue his conquests".(58)

Besides negotiating for men, Shelikhov and Bentham also seem to have made some arrangements regarding ship-building and the fur trade. Again writing Vorontsov, on November 14, this time from Irkutsk, Radishchev states: "I have made the acquaintance of Mr. Shelikhov, who has just returned from Okhotsk, where he goes every spring to meet his ships returning from America... In company with Colonel Bentham, he has built and equipped a ship for commerce in America, but it has proved a failure, and Shelikhov has taken action against the captain, an Englishman".(59)

More information on Bentham's Russian sojourn clarifies his relationship with Shelikhov. Bentham (1757-1831), the younger brother of the famous legal philosopher, Jeremy Bentham, and as talented, though in a different direction, served in Russia from 1780, and September, 1782, made a tour of Siberia, going as far east as Kiakhta and Nerchinsk. In 1787, Bentham's battalion of soldiers, whom he had converted into shipwrights and sailors, was ordered south, and in 1788 saw action against the Turkish fleet. Subsequently, Bentham got his patron, Prince G. A. Potemkin, to send him to Siberia. After his earlier trip he had spoken to Potemkin "about the capability of the Amur River for navigation, and for carrying on an extensive fur trade with China, Kamchatka, and the northern coast of America". Potemkin now reminded Bentham of this, "saying a great deal about Kamchatka and the profits derivable from the fur trade there". Bentham was given command of two battalions in Siberia, one occupying a segment of the Kirgiz line, the other on the Chinese frontier south of Lake Baikal. During this time, says his biographer, Bentham at his own expense enabled a party of English sailors to build and fit out some vessels at Kamchatka, from thence to explore the northwest coast of America, and if practicable to carry

(58) Letter, Radishchev to Vorontsov, from Tobol'sk, ca. 8 May 1791. Arkhiv Kniazia Vorontsova, v. 5, p. 312.

(59) Letter, Radishchev to Vorontsov, November 14, 1790, in Polnoe sobranie sochinenii A. N. Radishcheva (M. 1907), v. 2, p. 507; and Arkhiv Kniazia Vorontsova, v. 5, p. 330.

on a trade in furs. Years later, in 1808, one of the men, unfortunately one of the least intelligent, returned to give a vague report that the vessels had been built, and they had landed in America, where they built a wooden fort some-where on the coast, and engaged successfully in the fur trade.(60)

The proposal that Bentham would supply Shelikhov with a hundred men would have required the Empress' sanction. With the mighty Potemkin behind it, this might have been obtained, but for some unknown reason the plan was laid aside. However, the vague story of the English sailors building ships in Kamchatka and setting out for the North-west Coast may refer to some arrangement between Shelikhov and Bentham. It may, in fact, concern the entry into Shelikhov's service, along with several comrades, of Second Lieutenant Iakov Egorovich Shilts (James Shields), an Englishman in the Ekaterinburg regiment with earlier training as a shipwright. Shields built the company ship Severnyi orel at Okhotsk, took it to Kad'iak in the fall of 1791, and thereafter took part in the building of the Phoenix at Resurrection Harbor (now Seward) for Baranov.

Besides troops, Shelikhov sought to have clergy assigned to the colonies. It seems likely that this was intended mainly to help gain the favor of the Empress, but it was hoped also to help establish a more orderly way of life among the Russian hunters, and to pacify the natives. In this effort Shelikhov was finally successful, for by an ukaz of June 30, 1793, the Empress ordered the petition granted.

At the same time, Shelikhov asked the Governor-General of Irkutsk to use his influence with the crown to procure a number of exiles, skilled as blacksmiths, locksmiths and foundrymen, and ten families of serfs for the development of agriculture. This request was granted by an ukaz of December 31, 1793.(61)

In the summer of 1794, both the clergymen and colonists were assembled at Okhotsk, and dispatched for America on the Three Saints and the Ekaterina. The two

(60) M. S. Bentham, The life of Brigadier-general Sir Samuel Bentham, K.S.G., formerly Inspector-General of Naval Works, lately a commissioner of Her Majesty's Navy, with the distinct duty of civil architect and engineer of the Navy (London, 1872), pp. 91, 93-94.

(61) Tikhmenev, op. cit., I, p. 36. The same, quoted in letter, Pil to Shelikhov, Irkutsk, 12 May 1794, in Yudin Collection, Box 1, Folder 4, translated in D.R.A.H., v. 3, pp. 161-163.

vessels arrived at Kad'iak in August, with 192 persons on board including 52 craftsmen and peasants, and 10 clergymen, led by the Archimandrite Ioasaf. With them came provisions, stores, implements, seeds, and cattle, and lengthy instructions and admonitions to Baranov regarding establishment of an agricultural colony at Yakutat Bay. With a cool disregard for the realities of life in the colonies, and for the inhospitable conditions in the proposed location, Shelikhov urged that the new settlement be made "beautiful and pleasant to live in...everything must be impressive and look important, especially when a foreign ship arrives".(62)

In the end, none of these plans worked out. The clergy, in spite of claims made within six weeks of their arrival of "7,000 Americans baptised, and over 2,000 marriages performed", made little impression on either the natives or the Russian promyshlenniks and were in constant friction with the rough and ready Baranov.(63) A quarter of a century was to elapse before the Russian Church was firmly established in the colonies. The agricultural settlement at Yakutat was a failure, and in 1803 was wiped out by natives.

In 1791, Shelikhov's account of his voyage was published. It was simply his report of 1787 to Iakobii, slightly revised, but it gained wide notice in the capital, helped insure his fame and gave rise through additions made in subsequent editions, to problems of authorship and bibliography which are debated to this day.

At about this time, Shelikhov made the acquaintance of Nikolai Petrovich Rezanov (1764-1807), his future son-in-law, destined to be of great influence in carrying on and developing his enterprises. Although he was the son of Petr Gavrilovich Rezanov, long a highly respected judge in Irkutsk, Rezanov had spent most of his years in St. Petersburg, where like other well-born young Russians of the time he had become westernized in his manner and outlook. His rise had been rapid, from the Treasury to the Admiralty, then to the post of chief clerk for G. R. Derzhavin when the latter was head of the Bureau of Petitions, and from there to the suite of Prince Platon Zubov, by whose favor he had been sent on special missions for the Empress.(64)

---

(62) Letter, Shelikhov and Polevoi to Baranov, Okhotsk, August 9, 1794, in Tikhmenev, op. cit., II, Documents, pp. 55-56.

(63) Letter, Archimandrite Ioasaf to Shelikhov, May 18, 1745. Ibid., pp. 77-85; The Russian Orthodox Religious Mission in America, 1794-1837... (Kingston, Ont., 1978), pp. 51-52.

(64) "Rezanov, Nikolai Petrovich", Russkii biograficheskii slovar' (St. P., 1910), v. 15, p. 539.

1795

Exactly when and why he came to Irkutsk, and when he
married Shelikhov's daughter Anna is uncertain, but if we
again turn to biological evidence, Anna was born on
February 15, 1780, and was married before her father's
death (in 1795), when she was still barely fifteen, it
could hardly have been long before the latter date.

Shelikhov's old dream of the Kuriles and Japan, never
abandoned, also took new shape at this time. Probably it
was clear that the Kuriles themselves promised little, but
they were stepping stones to trade with Japan, which could
have incalculable value.

Shelikhov was not alone in eyeing Japan. In 1791,
Erik Laksman, a Swedish savant residing in Siberia, went
to St. Petersburg with the Japanese merchant Kodai, who
had been shipwrecked in the Aleutians. Probably at
Laksman's urging, the Empress authorized an expedition to
Japan, to be led by Laksman's son, Adam. Ostensibly to
return the shipwrecked men, the real motive for the
expedition was to open trade and diplomatic relations. On
September 13, 1792, the younger Laksman and 40 men left
Okhotsk in the Sv. Ekaterina. In May, 1794, Adam returned
to Irkutsk, to report that he had been received cordially
by the Japanese, and had been given permission to send
another embassy. Erik Laksman brought his son's reports
and a collection of Japanese art objects to St. Petersburg.
Both father and son were honored, and plans were made for
a second expedition.

Shelikhov had meanwhile followed the progress of the
expedition closely, and had reported on it to the heir to
the throne, Paul.(65) Evidently striving to further his
own interests, he himself sent an expedition to the Kuriles
in 1794 to establish a colony on Urup Island, delaying as
long as he could the dispatch of the second Japan expedition.
Finally, in May, 1795, it was decided to equip an expedition
in which Laksman would organize the scientific part, and
Shelikhov the trading part.(66)

And then, on July 20, 1795, at the height of his
career and expectations, Shelikhov died. He was only 47.
The cause of death is uncertain, but already on June 30,
evidently knowing that his days were numbered, he asked
the government in case of his death to extend material aid
to members of his family, namely to his wife Natal'ia
Alekseevna, and their son and two unmarried daughters, Ekaterir

---

(65) Tikhmenev, op. cit., I, p. 456 n.

(66) "Laksman, Erik", Russkii biograficheskii slovar',
v. 10, pp. 47-50. Wilhelm Lagus, Erik Laxman, hans Lefnad,
resor, forskningar och brefvexling (Helsingfors, 1880),
pp. 233, 243 ff.

and Avdot'ia.   *state affairs* - muddled

He had cause for worry, for his affairs were in a
muddled state. The Russian-Chinese trading center at
Kiakhta, closed since 1786, had reopened, but instead of
finding a ready market for his accumulated furs,
Shelikhov found that the price had dropped sharply,
probably because of imports by British and American trading
vessels in Canton.[67]

Shelikhov may also have had personal problems. For
this we have the testimony of Baron Vladimir Ivanovich
Shteingel (1783-1862). His account is defective but
nevertheless deserves attention for want of other evidence
in this sphere. Shteingel was born in the Perm region in
1783, the son of a captain ispravnik, or chief of police.
His father soon was transferred in the same capacity to
remote Nizhnekamchatsk, but two years later lost his
position and for a time the family lived in Kamchatka in
great poverty. When the elder Shteingel was transferred
to Irkutsk, the son studied in the gubernia school, and
at ten years of age entered naval cadet school first at
Kronshtadt and later at St. Petersburg. In 1799 he
finished as a midshipman, served with the fleet in various
operations during the Napoleonic wars, and later was
associated with Kondratii Ryleev. In the purge of
conspirators and their associates following the December
1825 revolt, Ryleev was hanged and Shteingel was sent to
Siberia, where he remained until 1858 when he was pardoned
by the new Emperor, Alexander II.

Shteingel wrote extensively, and in one of his articles
tells the following curious tale:

> I heard this anecdote during my stay in
> Okhotsk later on, from the eye witness Evstr.
> Delarov, who was a director of the American
> Company, and from several other sources. This
> is what they told me: Shelikhov, setting out
> for America in the 1780's, left his wife in
> Okhotsk[!]. Here she did not delay having an
> affair with one of the officials (I forget his
> name), and meanwhile sowed in Okhotsk, perhaps
> believing them herself, rumors that Shelikhov
> had died on the way from American to Kamchatka.
> Aided by his brother Vasilii, his wife was
> ready to marry the official when suddenly,
> inopportunely, came a letter stating that
> Shelikhov was alive and would go from Kamchatka
> to Okhotsk. In this critical position the
> wife decided to poison him upon arrival, but

---

(67) Polevoi, op. cit., p. 124.

> Shelikhov was warned, all was revealed, and
> through his workers he had his wife and
> brother publicly punished. Not content with
> this, he wanted on going to Irkutsk to give
> his wife over to the criminal court, insisting
> that she be given the knut. But in this case
> Baranov, then his prikazchik [!], persuaded
> him to spare his name and forgive the
> guilty woman.(68)

What can be made of this? There are obvious
inaccuracies, as is often the case with Shteingel's lively
reminiscences. If he was only ten years old when he
entered cadet school at Kronshtadt, he was probably only
nine at the most when he and the family moved from
Kamchatka. But he would have known Delarov prior to the
latter's death in St. Petersburg in 1807 or 1808 and
could have heard the tale from "several other sources", and
"during my stay in Okhotsk later on", presumably during his
years of exile. Thus it is not just boyhood recollections
but a persistent rumor. Shelikhov did not leave his wife
in Okhotsk when he went to America in 1783, but took her
with him. If there is anything to the story it might refer
to the period from August 1786 to January 1787, in which
Mrs. Shelikhov had already arrived in Okhotsk while
Shelikhov had to make his way there from Kamchatka.

The candid Shteingel then goes on to claim that many
in Irkutsk attributed Shelikhov's sudden death to his
wife.(69) This, too, could be dismissed as gossip, were it
not for partial corroboration through a document discovered
in 1953 in the Soviet archives. A resident of Irkutsk who
knew Shelikhov's family well wrote that Shelikhov had had
a painful death. "He suffered great pain in his stomach,
and had such an inflammation that in an instant, to alleviate
the fire, he swallowed a whole plateful of ice". This could
have been a perforated ulcer or a stomach cancer, but the
eyewitness of his agonies asserts further that Shelikhov
died of his own doing, "by suicide", apparently having taken
poison. The family then may have concealed the fact in
order to obtain full rites of church and avoid attracting
a swarm of creditors fearing a collapse of his affairs.(70)

Was Natal'ia Shelikhova a northern Lucretia Borgia or
a loyal helpmate? A correct conception of her personality,

---

(68) V. I. Shteingel', "Zapiski...", in Semevskii,
Obshchestvennye dvizheniia v Rossii v pervuiu polovinu XIX
veka (St. P., 1905), v. 1, pp. 342-343.

(69) Shteingel', op. cit., p. 343.

(70) Polevoi, op. cit., p. 125.

of her relations with Shelikhov, and of the nature of his death must await further research. (See Appendix 9.)

Shelikhov was buried at the cathedral church in the Znamenskii convent in Irkutsk. A florid epitaph was composed, with verses by Derzhavin and Dmitriev. In 1800 it was inscribed on a marble obelisk, brought from Ekaterinbrug in the Urals (the Demidov connection again?) and erected by his heirs and associates, where it is still to be seen. The cost of the monument, also inscribed on it, with evident pride, was 11,760 rubles, a large sum.

After his death, the Empress expressed appreciation of Shelikhov's labors and victories by giving his widow and descendants the right of hereditary nobility, with the right to engage in trade. His projects and possessions, however, underwent the usual drastic selection process as posterity determined what was viable and what should be abandoned. The expedition to Japan never took place--Laksman died in the same year, and the Empress in the year following, leaving no one to pursue the matter. The colony on Urup failed; the survivors were taken off in 1805. But the American enterprise, destined to be Shelikhov's principal monument, was held together by the iron hand of Baranov and expanded.

Under the new sovereign, Paul, other traders tried to wrest control of the company from Natal'ia Shelikhova, and the Emperor, disgusted by reports of abuses against the natives of the Aleutian Islands, was about to abolish the company's privileges. However, Natal'ia's determination, and the efforts of her highly placed son-in-law, Rezanov, saved the day. Rezanov, whose wife's inheritance consisted mainly of Company shares, worked hard behind the scenes, and was able to swing Paul over to the idea of a monopoly.[71] By a decree of June 8, 1799, the Russian-American Company was formed, destined to endure for nearly seventy years. Thus Shelikhov's dream was fulfilled. Whether the Company was the best solution for governing and exploiting such a remote and problem-filled territory, or whether it could have been more successfully handled in some other way, is debatable. As for Shelikhov, a contemporary opinion is provided by Radishchev, who, in informing Vorontsov of Shelikhov's death stated: "I cannot speak of his moral qualities, but he was a useful man".[72]

(71) A. Sgibnev, "Istoricheskii ocherk glavneishikh sobytii v Kamchatke", Morskoi sbornik, 1869:7, p. 43.

(72) Letter, A. N. Radishchev to A. R. Vorontsov, Ilimsk, June 9, 1796, in Polnoe sobranie socheniia A. N. Radishcheva (M. 1907), v. 2, p. 470.

There is need for a more complete biography of
Shelikhov. Some examples have been given here of how even
sources published long ago can yield additional information.
Archival research in the U.S.S.R. ought to yield a great
deal more. A number of avenues could be explored:
Shelikhov's origins and family ties; the true nature of
his activities--not the glossed over, idealized version
so far available--regarding the natives under company
rule, and toward his workers; the origins and role of
Natal'ia Shelikhova; and the roles of Golikov, the
Zubovs, Bentham, and Potemkin. Additional information should
result in a figure who is in many ways less creditable, but
more credible, and in a better appreciation of his times
and milieu, the problems which he faced, and his undoubted
talents.

Grigorii Shelikhov's book, here published in translation, helped to secure him reknown down to the present
day. It was first published in 1791 by the St. Petersburg
publisher and bookseller, V. Sopikov, under the formidable
title "The Russian merchant Grigorii Shelekhov's Journey
in 1783 from Okhotsk over the Eastern Ocean to the American
shores, with complete information about the discovery of
the islands of Kyktak and Afagnak newly acquired by him,
and with publication of a description of the way of life,
manners, customs, dwellings and dress of the peoples there,
now subjects of the Russian sovereign: also the climate,
annual changes, animals, domestic animals, fish, birds,
plants, and many other curious things found there, all
truly and accurately described by him. With a map and a
depiction of the seafarer himself and the savage peoples
he found there" [Rossiiskogo kuptsa Grigoriia Shelekhova
stranstvovanie s 1783 po 1783 godu...]. As stated before, it
was essentially the report he made to Governor-General
Iakobii in 1787, slightly revised.

That Shelikhov must have had a hand in preparing the
manuscript for publication seems likely. There are some
added details of the journey from Kamchatka to Okhotsk,
and expressions of gratitude to certain officials, which
he must have provided. Yet, Alexander Radishchev, in a
letter to A. R. Vorontsov written on November 14, 1791,
from Irkutsk, wrote: "Your Excellency knows him
[Shelikhov] and has read the account of his Voyage, just
published in Moscow, and with which he is dissatisfied".(73)

The dissatisfaction thus centered around the first
edition. Why was Shelikhov dissatisfied with it? There
is no ready answer, and the question, complicated by

---

(73) Polnoe sobranie sochinenii A. N. Radishcheva (M., 1907),
v. 2, p. 507; Okun', op. cit., pp. 23-24 n.

association with later editions, and attitudes of Shelikhov's posterity, has been reviewed by several authors.[74]

Taking the matter in sequence, one notes that a second volume, "A sequel to the voyage of Grigorii Shelikhov", appeared in 1792, a year after publication of the first.   It comprised the journal kept by Shelikhov's subordinates Izmailov and Bocharov on their voyage to Chugach Bay in 1788. It included descriptions of the secret burial places of copper plates stating that the land was "Russian territory". Shelikhov had not made the voyage, but it was associated with him.   In 1793 both works were included in one volume along with a new section entitled "An historical and geographical description of the Kurile, Aleutian, Andreianov and Fox Islands..."

The extent and nature of Shelikhov's "dissatisfaction" with the volume is still unclear.   The Soviet historian S. B. Okun' points out that the two editions of his book came out during Shelikhov's lifetime, and that until 1798, other than his "dissatisfaction", there seems to have been no protest by either Shelikhov or his heirs.   Yet "A memorial for the permanent establishment of the American Company", by Natal'ia Shelikhova, dated October 7, 1798, states that the publication was contrary to Shelikhov's desire to conceal company operations in America "so that foreigners will not learn so soon of the activities there".   This view is corroborated by "secret" instructions sent by the main office to Baranov in 1802.   They state that the book "is nothing but the journal he sent to former Governor-General Iakobii and stolen from the chancellory of (Governor-General) Pil' and printed in Moscow without (Shelikhov's) consent.   Thus ignorance sacrificed a state secret for the sake of base profit.   You can see for yourself then that the placement of the plates must be changed".

Thus it was not the first (1791) edition which was now causing displeasure, but the sequel of 1792 or the 1793 edition as republished with the 1792 sequel, telling of the secreting of the plates.   Okun' suggests that Natal'ia Shelikhova's statement of 1798 was merely an exaggeration, intended to prevent privileges being given out to a rival private company, on the grounds that this might lead to disclosure of state secrets.   He concludes that Shelikhov's own dissatisfaction might have arisen merely from the form of the publication. This is not entirely convincing, because the small, crudely printed volume seems neither better nor worse in form than others of its time.   However, no better explanation has yet been put forward.

_____

(74)   S. B. Okun', The Russian-American Company, Translation (Cambridge, 1951), of M.-L., 1939 ed., pp. 278-280; Andreev (1948), op. cit., pp. 31-39; B. P. Polevoi, 1971, pp. 29-34; N. N. Bolkhovitinov, The beginnings of Russian-American relations, 1775-1815, (Cambridge, 1975), p. 375.

The third, 1793, edition would have caused a modern writer ample dissatisfaction, for it includes an essay which is arrant plagiarism. Already in the middle of the last century the Russian academician Karl Baer declared that the "Historical and geographical description" had been published originally in Academician P. S. Pallas' Neue Nordische Beyträge (v. 4, pp. 112-141, 1783). The Russian ethnographer Leopold Shrenk[75] declared that the section came from William Coxe, Account of the Russian Discoveries between Asia and America, London, 1780, or from the anonymous J. L. S., Neue Nachrichten von denen Neuentdeckten Insuln in der See zwischen Asia and Amerika... (Hamburg and Leipzig, 1776).

Who was responsible? H. H. Bancroft, who thought erroneously that the 1793 edition was the first, charged that Shelikhov had copied extensively from J. L. S.' work. However, this was disproved by Avrahm Yarmolinsky, of the New York Public Library, who pointed out the existence of the earlier edition of 1791. Shelikhov could hardly have been responsible, being too busy with his affairs in eastern Siberia to engage in literary activities. Instead, the essay was evidently added by some unknown compiler in St. Petersburg, probably at the behest of the publisher, Sopikov.[76] But many writers unacquainted with the bibliographic intricacies of the matter have assumed the essay to be Shelikhov's.[77]

The key to the mystery is provided by A. I. Andreev, who points out that there is a direct tie between the description of the Kurile Islands in the Shelikhov volume and an analogous description in the Mesiatsoslov, or "Historical and geographical almanac" of the Academy of Sciences for 1785 (pp. 73-114) and then reprinted in the Sobranie sochinenii..., or "Collection of works from the almanacs of

(75) Leopold Shrenk, Ob inorodtsakh Amurskogo Kraia, 3 vols., (St. P., 1883, 1889, 1903), v. 2, p. 33.

(76) Avrahm Yarmolinsky, "Shelekhov's voyage to Alaska, a biographical note", New York Public Library Bulletin, v. 36, 1932, pp. 141-148.

(77) E.g., A. Adamov, in biographical sketch appended to Shelikhov na Kad'iake, povest' (M., 1948), p. 119, and the almost identical "Grigorii Ivanovich Shelekhov (1747-1795)", Sovetskaia etnografiia, 1948:1, pp. 189-201. Adamov corrects this in his subsequent G. I. Shelikhov--zamechatel'nyi russkii moreplavatel' i issledovatel' (M., 1951), p. 21, and revised edition of the same, G. I. Shelikhov (M., 1952), p. 29

various years" (Part 4, pp. 63-103). This description of
the Kurile Islands was compiled by Second-Major Petr Tatarinov, and communicated to the Academy of Sciences by F. I.
Klichka. The Tatarinov article states that it was based
on a description of the Kuriles made in the 1770's by the
cossack sotnik Ivan Chernyi, and by reports of Ivan
Ocheredin and Ivan Antipin. And even part of this account
seems to have been drawn from S. P. Krasheninnikov's
Description of the Land of Kamchatka (1755) and an account
of the Kuriles by Timofei Shmalev.(78) B. P. Polevoi sees
omission of references to Ocheredin and Antipin in the
1793 edition of Shelikhov's book as indication that it was
not Tatarinov's composition which was used but some earlier
account by Ocheredin and Antipin. It seems more likely
that the compiler omitted the names simply in order to
obscure the fact that the composition was of other, earlier
authorship.

After the account of the Kuriles comes a description of
the Aleutian Islands. This comes from the Mesiatsoslov
for 1781, or the 1790 reprint of it. Here there is omission
of references to the explorations of Andreian Tolstykh in
1760, and of other early voyagers. Again the compiler
evidently wished to conceal the antique nature of his
material. The first part of the description of Kodiak
cannot be identified as to its origin, but there follows
a lengthy passage which appears to be from the account of
Solov'ev, as presented in the Mesiatsoslov, with abridge-
ments and additions, either from J.L.S., Neue Nachrichten,
or from the translation of that work into English by Coxe
in 1780. Finally there is a short paragraph from the
account of Krenitsyn's voyage of 1768-1770, as presented
in the Coxe work, 1787 edition, p. 217).

The third part of the Shelikhov book is from Bocharov
and Izmailov's journal of their voyage of 1788. The first
and third parts of the book are therefore first-hand, and
worthy of careful study. The "Historical and Geographical
Description" on the other hand, is a compilation of
compilations, and has been sailing under false colors. It
deserves to be translated in its entirety, with authorship
properly ascribed, and published as a separate work.

Nevertheless, in spite of their varied origins, the
parts of the Shelikhov book were brought together, the book
was widely read, and was generally accepted as Shelikhov's
work. It is an important book in that it helped to inform
contemporaries about the Russian explorations and acquisitions
in the Pacific, and indicates Shelikhov's important role
in the establishment of the Russian colonies in Alaska and
in the introduction of European ways to the peoples of the
Northwest Coast of North America.

---

(78) A.I. Andreev, (1948), p. 61; B.P. Polevoi, op. cit.
p. 30-31.

1.

THE VOYAGE OF G.I. SHELIKHOV, 1783-1786

Having built three galiots on behalf of the Company
in Okhotsk and having named the first in honor of the
Three Saints (Tri Sviatitelia), the second in honor of
St. Simeon the God-receiver and Anna the Prophetess
(Sv. Simeon Bogopriimets i Anna Prorochitsa) and the third
in honor of St. Michael (Sv. Mikhail) we set sail, with
192 workmen, on August 16th, 1783 for the Eastern Ocean
from the mouth of the Urak River which flows into the sea
of Okhotsk. I was on board the first galiot with my wife,
who accompanied me everywhere and shared all the hardships
[1787: and two children]. In case the vessels should be
separated by contrary winds, I named Bering Island as a
rendezvous.

Overcoming various difficulties which hindered our
voyage, we reached the first Kurile island on August 31st,
but contrary winds prevented us landing until September
2nd, on which date, having anchored, we landed on the
island, took on fresh water and on September 3rd continued
our journey. On the 12th a storm which lasted two days
separated all the vessels. The storm was so violent that
we almost lost hope of living through it, however on the
14th the first two galiots met and [1812: on September
24th] reached Bering Island. It was decided to winter
there, to await the third galiot with 62 people on board,
and also taking into consideration the contrary winds.
However, throughout the time we stayed on the Bering
Islands we did not see the third galiot. On September 25th
I sent several men from each vessel to circumnavigate the
island in baidaras which we had brought with us, being
curious whether they would find anything remarkable. The
men returned on the 27th of the same month without having
found anything.

We took no furs on the island all winter with the
exception of a small quantity of arctic fox [pesets]
because there were no other wild animals.

Food obtainable on the island consists of salt water
fish, of which there are many varieties, meat from sea
animals such as sea lion, sea bear and seal. Birds
include geese, ducks, swans, cormorants, seagulls, murres
and partridges. In addition kutagarnik and sarana roots
are used and are considered edible. The winter continued
with strong winds, mostly from the north and east. We
had snow or snow storms almost every day.

The seamen were unable to avoid scurvy and it was
necessary to seek methods to cure it, so during the snow-
storms they walked by the sea and on sunny days went for
long distances into the hills on skiis.

We found that the magnetic variation here is
1 1/4 rhumb east.

We left this island on June 16th, 1784 [1793: July
16th] having arranged to meet at Unalashka should we be
separated. (For a description of this island see below.)
It is one of the islands in the Fox Chain. In order that
the third vessel, which was late, would know of our
arrangement and go there also, I wrote [i.e., left] a
letter for them on Bering Island.

Up to the 19th we were delayed by lack of winds or
met contrary ones, so that we moved rather slowly. On
the 19th we lost sight of the other galiot, the Sv. Simeon,
due to heavy fog and on the 20th our single vessel reached
Mednyi [Copper] Island, where we procured fresh water
and fur seal meat, leaving on the 23rd. On July 6th we
passed Atkha Island, one of the Andreianovs, on the 7th
we passed Amliia Island, on the 8th and 9th were in sight
of Siugam [1787: Saugam] and Amukhta Islands and later
the Islands of the Four Mountains. On the 10th we passed
through the strait between the Four Mountains going from
the south towards the north. On July 12th, some distance
from the islands, toward the north, we met with the other
galiot, the Sv. Simeon, and, continuing our journey, on the
13th reached Natykin Bay on Unalashka Island. On the
14th we took the vessels into Captain's Bay [Harbor] where
we unloaded and remained until the 22nd putting in
necessary provisions.

In passing the above named islands we were only able
to observe that the Aleutian Islands chain (see the
description further on) begins with Bering Island and ends
with Kykhtak Island which will be discussed below. [These
islands] consist of high rocky mountains, many of which are
active volcanoes. There are no forests whatsoever; the
only plants are creeping types which spread on the rocks,
such as willow, alder, and mountain ash and even these are
not found everywhere. The natives gather various types of
driftwood for fuel and construction.

Having finished all necessary business on Unalashka and
taking with us two interpreters and ten Aleuts who had
volunteered to work for us, we left on July 22nd to continue
our journey without waiting for the third galiot, leaving
instructions for the galiot Sv. Mikhail to proceed to the
island called Kykhtak, also known as Kad'iak, which was
designated as our general rendezvous. We passed through
the Fox group of islands from north to south by a strait
between Unimak and Akun islands. This passage offers no
obstacles to navigation as it is unobstructed and spacious,

however during flood and ebb tides the current is very
strong.

On August 3rd we reached Kykhtak and took the galiots
into harbor from the south, where we anchored. On the 4th
we sent out baidaras in pairs, with workmen to see if there
were any inhabitants on the islands. Two baidaras returned
the same day from one direction and reported that they had
seen no islanders. They were followed by one of the last
two baidaras which had been sent to inform us that they had
met a number of inhabitants; later the remaining baidara
returned [1793: on the 20th], bringing along one of the
islanders. I entertained him to the extent I felt it was
necessary, presented him with gifts and after several
conversations sent him back the following day. He returned
later and remained with us right up to my departure
accompanying us on all our trips, never once betraying us
and even warned us against some wicked residents of the
island who had planned to take our lives.* Their wicked
intention could be seen from their actions, which will be
described further. On the third day after our arrival
[1787: the day after] at the island, three men from the
group of people we had seen for the first time, and who
are called Koniagas, came to us in three baidaras. We
welcomed them on board with signs of friendship and
pleasure and exchanged some furs for goods which they needed.

During their stay on board on August 5th [date omitted
in 1787 account] there was an eclipse of the sun which
began at 2 o'clock in the afternoon and lasted 1 1/2 hours.
The Koniagas, like other people who have no idea of the
cause of this manifestation, were greatly amazed, however
nothing untoward happened at the time.

On August 7th I once again sent four baidaras with
workmen to examine possible hunting sites and also the
island itself, instructing them to go as far as possible.
On August 9th, approximately 40 versts from the harbor,
they saw a great number of savages gathered on a single
large rock which was inaccessible from the seaward side because
of steep cliffs. This rock was five sazhen high on one side
and more than seven on the other. The men I sent tried to
persuade them [1787; 1793: the savages] to be friendly
towards us, but they paid no attention to this and
threateningly ordered us to leave their shores if we
wished to remain alive and never to dare sail past them in
the future. Having been informed about this I immediately
proceeded to the spot with the workmen who were with me,
and attempted to persuade them to stop this resistance
and agree to friendly relations, assuring them that we on

---

* This native collaborator, so useful for Shelikhov's cause,
may have been Kashpak, referred to in a traditional
account. (See p. 13.)

our part did not come to quarrel or hut them, but on the
contrary to gain their good will, as proof of which I
promised to give them presents of articles they liked in
so far as I was able. There was a great number of them
there, at least 4,000 people, and despite my assurances
they began to shoot at us with bows and arrows so that
I was obliged to move away, exceedingly worried about the
uncertainty of the outcome of these difficulties. Noting
their stubborn attack and seeing their desire that we
leave their shores or be killed, I took care to take all
possible precautions against a surprise attack. On
[August] 12th, right at midnight, when the workmen were
changing guard, a great number of the Koniags [1793: these
savages] left their rock and attacked us so viciously that
it was possible to believe that they might fulfill their
intention. In truth it would not have been difficult for
them to achieve this if we had been less cautious and more
fearful. The probability of imminent death gave us vigor,
yet even then, defending ourselves with our firearms, we
barely managed to make them retreat. The battle lasted
about another hour. When the sun rose we saw none of the
attackers near us, not even the dead, for they had carried
them away. We, on the contrary, were so fortunate that none
of our number were killed or wounded, which I attribute
solely to God's providence.

Afterward a fugitive came to us, who had been a
captive of the Koniags [1793: the savages], the natives
of Taiagu [1793: Tagagu] (whom the Russians call Fox
Islands Aleuts). He told us that for the past few days the
savages had been expecting reinforcements from Kiliuda,
Ugashin, Ugatak, Chinigak [1793: Iliuda, Ugashik, Ugaatak,
Chinnigak] and many other places in great numbers and after
joining forces they intended to attack us from all sides,
both there and on the ships in the harbor, killing each and
every one of us. He said that the reverse they suffered
had not frightened them, but on the contrary had stimulated
them to greater efforts to defend themselves. They had
decided that should any of us remain alive we would be
divided amongst them and made slaves, and our property
shared as well as the timbers of our vessels which they
consider precious and expect to seize.

Seeing our danger and the ferocity we faced [1793:
from these savages] we decided to forestall their intent
and seize the rock previously mentioned on which they had
settled as in a fort, before their reinforcements arrived.
In the meantime the Koniags [1793: the savages] kept on
raiding us. This, together with the fact that our numbers
were in no way equal to the multitude of theirs, forced
me to approach their stronghold with all my men with the
intention of dislodging them and [we opened fire] but as
it did them no harm and they repulsed us with a vicious
barrage of arrows, I then found myself obliged to use the
five 2 1/2 pound guns [1793: 2 pound guns] we had brought
with us. I gave orders to aim at their dwellings and the

sharper rocks, so that in damaging them we would frighten the
savages to a greater extent because they were unfamiliar with
this type of weapon. In truth this novel and unusual
occurrence, more than the actual harm caused, soon frightened
and horrified them and caused them to come to absurd
conclusions about us. They then ran away, abandoning their
fortress to us without us losing another man, although five
were severely though not mortally wounded. Although I had
made every effort not to shed blood I cannot believe that
we did not kill some of them. I tried to verify this, but
in vain, as they carried their dead away with them or threw
them into the sea. We captured more than a thousand of
the Koniags [1793: of the savages], while the rest, of whom
there were no less than 2,000 [1793 and 1812: 3,000]
scattered. We brought more than 400 captives to the harbor,
freeing the rest. I chose one leader from the prisoners,
whom the Koniags call a khaskak, then placed all the others
under his command. I supplied them with a baidara,
baidarkas, nets and all other necessities, but took 20 of
their children as hostages as a pledge of their good faith.
These captives wanted to settle within 15 versts of the
harbor, which I permitted. Time proved them to be faithful
allies and through them we leanred that we had been in grave
danger with the possibility of total annihilation by the
reinforcements the Koniags were awaiting from other settlements. A great multitude of these savages were nearing the
fort when they were met by those running away. The latter,
grossly exaggerating, assured them that we had all changed
into flames and were destroying their dwellings and rocks
with our arrows. They awed the newcomers so much that they
too fled.

Yet, despite this they soon tried to attack us again,
with the exception of the captives whom I had settled. One
windy and rainy night an enormous number of them gathered
and violently attacked the baidaras standing in Ugatatsk
[1793: Igatatsk] Bay. They attacked from all sides with
arrows and spears, but gunfire repulsed them again. Whether
any of them were killed is unknown. On our side, although
six men were wounded, they rapidly recovered. One cannot
say that our baidaras escaped unscathed, as the Koniags
pierced them with spears. There were so many such hits that
some baidaras had up to a hundred punctures. Their direct
attack was just as ferocious.

I had already been warned about the aggressiveness of
the Koniag people and why they had been able to repulse or
annihilate all traders visiting them. However, my zeal for
the interests of the Highest Throne [1793: of my fatherland],
encouraged me to overcome the fears instilled in me by those
who had been here previously, the news of those who had
visited the Cape on this island, called Agaekhtalik, and
hunters I had met in the course of business, who had themselves suffered from their cruelty. I disregarded all the
warnings about them and as the general agreement with my

partners, Captain Mikhail Sergeev Golikov* and the Kursk merchant Ivan Larionovich Golikov, stated that the first duty was to pacify the savages in the interest of the government, I persuaded my workmen to engage in my enterprise. The Koniag expected not only to drive us off Kykhtak Island with ease, but not to leave a man alive, should we resist them with determination, or otherwise to parcel us among themselves as slaves, as they usually do in their incessant wars between various kin groups [pokolenii, or tribes]. The war captives are used for various labor tasks, their captors considering that they have become their property in perpetuity. They took into consideration 1) our small numbers - 130 people in all. 2) The success they had in 1761 when a hunting vessel belonging to another company had accidently anchored at Cape Agaekhtalik intending to winter there. Not only had the savages kept these men within a five verst limit of their vessel, but having deprived them of any possibility of hunting succeeded in forcing the vessel to leave ahead of time.** 3) In 1776 they drove off a vessel of the Kholodilov company, which had also anchored there, in eleven days. 4) In 1780 on the same Cape Agaekhtalik, a vessel of the Panov company under the command of navigator Ocheredin passed this way and although the crew had intended to spend the winter here, they were finally forced to flee to save themselves, after great suffering and loss of many men. 5) In 1783, some 300 hunters from various companies based on the Fox Islands outfitted three vessels and set off for the North American coast under the command of navigator Potap Zaikov. They reached the North American shores in late August and decided to winter in Chugatsk Bay, called by Cook "Sandwich Sound". Because of their numbers they thought they would be able to withstand the savages, but discovered their mistake. The inhabitants did not let them get near anything to hunt, nor were they able to go even one verst in small groups and without arms. No sooner was the winter over than they fled, forgetting all their plans and having lost a number

---

* [1793 ff.; not in 1787 ms.]: Captain Mikhail Sergeev Golikov died in St. Petersburg 27 January 1788 at the age of 41. On his tombstone in Bol'she-Okhtensk cemetery was placed a marble headstone on which among other things was stated in verse that he:

For the benefit of society expending his fortune
Through exploration increasing the Honor of Russia,
Built ships which found the [passage] way from Okhotsk
    to Northern America
He left a map of these places on a copper plate
Which testifies to the glory of Golikov's and his
    companions' labors.

** This lends credence to Kodiak having been discovered by Pan'kov (with the ship Vladimir) in 1761, rather than by Glotov (Adrian i Natal'ia) in 1763. (R.P.)

of men who died from starvation. These men, hearing of my intention to go to Kad'iak Island, did all they could to frighten me off, describing the natives as bloodthirsty and unreconcilable. They [mentioned] the past episodes as well as their own experience on Cape Chugatsk at the hands of inhabitants who are of the same origin as the Koniags. However, I paid little attention to all this and scorned all the dangers in order to fulfil the company's aims and my own.

The attacks upon me, described above, gave us little hope that we would be safe in future, especially as they never failed to attack our baidaras sent out to explore, even though they sent us hostages after each attempt. As we intended to spend the winter on the island inhabited by them, demonstrating through our generosity, hospitality and gifts that their own savagery was responsible for their lack of peace and killing one another, and also to show them a mode of life of which they were ignorant, we made every effort to build houses and a fort, even though it was of wattles to begin with.

We were successful after much labor, but as they continued to attack the baidaras I sent out to survey and describe the area, and ourselves, I decided that in order to avoid much bloodshed and protect ourselves, we should demonstrate the power of our gunpowder. I had a hole bored in a huge rock, filled it with gunpowder, attached a musket lock, tied a very long rope to it, led under another rock for the protection of the one who was to manipulate it, and then before a great number of peaceful Koniags, simultaneously with one musket shot, blew it to bits. The rumor spread everywhere about the amazing strength of our arrows.

After this demonstration and other marvelous yet frightening incidents which they could not explain, the Koniags of the island abandoned their efforts to force us out. I explained to them that I wished to live in peace and friendship with them, not carry on a war, and that had my intentions been otherwise they would not have escaped the force of my arms. Besides, our most gracious Sovereign wished to protect them and given them a safe and peaceful existence. This, together with numerous examples of kindness and small gifts, pacified them completely.

Through the interpreters I tried to instill in every way possible a realization of peacefulness, greatness, power and beauty of everything in Russia and the clemency of our Empress. Taking note of the reports about all this that had been spread, and their curiosity, I increased my efforts to assure them, sometimes verbally, and sometimes showing them things which they were prepared to worship had I not explained them, gradually getting them to understand the ignorance in which they were living. Thus, slowly, I earned their goodwill to such an extent that they finally

began to call me their father. Showing these signs of
their faith in me they willingly put themselves under my
authority.

They considered miraculous the speed with which our
houses were built, because they labor for several years
over the building of one hut, planing the boards with
sharpened bits of iron, and value them highly. Their
ignorance is so great that when we set out a Kulibin
lantern* on dark nights, they thought it was the sun which
we had stolen and attributed the overcast days to the same
reason. I was saddened by such incomprehension and did not
wish to leave them under so erroneous an impression. I
tried to the best of my ability to explain to them that it
was made by people just like themselves except that they
would remain in ignorance until they became peace loving
and copied our customs and way of life.

I showed them the utilities and advantages of Russian
houses, clothing and dietary practices. They saw the
labors of my workmen when they dug up the vegetable
garden, and sowed and planted seeds. When the produce
ripened I ordered it to be distributed among them, but in
using the foodstuffs they exhibited no other reaction than
surprise. I ordered many of them to be fed on food
prepared for their own use by my workmen, to which they
are very partial.

My conduct towards them increased their devotion by
the hour, and they did not know what to do to please me.
They brought me a great number of their children as
hostages, even though I neither asked for them nor needed
them. However, so as not to make them discontented I
accepted many of them while I gave suitable gifts to others
and sent them back.

When they had become so devoted to me I tried to find
out something about their divine services. I found their
hearts were not contaminated by worshipping idols. They
recognize only two beings in the world, one good and one
evil, to whom they attribute all sorts of absurdities in
keeping with their ignorance and wild state. Learning of
this I experimented in telling them as simply and clearly
as possible about our law [1793: ~ about our Christian law].
Noting their great curiosity in this matter I decided to
make use of this opportunity in my free time and so began
to teach those interested [a true understanding about our
law, trying to lead them to the path of truth. So
successful was I in touching their hearts that before my
departure I had converted forty people to Christianity],

---

* A lantern with a reflector, which amplified a weak source
  of light, invented in 1779 by Ivan Petrovich Kulibin
  (1735-1818).

who were baptised according to such ritual as is permitted
without the participation of a priest. I noted that these
converts began to despise their brothers and what is most
amazing is that having accepted the customs and manners
of the Russians they began to mock the other savages,
considering them ignoramuses compared to themselves.

As I received many of them in a room we had built
there, they saw the portrait of Her Majesty our Noble
Sovereign and several books which I used. Noting their
desire to know that which seemed amazing to them, I tried
to explain with all suitable reverence about Her Majesty.
I told of Her kindness, power and might and how fortunate
those people consider themselves who follow Her orders and
are protected by Her laws and how unfortunate are those
who try to escape these laws or act contrary to Her orders.
I particularly tried to instil in them an understanding
of the peace and safety of every individual, that all can
go anywhere they wish alone without fear that they might
be attacked or their property seized.

I chose these words, or rather this unimportant
example so that they could understand easily. And in fact
it impressed them so much that they asked me to drive off
anyone who might come to the island, and entrusted themselves to my protection, promising to hear and obey me in
everything. These poor people, coming to my settlement and
seeing the obedience of my workmen who obeyed my orders,
thought there could be no one greater than I. I led them
away from this unfortunate misconception, making them
understand that I was the lowliest of Her Majesty's
subjects; there are others whom She invests with the power
to watch and see that no one is hurt or oppressed. I
explained in every way possible how fortunate they will be
if they learn to love Her Majesty our gracious Sovereign
and are faithful to Her, and how She could punish them
should they act otherwise.

Frequent conversations regarding the order among
those living in Russia and our buildings aroused so much
curiosity that forty people of both sexes expressed a wish
to see the Russian settlements. This number included
children whom the savages gave me on my departure in order
that at least they might see everything to be found here
even though they themselves, the adults, were unable to do
so. All the above sailed with me to Okhotsk, fifteen of
them went on to Irkutsk and the remainder, having been
clothed and given suitable presents, went back on the
return voyage of my vessel.

As regards books I was unable to make anyone understand, but occasionally I sent them with written orders to
my artels at other points on the island, and when my orders
were filled according to what I had told them before they
left they thought it was superhuman. [Added to original
1787 account] For instance I sent one of them with an

order to my clerk for prunes and other dried fruit. The
messenger in tasting them on the return journey, ate half.
I saw this from the receipt and told him about it. He was
very surprised and said that this paper had indeed watched
him very carefully while he was eating but that in future
he would know how to prevent this. Wishing to test his
simplicity I sent him for the same items a second time and
seeing from the weight shown on the receipt that half was
missing, again told him so. He admitted having eaten them
but said he was amazed I should know because he had buried
the paper in sand while he was eating and evidently the
paper could see even through sand.

A second example. There was a large mirror standing
in the room I had built. When the savages came up to it
they were amazed to see people so much like themselves in
it and could not understand who these people might be,
saying it was sorcery which they could not understand.
[End of added passage.]

In this manner I began to lead them to an understanding
of books, promising to teach their children should any of
them be willing. Several brought their children,
entrusting them to me so that they could learn what they
considered great wisdom. I must give credit to these
people on the keenness of their mind, for the children
learned their lessons quite quickly and some of them learned
to speak Russian so well that at the time of my departure
there was no difficulty in understanding them. When I
left there were 25 boys learning to read who were much more
willing to be with the Russians than with their savage
fathers. Thus I tried to lead them to an understanding
of their own ignorance. I continually battled my workmen
who were always ready to pick a quarrel, and finally
succeeded in showing them the benefit they themselves derived.

The savages, having learned of the power of my written
messages asked me for what might be called tickets when
going to distant hunting grounds, in order to show them to
any of my artels they might encounter as proof that they
were friendly and peaceful.

Protecting them with my men from attacks by savages
from other places, I gave them an understanding of how
pleasant it is to live in peace, for after that their
enemies did not dare to make further attacks. When they
saw that their services did not go unrewarded they wanted
me to reamin with them forever. I can say, and am proud
of it, that when they heard of my impending departure they
grieved as if they had lost everything. However I had
entrusted all the affairs to my manager, the Eniseisk
merchant, Samoilov, whom I left behind trusting that he
would follow my example, and in addition supplied him with
many written instructions.

According to information received from the savages
prior to my departure, although they cannot give any

absolutely precise account of the number of peaceful
Koniags, who are completely well-disposed towards me from
their stories and from the conclusions I have drawn
myself, one can almost certainly count on over 50,000
persons of both sexes devoted to Her Majesty.

I had never mentioned the payment of iasak [a tribute
in furs] to them so as not to arouse their suspicions or
cause a stumbling block. I only tried to give them a good
opinion of the Russian people and gradually introduce our
customs, so that the natives should not be repulsed by
them, but, on the contrary, accept them, leaving it to the
decision of higher authority to decide how to act in regard
to the collection if iasak.

In 1785 scurvy was noticed among my workmen, which
finally became so acute when winter was only half over they
began to die and the remainder became very weak. News
of this spread all over and it was noted that distant
savages began to hold gatherings. We received this information from friendly Koniags, who added that these natives
were planning to attack us and so without waiting further
instructions from me they had dispersed them, bringing the
ringleaders to me who admitted their guilt. I then
decided it was necessary to keep them here under guard.
On April 9th I sent one of the Russian workmen [1793:
sent the Russian Rasetnyi] with 1,000 peaceful Koniags
(who in their zeal to serve me had volunteered to accompany
this man to insure his safety) to the Unga Islands, called
by Bering the Shumagins. I asked him to contact the
companies located there, notifying them by letters about
the outbreak of scurvy among us and all other mishaps and
asking them for any aid they could give. However, after
my messengers left the scurvy began to abate.

On May 2nd I sent 52 Russian workmen in four baidaras,
11 Fox Island Aleuts and 110 Koniags in baidarkas to the
east with the intention of becoming acquainted with the
people living on the islands lying along the American coast
up to the Kinai and Chugatsk Bays, instructing them to
investigate possible resources, make necessary descriptions
and then to continue the journey as long as summer made it
possible. [In 1787 edition, omitted in later editions: The
enclosed plan shows how far they got.]

This party returned towards the end of August, having
sailed along the north side in the strait between the American
coast and Kykhtak Island. Throughout the summer they were
attacked either by the Koniags, the Chiugach or the Kinais,
and these peoples even gave them 20 men as hostages. As
regards trade, at that time it was practically insignificant
because the inhabitants of that area, being unacquainted
with us, were afraid to make any transactions, even though
they had given hostages. Having reached Kykhtak Island,
this party settled down to spend the winter, choosing the

Karlutsk locality, a well-populated spot. During the
winter they travelled in baidaras along the northern and
western coasts of the island, and along the American coast
from Katmak [1793: Iukat] to Kamyshatsk Bay. By their
peaceful dealings with the inhabitants and constant
kindness accompanied by treats and gifts they made them
allies, took hostages and traded with them in such a
manner that there were no disagreements whatsoever.

All winter long I sent out of the harbor parties along
the southern and eastern shores of Kykhtak Island and to
the islands lying along these shores. They made friends
of any Koniags by kindness and trade, took hostages, and
made firm their acceptance of subordination to the Russian
state.

Towards the end of December I sent two of my men with
an interpreter to Kinai Bay, under the guise of traders,
to gather information. I gave them some trade goods to
exchange and entrusted their safety to the toion or kaskak
hostage from Shuekh Island [1793: to the hostage Askak].

On January 10th, 1786, I sent eleven workmen from the
harbor to go to the east side of Kykhtak Island to a spruce
forest about 160 versts from the harbor, close to the
Chinigatsk [1793: near Kinaigatsk] settlement, to make
boats [shliupki]. These men, first building winter quarters,
completed their assignment, purchased a quantity of furs
and returned to the harbor on May 1st.

On February 25th I received a letter dated February 19th
from the Greek Evstrat Delarov of the Katmatsk [Katmai]
settlement advising that our company's galiot Sv. Mikhail
had sailed from the harbor of Unalashka Island on May 12th,
1785, according to my instructions. Contrary winds kept
it near Unalashka for six weeks, then having lost a mast
broken below the crosstrees during a storm, it was obliged
to return to Unalashka. After the mast was repaired the
vessel set sail again in August, only to suffer another
accident as soon as it put out to sea. An error by the
assistant navigator caused the galiot to be damaged on
rocks, forcing it to winter in Unalashka. However, 30 men
in baidaras were sent to our assistance. These were also
delayed by storms, and spent six weeks on the American coast
where six died of cold and hunger. The rest, as the above
mentioned Greek Delarov states, were saved by the men sent out
by our company, but upon arrival in the harbor five of these
died.

While preparing to leave America, on March 7th I sent
a party of 5 Russians, accompanied by 1,000 Koniags of
Kad'iak and adjacent islands and 70 Fox Island Aleuts,
serving voluntarily for pay, towards Cape St. Elias to
complete the survey begun the previous year, and to build
a fort on that cape. Serving voluntarily for pay, [those
in the party] are to aid the Russians in everything, including

the persuasion of the local inhabitants, down to 47 degrees,
to live in peace. I instructed them to place crosses along
the shore, and to bury broken pottery, birch bark and
charcoal in the ground.

The men I dispatched sent me two men from the Chingatsk
settlement in the latter part of March informing me that the
toen of Shuekh had turned traitor and had killed the workmen
and interpreter I had entrusted to his care, who were to
have surveyed Kinai Bay. [They] asked me for men to help
defend themselves against up to 1,000 Kinaitsy, who had
come from the American coast to Shuekh. Upon hearing this
news I sent out from the harbor two parties, the first
consisting of 30 Russian workmen with one man in charge, the
second with a special [manager] consisting of Koniag and
Fox Aleuts who were serving us voluntarily, instructing them
to occupy a position suitable for a harbor on Afagnak
opposite Shuekh Island and build a fort according to a given
plan. In the meantime at the harbor the galiot Three
Saints was to be readied for a voyage.

On May 19th I received information from Afagnak and
Shuekh Islands that following the joining of our forces the
enterprise of the Kinais was annihilated. The fort on
Afagnak was begun, and finally following my instructions
another at Kinai Bay, after which they proceeded along the
American shore to Cape St. Elias and beyond [1793: omits
"and beyond"]. A special party of men was left behind to
complete the buildings.

Afagnak Island and the American coast opposite it as
well as Kad'iak Island have the best harbors, the land is
fertile, there are many fish and birds of all kinds, the
fields are covered with grass and pasture lands, there is
plentiful timber suitable for shipbuilding and other
construction on Shuekh Island and the American coast nearby.

This year a far greater number of Americans and island
residents visited all our artels, paying either ceremonial
visits or just dropping in. No opportunity was lost to
demonstrate our friendship and peaceful intentions.

This year the strongest winds blew from the north and
west; there were very weak winds from the east while there
were practically no southerly winds at all during the winter.
Very little rain fell during the winter; most of the time
it snowed. Where there was shelter from the winds it lay
more than one arshin thick, however where the winds could
blow it off it did not stay.

On May 22nd I put to sea on the galiot Three Saints
escorted by the toens of Kykhtak, the American and other
islands and the best men of the Koniags. Just then we
saw our company's galiot Sv. Mikhail moving under full sail
towards our harbor. I approached it and replacing the
skipper [morekhod] instructed it to proceed into the harbor,
giving instructions to the manager, who was then on Shuekh

and Afagnak Islands, that upon his return he was to take the galiot to the harbor at the fort on Afagnak Island. Here I must mention the galiots and the premise on which they were to remain there. I instructed my representative Samoilov that one should sail in the open sea from longitude 40 to 73 degrees, counting from the meridian of Okhotsk, which I placed first in my calculations, and from latitude 60 to 40 degrees. The second was to sail north-wards, where the two parts of the world draw together, in search of undiscovered places and islands. The third, on which I sailed from Kadiak, has been converted into a transport, by means of which I shall consider it a pleasant duty to report to the government annually on the business in this area.

We then set sail from the American coasts with the intention of passing 45 degrees latitude and to sail west along this line until opposite Kamchatka Cape, then turn towards it and after passing through the Kurile Strait, sail towards Okhotsk. I intended to do this in the hope that I might come upon some unknown islands along the route between 40 and 50 degrees. Unfortunately, however, all summer long the winds blew continuously between southwest and west,* which prevented me from carrying out my plan and I therefore had to sail as directly as possible towards Okhotsk. However, even there contrary winds were against us.

During this voyage we saw the Islands of the Four Mountains and Amukhta. Because of active volcanoes the latter seemed to be enveloped in flame. Tacking we saw Siugam [sic], Amlia, Atkha and other Andreianov Islands. On July 30th we reached the first Kurile Island and there anchored for the first time. As twelve of my Russian workers were very weak from scurvy, all the duties of sailors were carried out by the Americans who out of curiosity had sailed with me to Okhotsk. On July 31st these men also brought 40 barrels of fresh water on board the galiot from the first Kurile island.

As for the sea, the only fact worthy of mention is that near the Kamchatka coast the current is very strong and the turbulence is so great that even when there is no wind, the vessel rolls so badly that the decks nearly touch the water.

On August 1st the galiot entered the first Kurile strait. Great winds delayed us here until the 5th, when we passed through the second Kurile strait into harbor. We left on the 7th, veering towards the Bol'sheretsk estuary, and anchored opposite the estuary on the 8th. I went ashore in a baidara and sent it back, remaining to buy

---

* Thus in 1787 version. 1793 and later editions omit "southwest" through error.

fresh fish. After performing this task I wanted to return
to the ship, but various matters prevented this. Meanwhile
strong winds tore the galiot from its anchor and the
weakness of the men on board made it impossible to come
about, which separated me even further from the vessel.
Finally I hired a boat [bot] and set off towards the
Bol'sheretsk settlement, which I reached on the 15th,
intending to go to Okhotsk overland with three horses
which I purchased here for 200 rubles.

However, at this time information reached Bol'sheretsk
that on August 9th an English vessel had anchored in
Petropavlovsk harbor and would remain there for no more
than twenty days. Wishing to find out where this vessel
was from and the reason for its voyage, and hoping to
obtain some information which might be useful to us, I
decided to postpone my trip to Okhotsk and visit
Petropavlovsk harbor.

I left on the 20th on horseback and reached my
destination on the 23rd. The Englishmen, noting my arrival
with several men, hurried to come ashore in a boat
[shliupka]. The captain and two officers treated us very
kindly and persuaded me to leave the customs house [kazennyi
dom] and go on board the vessel, where they showed me
samples of their merchandise and told me that they had
brought letters from the [East] India Company to the Kamchatka
authorities stating that they wished to commence trading in
Kamchatka and that the company requested permission from
Russia to do so. Without letting them know who I was, I
tried to find out where they had come from and where they
had sailed. They did not try to hide their maps from me,
and I found out that they had sailed from Bengal at
latitude 23 degrees north on March 20th by our calendar,
from Malacca on April 16th, reached Canton on May 29th, left
Canton [1787: June] on July 28th, reached the 2nd Kurile
Island July 25th, and Petropavlovsk Harbor on August 9th.
The ship's officers were three Englishmen and one Portuguese.
The sailors were Englishmen, Indians, Arabs and Chinese.
The total crew was seventy men; the vessel was made of
red wood [krasnogo dereva - mahogany?], covered with brass
as far as the main wales, had two masts, 28 sails, was 65
feet in the keel, loaded 9 1/2 [1793: 5 1/2], and had 12
guns on deck.

While I was on board I was treated to various drinks
up to supper time and after supper at 10 o'clock the captain
of the ship, William Peters, and his officers accompanied
me in their boat as far as the customs house. He postponed
any bargaining until the arrival of the Kamchatka commandant.
On the 25th Baron Shteingel', the Kamchatka ispravnik
[Chief of Police] came, and on the 26th and 27th an agreement regarding duty payable was made through him in the
French language to the effect that whatever duty was decided
upon by the higher authority would be paid without any
argument, and trade commenced. On the 28th agreement was

reached about goods to be brought to Kamchatka in future
and what goods would be received in return and at what
price. On the 29th, 30th and 31st I took delivery of the
goods I had bargained for from the Englishmen and on
September 1st the delivery and accounting were completed.
All in all I had taken goods to the value of 6,611 rubles.
On that date I paid them 1,000 rubles and drew a bill for
the balance, to fall due in two months time, payable in
Moscow at 6% interest per annum. On the 3rd, I bade the
Englishmen goodbye and left the harbor by boat [v batakh].
The Englishmen intended to leave on the 4th. I arrived
in Bol'sheretsk on September 8th and sold all the goods I
had purchased from the Englishmen to the clerks of the
Tot'ma merchants, the Panovs and others. I received a
profit of 50 kopeks per ruble from these goods.

I left Bol'sheretsk on September 12th, and following
the Tigil coast reached Tigil fort on October 2nd, leaving
it by dog sledge on November 18th. I arrived in Okhotsk
on January 27th, 1787, in other words after the arrival
of the galiot in which I had sailed.

On February 8th I left Okhotsk with my wife once
again by dog sledge, to continue the journey, sometimes by
reindeer, in other places by horses and even oxen,
suffering untold difficulties and hardships. On March
11th I reached Iakutsk and left it the next day [1793:
on the 12th by sleigh].

[1793: the following passage added to 1787
version] After my departure from Kamchatka,
thanks to travel by dog and reindeer I was
subject to extreme and unbearable difficulties
in many wastelands where my life was seriously
endangered and I suffered paralyzing fear.
Firstly, because the Koriak bands [ordy]
between Tigil and Inzhiga seemed to us to be
extremely unreliable. Secondly, the winter
with almost no exception proved to be extremely
harsh and cold, with the cruelest north winds.
We were often caught in such severe blizzards
[purga. Note in 1793 edition: Purga, in
Russian v'iuga or metelitsa] in the wilderness
that it was impossible to travel even tied
together and we were only able to save ourselves by lying in the snow for two, three
and even five days in the same spot without
water or cooked food. As it was impossible to
light a fire, we used snow to quench our thirst
and chewed biscuits or iukola to still our
hunger while lying in the snow.

Because of such difficulties when using dogs
and reindeer and during the last part of the
journey from Aldan to Irkutsk because of the
exhaustion of the horses, which often fell,
I journeyed on foot [end of added passage]

and finally successfully reached Irkutsk at noon on April 6th.

> [1793: the following passage was added to the
> original] I consider it my duty to express my
> thanks to two worthy gentlemen who have faith-
> fully served their country and fatherland for
> many years, the brothers Timofei and Vasilii
> Shmalev, both captains, who guarded me from all
> dangers from the natives, the one stationed
> in the Tigil fort and the other between Tigil
> and the town of Inzhiginsk, where they were in
> charge of controlling Koriak and Chukchi orda
> in the Kamensk settlement. In addition I was
> greatly assisted in the success of my journey
> by Corporal Nikolai Popov of the Tigil detach-
> ment and the Koriak interpreter cossack Ivan
> Suzdalev, who accompanied me as interpreter from
> the Tigil fort to the town of Inzhiga. As Popov
> and Suzdalev have Koriak relatives I was able to
> travel in safety, for which I am much obliged
> to the gentlemen captains the two brothers
> Shmalev, Corporal Popov and interpreter Suzdalev,
> and take this opportunity of expressing my
> thanks to them, for they protected my life.
>
> I have written as much as I am able during
> my short stay in Irkutsk about my ocean voyage,
> and all measures taken to ensure benefits.
> Now I must describe the places I saw, the people
> who live there, their customs, and the animals
> and birds to be found there. The description
> follows: [End of added passage. The last
> phrase is repeated in 1793 and later editions].

Now I must describe the American islands, the people who live there, their manners, customs and clothing, and the animals and birds to be found there.

The islands lying along the American coast and extending from Kykhtak to the east and to Northeastern America are mainly rocky and mountainous. However, there are also good lands suitable for agriculture, which was confirmed by my own experiments having planted barley, millet, peas, beans, pumpkins, carrots, mustard, beetroot, potatoes, turnips and rhubarb. Everything came up very well except that the millet [1793: peas], beans and pumpkins did not develop seed and that only because they were not planted in time. There are meadows suitable for making hay, and many types of grass, and in places cattle can subsist through the whole winter without hay. I did not see any great forests; however, there are many small ones. The plants

which the inhabitants usually use as food are roots,
namely sarana, makarsha, yellow fern and dog cabbage. The
latter deserves particular mention because on islands where
there are no mice it is very tasty, whereas where these
animals exist the root is so bitter that it is inedible.

The following berries are plentiful: raspberry,
blueberry, blackberry, cloudberry, partridgeberry, guelder
rose, cranberry and brambleberry. As regards trees I found
five varieties growing from the middle of Kykhtak Island
and along the American coast eastwards, namely alder,
willow, birch and mountain ash, and to the east on the
islands and along the American shore along the bays spruce,
larches and those previously mentioned.

The following birds are to be found: geese, various
types of ducks, crows, jackdaws, black canaries called
napoiki and magpies. The call of these birds does not
resemble that of the birds of this type known in Russia;
they sing quite well though not loudly and almost sound
like a bullfinch. There are gulls, cranes, herons, snipes,
glupysh, tufted puffins, murres, cormorants and loons.

Sea animals include: sea otter, sea lion, whales,
[hair] seal; fresh water: beavers, otters. Land animals:
foxes, wolves, bears, ermine, deer, sable, hare, wolverine,
lynx, marmot, ground squirrel, wild sheep and porcupine of
special variety. Ocean fish caught: halibut, cod,
herring. The following come into the rivers: king salmon,
dog salmon, [keta] Dolly Verden (gol'tsy), khaiko
salmon, nerka salmon, loach, cuttlefish, dog salmon and a
strange type of crayfish.

The Koniag people are tall [sic - roslyi], healthy,
well-fleshed. The majority have round faces though some
have elongated oval faces. They are dark complexioned,
with black though occasionally dark brown hair; both the
men and women cut it into a ring. The wives of the leading
men differ from the ordinary women by brushing some hair
forward, trimming it to their eyebrows and having plaits.
Some have beards [i.e., tattooed chins], others have their
breasts and shoulders tattooed instead of wearing shawls.
Men, women, and girls [1787 version omits 'men'] pierce
the cartilage in their noses; they also pierce their ears and
lower lips. Some of the men, though not many, have tattooed
necks. Every man has a slit lower lip so that at first
glance it appears as if they have two mouths. Into the
hole made in the nose cartilage they insert a long bone;
those who have beads [biser] or corals [korol'ki] hang
them in their ears, nose and lips, and consider this to
be the very best decoration. They do not trim their beards,
none have shirts, they walk barefooted and at home
completely naked except that they tie a shred of animal fur
or flowers and grass in front. They wear parkas made from
sea otter, fox, bear, birdskins, ground squirrel, marmot,
otter, sable, hare, deer, wolverine and lynx. The kamlei,

a type of parka, is made from the intestines of sea lion, seals and whales. On their heads they wear hats woven from spruce roots and grasses, also curved caps from hollowed wood.

In hunting sea animals they use arrows which they throw from boards, while in war they have bows and spears tipped with iron, copper, bone or stone. They have iron axes of special type consisting of a small blade. Their pipes and knives are of iron and bone, and their needles of iron. Before we came the women made their needles themselves, and used sinews for thread; dishes are of wood, horn of wild sheep, clay or hollowed out stone. Their baidaras and baidarkas are completely covered over the ribbing with skins instead of boards, leaving but a hatch. They use them when fishing and hunting sea animals, when performing various domestic chores and travelling. They catch fish in the ocean with bone hooks with long lines made from dry kelp, one piece of which can be up to 40 sazhen or more in length. In the rivers they catch fish by making stone weirs. They spear the fish with gaffs similar to spears, in the blunt end of which is a hollow into which is placed a barbed point from bone, stone or iron, tied with sinew to the shaft. In the bays and harbors they kill red fish [blueback salmon] with arrows when they jump from the water.

They obtain fire by friction, from wood [i.e., a fire drill]; for illumination they use stone dishes filled with seal, bear, sea lion, whale or fur seal oil into which they insert grass wicks.

I know nothing about their weddings, nor anything about newborn children except that they are given the names of whoever or whatever is first met, be it an animal, bird or the like.

Funeral rites differ among the various Koniag kin groups. I did not see any rites myself and so can say nothing about them; however, one thing is correct, that some place their dead into a baidarka with his best possessions and cover this with a mound of earth; others bury the dead in the ground together with a living captive who had been the man's slave. The Kinais burn the bodies of the dead together with animal skins, brought by the deceased's relatives.

When mourning the dead they cut the hair on their heads and paint their faces with black paint. They do this for relatives, i.e., father, mother, brother, sister or other close and loved kin, and often for an unrelated person with whom they lived in friendship. However, if the dead person was disliked or was not on friendly terms, even though related, they will not wear any signs of mourning.

They do not appear to have communicable diseases, with
the exception of venereal disease which has been observed;
they know nothing of smallpox and it has never occurred
there. The people are of a rather strong build and live
up to 100 years.

They greet arriving guests covered in red paint and
dressed in their best finery, beating drums and dancing
with weapons in hand, while the guests approach as if
ready to do battle. As soon as they near the shore the
hosts rush into the water to their chests. The baidaras
and baidarkas are carried out of the water with all
possible speed and then they rush to take out the guests,
carrying them out one by one on their backs to a place
which is designated for games. There, having seated them
in their appointed places, they remain silent until all
have eaten and drank. The best and greatest honor consists
of serving cold water, after which boys serve food, oil,
tolkusha, consisting of blended fat of seal, whale and
sivuch or so called sea lions, and crushed berries, i.e.,
partridge berry, cranberry, blackberry, brambleberry, etc.
to which are added various roots and plain berries. Also
dried fish which is called iukola, and flesh of animals
and birds, whatever one happens to have best. Salt is
unknown to them. The host must eat every dish and beverage
first. Until he begins, the guests will not take anything,
which leads one to suspect that sometimes they mix in
poison. The host, having tasted a dish, passes it on to the
most important guest who, having served himself, sends it
on to the next until it finally reaches the last one. All
the remnants are returned to the first, who places them
all together, and upon their departure the guests take it
all away with them.

When the meal is finished they continue to converse,
then the games begin with drums and rattles. Some don
various and strange masks made from wood painted in various
colors, then they carry their guests into a specially made
large kazima [house] which is capable of holding many
people. This kazima resembles a small temple of crude and
barbaric architecture. Here they carry on games with all
the usual ceremonials. As long as the guests remain
there the games continue day and night without ceasing.
When exhausted the participants fall asleep where they are
and upon waking rejoin the games. When the guests decide
to leave, the games come to an end and both sides exchange
gifts and trade things. In these kazimas councils are
held and agreements and settlements made. When important
councils are held women are not permitted into the kazima.

The Koniag and Chiugach have the same language, while
the language and customs of the Kinais are completely
different.

They live in dugouts [zemlianka] with walls lined
with wood; the windows are on top, the panes made of

intestines and bladders of various animals, small or
narrow pieces being sewn together with sinew; entrance is
from below. There are no stoves nor do they light fires
because they are sufficiently warm without this. Their
bathhouses are in the same type of huts where they steam
themselves, using grasses and birch twigs. They are
heated by rocks which have been made hot in the kitchen
and brought in. The heat is intense and there are no
fumes. They are extremely fond of steam baths. They have
a communal kitchen with doors or entrance holes [laz] all
round it.

In general they live like bandits; whoever is the most
successful in thievery gets the greatest praise. They do
not have many wives, very few have two, on the contrary
a good skilled woman might keep two or three husbands; there
is no jealousy among the husbands and they live amicably
together. None of them have overland transportation nor are
there any animals suited to it. Although they have many
dogs they are not used. The inhabitants of the American
coast and other islands travel by rivers, streams, and
lakes in their baidarkas; I know nothing of the people who
live in the American interior.

They have no conception of Divinity, although they say
that there are two beings in the world or two Spirits, the
one good and the other evil. However, they have no images
of them, nor do they worship them; in other words, they
have no idols. All they can say to describe the two
spirits is to say that the good one taught them how to build
baidaras and the evil one how to damage and break them.
One can judge from this how narrow is their understanding.
In addition they frequently use sorcery and shamanism. Not
only is there no proper justice or punishment--it hardly
exists at all.

From all the above one can clearly see that they lead
lives very little different from those of cattle. Their
blood is exceptionally hot, which one can feel in coming
close to any one of the inhabitants; the women in particular
appear to be aflame. By nature they are cunning and enter-
prising, and vindictive and vicious when slighted, although
they appear to be meek. Of their general faithfulness and
righteousness I can say little because of the short time I
was there. I saw great proof of loyalty and faithfulness
on the part of many; I have also seen the opposite. When
they have an opportunity to do something which will be
profitable they willingly undertake the labor, although it
may not be familiar to them and do not shirk if they are
sure of gain. In general the people are merry and carefree.
Proof of this is their day-long games; and because of this
they live in such unbounded and continuous immorality;
household affairs are neglected, and they have no notions
of husbandry, and for this reason they have frequently to
suffer hunger and nakedness.

Regarding detailed descriptions of sea and air phenomena during our voyages and in the places where we stayed, detailed notes were kept daily. Upon my arrival in Okhotsk these were retained by the regional commandant Mr. Kozlov-Ugrenin, who I am sure will not fail to send them on to whoever they may concern if there should be anything of interest.

2.

AN HISTORICAL AND GEOGRAPHICAL
DESCRIPTION OF THE KURILE [AND THE]
ALEUTIAN, ANDREIANOV AND FOX ISLANDS, EXTENDING
FROM KAMCHATKA TOWARDS AMERICA
IN THE EASTERN OCEAN

[This portion of the 1793 edition of Shelikhov's Journey
was added, evidently by the publisher, to Shelikhov's own
account (his report of 1787), and that of his
subordinates Bocharov and Izmailov (the journal of their
voyages of 1788). Most of it is taken word for word from
articles in the periodical Mesiatsoslov which are based
on accounts of earlier voyages.]

THE KURILE ISLANDS

[From pp. 63-99 of "Opisanie Kuril'skikh ostrovov
(Description of the Kurile Islands)" in the periodical
Mesiatsoslov for 1785, reprinted in 1790, ch. VI, 63-103.
References to the original will be indicated by 1785 in
brackets.]

    [I] Shoumichu. This island is about 50 versts long
from the northeast to the southeast, 30 versts wide, and
low. In the middle of the island along the eastern shore
beside the sea is a deep ravine and rocky crags, while close
to the shore there are many kekurs [defined in footnote in
1785 version, and in 1793 and subsequent editions:] the
name for a high rock like a wall or pillar standing off-
shore or at the shoreline itself. Various metals have
been noted on the island, including silver ore which was
worked at some previous date. On the same side a river
flows into the sea. Along the northside the shore west-
ward is sandy with rock outcroppings. There is a lake in
the center of the island about five versts in circumference
from which a small river flows into the sea. In addition
to this main river there are many other shallow streams
which flow into the sea: salmon, humpbacked salmon, loach,
and [1785:] kuizhi [1793: kurizha. Probably a misprint
for kundzha, kunzha or kumzha, a type of salmon.]. When
the weather is calm, mackerel, cod and riamzha are caught
in the sea with rod and line. There is no rounded wood
[i.e., woody growth borne by a trunk] with the exception of

G. I. Shelikhov, ca. 1795

G. I. Shelikhov bust and painting

G. I. Shelikhov

РОССІЙСКАГО КУПЦА.

ГРИГОРЬЯ

ШЕЛЕХОВА

СТРАНСТВОВАНІЕ

въ 1783 году

Изъ Охотска по Восточному Окея-
ну къ Американскимъ берегамъ,

Съ обстоятельнымъ увѣдомленіемъ объ
открытіи новообрѣтенныхъ имъ острововъ
Кыктака и Афагнака, и съ пріобщеніемъ
описанія образа жизни, нравовъ, обрядовъ,
жилищъ и одеждъ тамошнихъ народовъ, поко-
рившихся подъ Россійскую державу : также
Климатъ, годовыя перемѣны, звѣри, домаш-
нія животныя, рыбы, птицы, земныя про-
израстѣнія и многіе другіе любопытные
предметы тамъ находящіеся, что все вѣр-
но и точно описано имъ самимъ.

Съ чертежемъ и со изображеніемъ самаго
мореходца, и найденныхъ имъ дикихъ людей.

ВЪ САНКТПЕТЕРБУРГѢ 1791 года.
Иждивеніемъ В. С.

Title page, 1791 edition

Колумбы Росские презрѣвъ угрюмый рокъ
Межъ льдами новый путь отворятъ на Востокъ,
И наша досягнетъ въ Америку Держава,
И во всѣ концы достигнетъ Россовъ слава.

Frontispiece, 1791 edition

Three Saints Bay, Kadiak, 29 June 1790

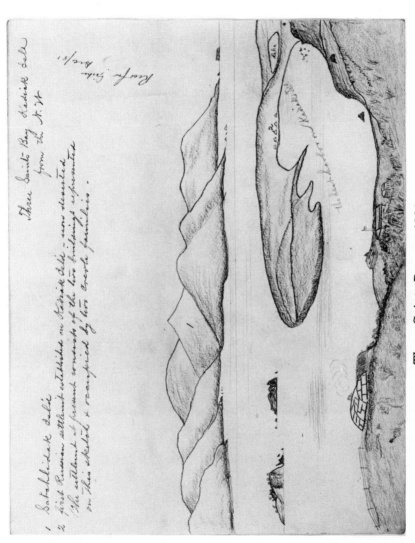

Three Saints Bay, ca. 1881

Tomb of Shelikhov, Irkutsk

small alder, willow, and creeping cedar which bears small
nuts. The waves throw whales and different sorts of
crustaceans onto the beach.

Sweet grass grows on the island which is made into
wine, kupren [probably kiprei - willow-herb or rose-bay],
and dog cabbage, also morkovnik [carrot root] which the
natives use for food, and nettles which the women make
into ropes and nets. There is a great variety of mice
which they call naush'chichi.

There are 44 iasak-paying people on this island.

[II] Poromusir or Poromushir is the second island,
separated from the first by a strait about two versts
wide, where a vessel could anchor in case of need but not
in complete safety, as the bottom of this strait consists
of rocky mountains. If through some mischance the vessel
is unable to remain at anchor it can be subject to extreme
danger because the shores there are steep and rocky and
it is impossible [to avoid] them because of the narrowness
of the channel. Such a mishap occurred in this strait
in 1741 when a government vessel perished there. This
island extends from the northeast to the southwest; it is
twice as large as the first, is mountainous, and has
many streams and lakes. There are no forests there at all
with the exception of creeping cedar and dwarfed spruce
which the natives use for firewood. For building their
yurts they gather all types of driftwood, among which
there are occasionally fairly large pieces of camphorwood.

The following grow on the island: sweet grass, kuprei
[in 1785 version, omitted in 1793], nettle, wood sorrel,
meadow sweet, chakicha and ranunculus whose roots they
steep, powder and smear on their arrows to poison animals.
The island has red foxes, wolves and a great variety of
mice of all types. There are 76 iasak-payers on this
island.

[III] Shirinki is about 20 versts from the second
island, separated by a strait which can be rowed across in
about 4 hours on a quiet day. The whole island is
surrounded by cliffs and crumbling rock so that there is
no place where large vessels can come alongside. One can
land on it on calm days using baidaras to hunt animals
for food and birds for clothing. The birds are called
ara [murres]. The island is about 40 versts in circumference and is about equal in length and breadth. There
is a round sopka [conical peak] on the island, sea lions
and seals are to be found, however, red foxes are only
brought there on ice floes from other islands. Sarana
root grows here, upiava, usut, kutash and sweet grass.
There are no berries with the exception of shiksha; the
timber consists of small creeping cedar and alder. There

are no flowing rivers, brooks or well heads, only holes
and furrows filled with rain water, which is used by the
Kuriles who come here to hunt. They are endangered by
rocks constantly falling from the cliffs, which not
only kill men but even birds, so for this reason the
island is uninhabited.

[IV] Makan Rur Asy [Makanrushi]. This island is about
60 versts from the third one, 20 versts long, 10 versts
wide. The shore is surrounded by mountains which form
ranges and among them in places are meadows. A quantity
of maroshka and shiksha grow here. There is no timber
other than cedar, alder, creeping cedar and mountain ash.
The following roots grow: sarana, upiava, mitu, kutash,
cheremsha [a type of onion] and sweet grass. Off the
island, there are a few sea otter, seal and red foxes.
There are no lakes or rivers but a large number of springs
along the shore. There is no suitable harbor for boats,
let alone large vessels.

[V] Anakutan or Anekotan is about 35 versts from the
fourth island, about 100 versts long and 15 versts wide.
There are [1785:] three [1793: two] peaks on this, the
first surrounded by smaller ones and ridges; the Kurile
people call it Asyrmintar, which means that it has
previously been burning. It stands on a cape towards the
second island surrounded by cliffs and high mountains,
here there are glupysh and murres. On the cape to the
east right in the strait is a large kekur where there are
also glupysh and tufted puffins. The second peak stands
in the middle of the island and is called [1785:] Amkausyr
[1793: Amkausar] which also was active at one time.
Beside this volcano is a lake 4 versts long, and 2 versts
wide; there are no fish in it. There is a third mountain,
called Toorusyr, close to the cape by the sixth island.
It stands in the middle of a lake about 15 versts in circumference; in which, as in the first lake, there are no fish.
There is no useful standing timber here with the exception
of creeping cedar, and small alder. Edible roots to be
found are mitu and usut; berries are shiksha, blueberry,
honeysuckle, mountain ash and cloudberry; meadowsweet
grass and a small amount of sweet grass. Sometimes there
is a fair number of red foxes on this island; however,
sea otters and seals are scarce. On the north side there
are six sandy coves, on the east side in the middle of the
island one; on the other sides are rocky bays and landing
places which baidaras can enter. Rocky streams flow from
the mountains and in the ravines on the island. At high
water golets and humpbacked salmon go in there.

[VI] Ar Amakutan, i.e., Sarannoi or Kharamokatan, is
the sixth island about 6 versts away from the one described
above. In the middle of the island is a volcano which was

formerly active. On the north side of this volcano is a
lake 5 versts long and 2 versts wide; there are no fish.
There are two rocky islands on this lake, on which are
seagulls and geese. On the eastern side of the volcano
are two small lakes which in Kurile are called Tontou and
Rui. The following roots grow there: sarana, mitu,
upech', kutash; sweet grass, meadow sweet and wild onion;
the berries are shiksha, cloudberry, and mountain ash;
the timber is creeping ceder, alder and small ash. There
are two streams on the island; the one on the north falls
into a sandy bay; the second flows west; neither has fish.
The shores of the island are rocky. There is a peak on
the east side towards the strait off the fifth island;
the base and top of it consist of white sand. On this
island there is a small number of red foxes, sea otter and
seal. Kurile natives come from other islands to hunt them
using nets made from nettle and shoot them with bow and
arrows. The crags on this island contain metal similar to
iron and also another sparkling metal imbedded in a white
rock.

[VII] Syaskutan or Shiiashkotan is an island about
50 versts away from the one mentioned above. The current
between them, caused by incoming and outgoing tides, can
be very strong. It is about 80 versts long and 5 versts
wide. There are two stony [volcanic] peaks on it; one is
in the northeast edge and in the Kurile language is called
Sinnarka. It was formerly active and is shaped like a
ridge where one can walk [? - kuda khodiat peshie]. Near
this volcano are tall stony mountains and rock strewn
places. The second volcano, a large one, stands near the
top of the northwest shore. It is stony on both sides and
from the very top to the shore is hilly. In the middle of
the island there are sandy coves on both sides, apart from
these there are no other suitable landing places nor are
there any low lying places among the mountains. From this
island, bypassing the next two, one comes directly to the
one called Mussyr about 35 versts away.

[VIII] Ikarma or Egarma. This island is about 12
versts from the previous one; it is about 8 versts long.
There is a volcano peak on it which is intermittently
active. Its shores are sandy in places and rocky in
others, sulphur springs are visible on the rocky shore and
one can land on the sandy shores by boat. There are neither
lakes nor streams on this island with the exception of some
springs. The following root plants grow there: upeg,
sarana, kutagarnik, sweet grass, meadow sweet. The timber
is small cedar, alder, willow and ash: the birds are
geese and gulls, and glupysh and tufted puffins are on the
rocks. Of animals there are only seals and sea otters
and those are scarce.

[IX] Chirinkutan or Chikurkotan, 30 versts from
Ikarma, is about 15 versts in length and breadth. On
the ocean shore it has a smoking volcano down whose slope
rocks come constantly. The whole island is surrounded by
mountains and rock cliffs, so that there are no suitable
landing places for baidaras. All kinds of grasses grow
on it; in places there are patches of small alder. The
following birds breed there: murres, tufted puffins, and
glupysh, also small black birds with red beaks and a high
feather on the top of the head, called kurikury, also
another smaller bird, also black with white eyes, red beak
and three feathers on the head like three little horns
called turutury. They sing sonorously and live in holes
in the ground where they hatch their young. Both these
birds are to be found on the cliffs and rock clefts. The
Kurile people come here from Syaskutan Island in the summer
to hunt them, using their skins for making clothing. They
especially prefer glupysh skins for this purpose. When
these birds are still young and unable to leave their
nests they are caught by hand. The fat is rendered and
stored for winter use; they are so fat that there is
practically no flesh on them. When the glupyshi are
hatching their young it is dangerous for a man to approach
the nests because they regurgitate and spit out fat as
if it was water, they also feed their young with it,
gathering it from the sea. Their nests are found on hill-
sides in thick grass. The toporok [alca arctica] weaves
its nests on cliffs, clefts or in the ground. When caught
they bite severely, they feed their young on fish similar
to herring, which they catch in the sea.

[X] Mussyr or Egakto. This island is separated from
the one above by a strait about 35 versts wide. It is 3
versts long and wide. Near it are two large rocks or
kekurs on which breed seagulls and cormorants, which the
Kuriles call chiromussyr [1793: churomussyr], and on the
other rock sea lions, which they call syaso [1793: syiago].
This island is rocky, and has neither streams nor springs;
water remaining after rains is dipped out of holes. The
landing there is rather poor. Near this island there are
many sea animals--sea lions which breed here. In June there
are many calves and the Kuriles come here to hunt from
various islands. The big ones are shot with arrows or guns
while the young are clubbed. Their meat is used for food
and the skin of the young for shoes and clothing. There is
no wood on this island so that the Kuriles bring both wood
and water for cooking food with them.

[XI] Rakhkoke or Rakhkoti, the eleventh Kurile island,
is separated from the one above by a straint of 120 versts;
it is about 20 versts wide and long. It is now uninhabited
and consists of one peak or [volcanic] cone; from former
descriptions it is evident that on it once grew grasses,
in which birds lived, that all of its cliff was strewn with

rocks and earth and almost a third of the cone was torn
away and scattered around the island. At the present time
some say that in 1777 it burned and the peak was scattered
from that. Where formerly was a depth of 13 sazhen, now
there are sandy shoals, on which lie and breed sea lions
in great number, but birds, not having nesting places,
have left.

[XII] Mutova, or Matousa Island is 45 versts from
the one described above; in length and width it is about
30 versts. On its south side is a very high smoking
volcanic peak, which often throws out hot stones; at the
north end are steep drifts or slopes and level places, on
which grow grasses as in fields: sweet grass, meadow
sweet, kutagarnik, kislitsa, shchavel'naia and other types,
and, as the other islands, various saranas. Moreover, on
this island grows grass higher than a man, its hollow
stem is thick, with round and wide leaves like a hat, so
that a man among them cannot get wet from rain. The
timber on this island is small alder, cedar and mountain
ash. Of animals there are only foxes. The sandy shore
of this island abounds in bays and baidara landings. Near
the island there are sea otters and seals. They are
hunted by the same Kurile peoples who hunt on the islands
mentioned previously. A variety of birds breed on the
cliffs. There are no rivers with fish at all. Next to this
island lies another one which is low without any ridges,
on which grow all sorts of different grasses. There are
also many sea birds. Geese moult here and are hunted by
the Kuriles, who dry them. On this island there are 63
iasak payers, 85 women, 14 children of male sex and 28
of female sex.

[XIII] Rasagu or Rashaua, the thirteenth island, is
about 40 versts from the one above, it is about 30 versts
long and wide. There are some high ranges on it surrounded
by steep cliffs; the shore is rocky, there are few sandy
places. Along the slopes and top of the range grow good
birches, alder and cedar, while below the hills and in
level places there are all types of grasses, including a
fairly tall one with large leaves. Except for a few foxes
there are no animals on this island; all kinds of sea birds
breed on the cliffs and rocks; there are sea otters and
seals near the island. The small number of inhabitants
living on the island resembles in manner and way of life
the Kuriles of the first islands and speak the same
language.

[XIV] Usasyr or Ushishir Island is separated from
the thirteenth island by a strait about 17 versts wide;
the width and length of the island is about 25 versts.
It consists of two small islands; the shores of the first
consist of cliffs, which resemble a ravine the surface

of which is flat with steep slopes. In places grow all
kinds of grass; in the center there is a quantity of
cloudberry; there are no animals of any kind. The side
of the other island nearest the strait is low and grassy,
changing then to high ranges. On the east and north
sides are cliffs, in places intermingled [with] kekurs.
On the south end there is a bay like a round lake; in the
center of it are two small islands with valcanic peaks,
while in the mouth of the bay stands a large kekur. Among
the grasses on this island is the tall one with large
leaves, sweet grass, meadow sweet, kutagarnik, wood sorrel
and various types of sarana. The shore around the bay is
sandy, near it and near the seashore are hot and boiling
springs side by side. Near the large springs is a deep
ravine where sulphur and saltpeter accumulates and breaks
off in large lumps. There is a lot of it strewn on the
shore. This island is treeless. Around, about the mountains
and ranges in low lying areas many different sea birds breed
such as murres, glupyshi, tufted puffins, cormorants,
kurukury, turutury, various gulls, grey geese and a bird
about the size of a sea swallow with greyish feathers on
its back and wings, white belly and crooked beak which
is called kacharka [1793: kagarka]. The Kuriles come
from different islands for the summer to hunt them and
live here until autumn. They dry the birds they take and
render fat from the glupyshi.

[XV] Ketoi is the fifteenth island and is 36 versts
from the aforementioned. It is 30 versts long and 10
versts wide. It has ridges and mountains with white cliffs.
Below the rigdes and slopes grow birches, alder, mountain
ash, cedar, creeping cedar and especially a thick reed with
joints and a strong wood similar to spruce, on which grow
red berries with pits similar to yew; the Kuriles call it
raima. Below the slopes on the low places, depressions
and along the shore there are various grasses, among
them a tall one on a thick stem with large round leaves,
meadow sweet, sweet grass, kutagarnik and plenty of sarana.
On this island are white foxes, silver, cross [sivodushki]
and red foxes; near the island are sea otter and seals,
but in small numbers.

[XVI] Semusyr or Shimushir, an island 30 versts from
the 15th, is 130 versts long and 10 versts wide. There
are 4 volcanic peaks on it, one of which stands close to
the cape facing the 15th island. It is called To-eto-kusyr
in Kurile; reeds grow thickly at the foot of it, and
birches. There is a bay cutting into the cape about 10
versts long and 3 wide; its mouth is about 200 sazhen wide,
only seals are to be found there. The second volcanic
peak, which the Kuriles call Itaikioi, is flat on top. It
was previously active, which is the reason why the creeping
cedar trees and edible roots at the foot of it have been
burned out. The third volcanic peak, called Ikaimikot, has

a ridge to the east, it is rocky at the base. The fourth
volcanic peak is Aneiusy; on it are found the stones
which are used as arrowheads instead of iron blades. At
its base stand mountains and tall rock cliffs. All along
the shore around the whole island are rocks and cliffs.
On the eastern side are three small sandy inlets, but
because of their shallowness and rough waters they are not
suitable landing places for baidaras. In the middle of
the north side there is a bay convenient for landing.
There are no lakes or fish bearing rivers with the
exception of some small springs; root crops, grass,
birch and small reeds are the same as on the previous
islands. Animals are brown foxes, cross and red but of
poor quality, and a few sea otters, seals and sea lions.
The berries are mountain ash, shiksha, and cedar nuts
annually. It is about 20 versts from this island to the
next through a strait.

[XVII] Chirpooi, the seventeenth island, is 25
versts long and broad and is divided by a strait about
4 versts wide. Here on kekurs breed murres and tufted
puffins. The first part of the island is locally called
Repunki Girkosy. It has a volcano which once threw rocks
all over the island. A cape of this island stretches
towards the strait of the sixteenth and is called
Tonukarasy, which means that from it one looks across
the strait. There is a sandy inlet here, but because of
the continually rough water it is dangerous even for
baidaras to moor here. There are few red foxes on the
island or sea otters and seals around it. There is
a sufficiency of edible roots and cheremsha as on the
other islands. There is no timber here except reedy
growth of mountain ash. There are no streams on this
island, only one spring, whose water tastes sour like
kvass, yet when it is heated the sourness disappears.

A small islet has separated from this island; it is
about 10 versts long. On it is a volcanic peak stretching
into a ridge. It is smooth; at the foot of the peak are
mountains and rocky cliffs. Because of the rocky shore
and constant high seas there is not a single landing place
for baidaras. Towards the strait of the eighteenth
island right on the cape stands a rock and there is a
small bay where there are many sea lions in summer. There
is no timber, or lakes or rivers with the exception of
small springs. There are the same type of roots and in
the same quantity as on the other islands. From this
island to the next the strait is about 25 versts.

At a distance of 30 versts from this island between
north and west is yet another islet, a round one called
Sivuchei; it is about 12 versts long. It has a peak
which has at its base high mountain ridges and very high
cliffs; the timber is creeping cedar, alder, willow and
mountain ash; each year there are abundant berries, cedar

nuts and the same roots as on the other islands. The shore
around the island is rocky and the cliffs are high, there
is a fair number of sea lions around the island but few
sea otters or seals. Along the cliffs live murres, tufted
puffins, glupyshi, sea gulls and geese in good numbers.

[XVIII] Urup, the eighteenth Kurile island, is 25
versts from the previous one; it is about 200 versts long
and 20 versts wide. High ranges and mountains are spread
all over this island; the surface is bare rock, rubble and
cliffs, between which are valleys and deep streams. On
the northern end of the island there is low lying area for
about 5 versts, where various roots grow; close to this
island are four small ones close to each other. Along the
ridges, in the valleys and above the rivers through the
entire island, as well as on the whole northern and
eastern shores, there are good tall stands of birch, alder,
mountain ash and willow. Among them grow raima and another
type of tree similar to the birch. The leaves are the
same but it differs in hardness and blossom, which is similar
to that of the cheremukha [bird cherry]. In all the
mountainous places grows creeping cedar and very thick
growing reeds in places, each reed of the thickness of an
ordinary cane. From the ridges flow good streams which
in the summer are entered by gol'tsy, kunzha and gorbusha
salmon. On the north side in the middle of the island is
a large lake with a river from it running into the sea.
Various species of sea fish enter it. Near the sea, in
the ravines, in the valleys and along streams grow tall
grasses; the high grass with a thick pipe [bamboo], sweet
grass, from which wine is made, kutagarnik, morkovnik,
meadow sweet, wild onion, various types of wood sorrel,
shore pypei and other marsh grasses, while in dry places
there are various flowers, zveroboi [St. John's wort], various
types of sarana and roots called mitu and chakicha in good
quantity. On the north side field peas grow in places, in
parts the soil is black and moist. The berries are
mountain ash, and a large sweet shipishnik [possibly
shipovnik - wild rose?]. There are red foxes and whitish
ones as well as very many rats. Near the island there
are bays in many places which can serve as landings for
baidaras, while on the south side of the island is one
where any type of vessel can anchor. Along the island on
the south end as well as in the north end veins are visible
in the cliffs similar to silver ore, while in other places
the veins are various, whitish and red. The nobleman
Antipin who was on this island took three rock samples
with him to Irkutsk and upon testing them Mr. Karamyshev
found one to contain copper pyrite [mednaia kolchedannaia
ruda] ore mixed with quartz which can yield 10-15 per 100.
Another was of steelbearing density, pure chalcopyrite
containing mainly [burnable] sulphur and some iron with
an admixture of flint quartz. This chalcopyrite can be
used to make sulphur, green vitriol and red paint. In
the third is grey sulphuric chalcopyrite containing a very

small amount of copper imbedded with gornosal'naia rock
with small admixtures. Around the island there are sea
otters and seals; they are hunted by hairy Kuriles
[mokhnatye] from the islands of Etortu, Kunasyr, Chikota
and others [1785: nos. 21, 21, 22]; they remain here
until August and some winter here.

        [XIX] Etorpu Island is 30 versts from the afore- ✓
mentioned. It is 30 versts in length and breadth. This
island is dotted with mountains, ridges and high volcanic
peaks, one of which on the northern end smokes continually
and sometimes throws out flames. The surface of the
ridges consists of bare rock, rubble and cliffs between
which are rifts and deep rivers. Along the rivers and on
all the rest of the island there are stands of thick
trunked birch, alder, mountain ash and tall willow;
between this grows raima and other trees similar to birch.
There are also reeds on this island, the thickness of a
walking cane [bamboo], along the level places grow
grasses and flowers. The soil is moist and black, which
would probably be suitable for growing every kind of grain.
In the fields and on the cliffs beside the sea grows a
variety of grasses, sweet grass, shalamoinik, kutagarnik,
wild onion, wood sorrel and a tall grass with large leaves
on one stem. On the south side almost from the middle of
the island along the mountains and in level places grow
larches; individual trees are not very thick near the
sea but further inland become suitable for construction.
There are quantities of black bears, sables, foxes, and rats
and other pests in the woods. The whole shore of the
island consists of wide inlets and bays with sandy headland with cliffs, streams fall into these bays from the
ridges, which are entered during the summer by the same
types of fish as mentioned on the previous island. The
streams which run to the north side are entered by all
types of fish in the summer and in September and November
have keta and silver salmon. On the same side near the
north end is a large lake with fish, with a stream
running into the sea. On quiet days the following fish
are caught by fishing lines from baidaras: cod, halibut,
rianzha and other fish. The bays of this island are
inhabited by large families of Hairy Kuriles, 92 men,
117 women, minors 28 males, 72 females. There are only
small numbers of seal and small-sized sea lions around the
island. The shortage of other sea animals is compensated
by whales and large killer whales which are thrown out
onto beaches.

        [XX] Kunasyr or Kunashir is an island about 40
versts from the above named. It is 150 versts long and
50 versts wide. Along the island are volcanic peaks and
high ranges; however, in the center there are level and
flat low-lying places. Along the ridges in the valleys
grow spruce, larch, birch, alder, mountain ash and willow,

and in places creeping cedar. Along the plains grow
spruce and larch; usable timber. In the low-lying areas
of the islands the wood consists of sparse bush growth;
there are all types of grasses, the fields would be suitable
for all types of grain. Along the shore the same type of
grasses as on the other islands grows in places; the sweet
grass is quite thick and tall. Of animals there are
black bears, sable and foxes, while in the rivers are
otters.

On the south end of this island, about 5 versts from
the ridges, is a low-lying place where pearl shells are
washed up from the sea. There are large numbers of them
lying on the sand and they are used instead of plates.
Past the headland of the bay is a large inlet from the
sea, like a lake, into which falls a stream from the
ridge. All types of fish enter it in the summer. Higher
above the cape and the low spot is a large lake from which
a stream flows into the sea. In the autumn a large number
of keta and silver salmon enter the lake through it. On
the northern side near the sea is another lake. Along
the shore the following fish are netted: cod, halibut and
others in good quantity. Among them is a type of fish
similar to sturgeon. Parts of the island are inhabited
by Hairy Kuriles: 41 men, 93 women, 27 children of male
sex and 33 of female sex. On this island a fort has been
built and surrounded by a moat.

[XXI] Chikota or Shigodan, the twenty-first Kurile
island, is 70 versts from the previously mentioned one.
It is 120 versts long, and 40 versts wide. It, like the
others, has mountains and volcanic peaks, streams and lakes.
The same types of trees grow here as on the previously
mentioned island. Along the streams and lakes live Hairy
Kuriles who catch fish in the lakes and the sea. Animals
to be found are foxes and sables. [In 1785, but not in
1793 edition: neither Ocheredin nor Antipin were on this
island because it lies on the side of Japan from the 20th.]

[XXII] Matmai or Atkis Island is 20 versts from
Chikota and 25 versts from Kunasyr. [1785: Ocheredin
and Antipin called this island Atkis.] The size of this
island is unknown and some Japanese [1785: coming there
for trade] think that it is part of the mainland, but
we cannot accept this as correct and are unsure as to
whether it is to be considered an island or part of the
mainland [1785: Edzo].

On the south end of Matmai is a small town of the
same name where the chief lives. The extent of the land
under power of the Japanese and Chinese is unknown.
Actually Matmai is possessed by the Hairy Kuriles, who
are not subject to either the Chinese or Japanese and
have their own laws. Each group of them has as headman

the eldest in the kingroup, who rule over husbandmen as
superiors, but whether they have over them a supreme head
is not known.

The Chinese and Japanese come to Matmai in ships to
trade with the Kuriles [1785: wine; 1793: vazha - mail?].
They bring clothing made from cotton and silk, laquerware,
rice, tobacco, swords, knives, kettles, axes, etc. and
in exchange get sea otter, seals and the pelts of various
animals, whales and other sea animal oil, fish, eagle
feathers, etc.

Along the shore of Matmai which we know, i.e., along
the cape stretching northward [In 1785 version, but not
in 1793: On Matmai, where Ocheredin and Antipin were in
baidaras, and where the place called Atkis is located,
the coast extends northward as a great cape...], there
are high mountains everywhere, stretching in a range
towards the east. In the middle of the island between the
ranges are valleys and wide slopes and a great number of
rivers falling into the sea. There are many bays and
inlets suitable for harbors. The following trees grow on
Matmai: oak, beech, elm and linden, birch, willow, and
many other trees unknown in Russia. On the ranges large
nuts grow, while in the fields are unknown grasses and
berries: wild strawberry, shiksha, cloudberry, wild rose.
In the woods there are black bears, moose, deer, wild
goats, small sable, foxes and hares, while in the rivers
there are otters. The natives shoot the wild goats with
bow and arrow or take them in drives. There are many
birds of all kinds on the lakes.

The Kuriles have no conception of an eternal being
[1793: of God], but they state that in ages long past
someone came down to earth from the sky in a fog. They
venerate the owl and have many small idols [bolvanchiki]
like the Mongols and Tungus. The dead are buried in the
ground and they believe that the dead live underground.

The Kuriles [1793: never shave] all grow beards
which cover their faces right from the eyes down; they have
fine hairs all over their bodies while on their chests the
hairs are thick and black. That is why they have been
called 'hairy'.

Their headmen and well-to-do people wear Japanese
and Chinese gowns [aziams] while the rest have clothing
made from bear skins or wild goat as well as clothing woven
from liak [linen]. The women sew the clothing. On the
last three islands, the people speak the same language.
When talking they often rub their beards and bellies, and
rubbing one palm against the other laugh [1785: 'ga, ga,
ga!']. They have no writing.

When eating, each householder or elder cuts up what is
placed before him, for instances, fish, etc. He puts the

first piece on his own plate, then divides the rest
according to seniority. During the meal everybody sits
meekly and silently while the elder laughs loudly during
the division.

The Hairy Kuriles on the last four islands live in
balagans [huts] built on stilts, lined and covered with
grass. If some one does in the balagan, they build a new
one in a different spot.

[The rest of the article from Mesiatsoslov, on a meeting
of the Russians with the Japanese, was omitted in the 1793
and 1812 editions.]

THE ALEUTIAN ISLANDS

[This section is from an article in Mesiatsoslov, 1781,
reprinted in 1790, p. 355 ff. References to the original
will be indicated by 1781 in brackets.]

Bering or Komandorskii Island is uninhabited; it is
low-lying and stony, especially on the southwest side.
It lies 250 versts straight east of the Kamchatka River
at 185 degrees longitude. This island is from 70 to 80
versts long, extending from northwest to southeast in
the same direction as Mednyi [Copper] Island, which got
its name because large and small pieces of copper are
washed ashore there from the sea. They are so plentiful
that it would be possible to carry on a profitable trade
with the Chinese, among whom this metal is quite
expensive. Some of these copper pieces look as if they
had previously been melted. Although this island is not
high it has many hills. The sea sometimes casts up
real camphorwood on this island as well as another wood
which is white and soft and scented. Mednyi Island lies
60 to 70 versts from the southeast end of Bering Island
and is about 50 versts long.

The number of the Aleutian Islands is unknown. [In
1781 version, but omitted in 1793 and later editions:
"however, all of those which the Aleut toion included
under the general term Khao or Sazin'ian must be included
among them. In our travel accounts their positions are
shown as follows:"] These islands lie almost 300 versts
from Mednyi Island and extend from east to south. Attak
[Attu] is the nearest. It seems to be larger than Bering
Island and lies from west to southeast; 20 versts to the
east lies Samiia [Shemya] Island while not far from the
east end lies another small island. On the south side of
the sea strait which separates these two islands is
Anatta [Agattu] which is in almost the same location and

is about 25 versts long. All these islands lie between
the 54 and 55 degrees latitude north. [The following
sentence, not in 1781 version, appears in 1793 edition:]
The inhabitants of these islands mainly eat dried fish
and other sea animals.

[The following, included in 1781 version, is omitted in
1793 edition: "But of the greater part of them we have
no information whatever. What is known is given above with
the description of the voyages of Adrian Tolstykh in 1756".]

THE ADRIANOV ISLANDS

[Subtitle in 1781 version; omitted in 1793 edition.]

    Beyond the Aleutian Islands are the Adrianov [sic]
Islands which extend right up to the Fox Islands and
supplement the chain of islands from Kamchatka to America.
These Adrianov Islands are so-called because Adrian
Tolstykh visited nearly all of them during his voyage in
1760.

> [In 1781 version, omitted in 1793 edition:
> "Past the Aleutian Islands are the Adrianov
> Islands which extend right up to the Fox
> Islands and supplement the chain of islands
> from Kamchatka to America. From these
> islands those that lie farther than the
> others to the northeast are so close to the
> Fox Islands that sometimes they too are
> regarded as part of the Fox Islands; and they
> without doubt belong to that section of
> islands which the Aleuts called Nego, and
> which the Russians call Adrianov Islands
> because Adrian Tolstykh landed on almost all
> of them during his voyage in 1760. In the
> description of the voyages of this navigator
> we have reported the description of the six
> islands almost exactly as given in his daily
> journal".]

[At this point the compiler of the 1793 edition turns back
to an earlier part of the 1781 source, pp. 325-329,
attributed therein to the account of Andreian Tolstykh,
who first visited that group of islands in 1760.
Similar information, probably also originating in Tolstykh,
appears in J. Staehlin, An Account of the New Northern
Archipelago (London, 1774), from reports made to the
Governing Senate by the offices of authorities in Irkutsk,
Kamchatka and Bol'sheretsk in the years 1765-1767.]

72

The island of Aiaga [Adak] is about 130 versts in circumference. There are many high and stony mountains on it, while between them lie bogs and tundra, but no high trees grow there at all. Vegetation is almost identical with that of Kamchatka. The berries are bear whortleberry [vodianitsa] or crowberry [shiksha], but blueberries [golubitsa] are found but occasionally. It is impossible to estimate the number of inhabitants because they continually move from one island to another in baidaras.

Kanaga lies west of Aiaga and is 200 versts in circumference. There is a high active volcano on this island where the inhabitants gather sulphur in the summer time. At the foot of this mountain are hot springs in which the natives cook their food. Otherwise this island has no fresh water and there are only about 200 inhabitants.

Chet'khina [Great Sitkin] lies 40 versts east of Kanaga and is 80 versts in circumference. There are many stony mountains on it, one worthy of mention being the so-called White Volcanic Peak (belaia sopka). In low-lying areas it too has hot springs, however, there are no streams with fish at all. Only four families live on this island.

Tagalak is 40 versts in circumference and lies 10 versts east from Chet'khina. There are few stony mountains on it and no running water with fish in it at all. Furthermore, no grasses suitable for food grow there. The shores are completely rocky, so that it is dangerous to approach them on baidaras. Only 4 families live here.

Atkhu [sic, in 1781 and 1793] lies 40 versts east of Tagalak and is up to 350 versts in circumference. Close by is a harbor where vessels can safely anchor. There are many mountains on this island with many streams running into the sea. In some of them flowing east there is quite a lot of fish. There are about 60 residents on this island.

Amlag [Amlia] is a mountainous island lying seven versts east of Atkhu and is about 300 versts in circumference. There are also 60 inhabitants here, but it has a fair landing place and is notably rich in edible roots. There are many small streams on this island, however fish are to be found only in one which flows north.

[Omitted: Besides these islands many others were visible in the east which, however, these seafarers did not reach.]

The inhabitants of this island live in underground caves [sic] where they do not make fire even in the winter. Their shirts or parkas are made from the skins of birds,

murres or puffins [Omitted: scientific names, given in
original], which they catch in snares. In rainy weather
they wear another type of garment sewn from the intestines
of seals and sea lion intestines. They
catch flounder with wooden rods and eat it raw. They
never store anything for future use so that when the
weather is stormy and they are unable to go out fishing
they are obliged to eat seaweed and snails which they
gather along the shore and also eat raw. They catch sea
otters during May and June in the following manner: on a
quiet day they go out to sea in several baidaras [sic, as
in 1781 version] and sighting an otter they fire harpoons
at it; then they draw in so close that it cannot escape.
They catch seals in the same manner. They do not change
their clothing even in the most severe cold weather.
Only when the cold is very great do they burn dry grass
and warm their clothing near it. Clothing for the women
and children is made from sea otter pelts in the same manner
as for men. Should they have to spend the night away from
their habitation, they dig a hole in the ground and lie
in it to sleep, covered by a cloak or a mat woven from
grasses. They never think of the future and are only
concerned with the present. They have not the slightest
conception of law and see no difference between decent
and indecent behavior. They differ little from beasts.

THE FOX ISLANDS

    The islands lie past the Aleutian and Andrianov
Islands. They are between latitude 53 and 55 degrees north
and between 210 and 218 degrees of longitude and so are
adjacent to America.

[The 1781 work adds: "...between 210 and 218 degrees of
longitude, and in all probability extend to America".
This is omitted in the Shelikhov volume, since it would
have shown the account to be of an earlier date. For
information on Unalashka the compiler then turns to other
sources. The wording follows closely the journal of the
voyage of 1772-1777 of the Sv. Mikhail, belonging to the
Tot'ma merchant A. G. Kholodilov. There are two versions
of this account, one of the peredovshchik Dmitrii Bragin,
in Neue Nordische Beyträge, II, 1781, 308-324, translated
by James R. Masterson and Helen Brower in Bering's
Successors, Seattle, 1948, pp. 67-73; and one by the
apprentice navigator Dmitrii Polutov, in Mesiatsoslov, 1783,
as reprinted in 1790, pp. 304-318.]

74

Unalashka or Agunaliaska is the most notable of the
Fox Islands. According to some informants it is 120
versts long and according to others it is 200 versts; it
is from 10 to 18 versts wide and lies at latitude 53
degrees 29 minutes north and between longitude 213 to 215
degrees. On the north side of this island are three bays,
one of which is called Udaga and extends along the northeastern and southwestern side almost to the middle of
the island. There are no trees here whatsoever with the
exception of creeping willow. There are about 200 tribute
paying and non-tribute paying residents. The men wear
clothing made from birds and intestines; their kamleis
and hats are of wood [sic], while those of the women are
made from fur seal. They wear bones in their lips and
noses, and beads and corals [korol'ki] of different colors
in their ears, but predominantly white. They cut their
hair in front and tie it in a bunch at the back; they
also loosen some hair at the temples. They build their
yurts from driftwood and dig them about a sazhen into the
ground. They take the following fish in the various
rivers, red, white, kizhich, golets or gorbusha salmon.
The edible berries are raspberry, shiksha, chernitsa;
there is also sarana, sweet grass, makarsha root, and
another yellow one similar to osolodka [probably sladkii
koren, sweet root]. On this island are cross and red
foxes, seal, sea lion, and a few sea otters. The
inhabitants of Unalashka go out to hunt the sea animals
and whales in baidaras in May in groups of about 100.
They shoot them with arrows from bows [sic] and with a
throwing board throw spears at them about 2 arshin in
length into which they insert a sharpened bone or stone
which serves as the blade. They tie bladders to their
arrows to prevent them from sinking.

Umnak is about 5 versts from Unalashka, it is 100 to
150 versts long, 7 to 15 versts wide. On the western end
of the north shore is a fairly large harbor and a bay in
which lies a small rocky island called Adugak. On the
south side is another one called Shemilga [Samalga].
There are no trees except creeping cedar. In the center
of the island is an active volcano, which generates hot
springs in low-lying places; the natives boil their
meat, fish and roots in them. The animals are black,
cross and red foxes, seal, a small number of sea otters.
There are 80 residents on this island, all friendly.

Unalga [1793 edition by error calls this Kigalga].
This island lies 5 versts east of Unalashka. It is no
more than 10 versts long and 1 verst wide. There is
no timber or rivers. For food there is sarana root,
sweet grass, and shiksha. There are foxes of the types
previously mentioned, and seals, but no sea otters.

Akutan is an island separated from the one previously
described by a strait 20 versts wide. It is 40 versts long
and 5-10 versts wide. It has high cliffs and no suitable

harbor. There is no timber with the exception of creeping
cedar. The animals are the same as on the other islands
with the exception of sea otters. One must assume the
same applies to the grasses and berries. There are no
fish in the streams. There are 40 inhabitants.

Akun Island is 1 verst from Akutan. It is 35 versts
long and from 10-15 versts wide. It has no harbor with
the exception of a bay on the northern side. The timber
is creeping cedar. Although there are streams on it there
are very few fish therein. Besides roots there are the
usual berries. The animals are foxes--black, cross and
red--and seals. There are no sea otters. There are 50
residents, including those who pay iasak and those who do
not.

Avatonok Island is separated to the east from the
above by a strait about 30 versts wide. It is about 20
versts long and 3 to 5 versts wide. There is no harbor.
The inhabitants, of whom there are 20, eat grass, roots,
sarana and berries. Although there are some streams
they have no fish. The animals are the same as on the
other islands. There are no sea otters. To the southeast
lies

Kigalka Island, separated by a strait of 20 versts.
This island is 20 versts long and 5 to 7 versts wide.
There are no harbors with the exception of an ocean bay
which is not suitable for vessels. There are no fish
in the streams. The inhabitants number 40, their mode of
living is the same as on the other islands. The animals
and vegetation are the same as on the others.

Ugamok Island is 5 versts from Kigalka. There are
7 inhabitants who live in the same way as the other
islanders. Of animals there are only red foxes and seals.

Kad'iak Island lies 800 versts northeast of Unalashka.
Because of the danger of attack by the islanders the size
of this island is not accurately known, however it is
supposed to be about 200 versts long and 20 to 30 versts
wide. On the east end of it is a bay with many streams
running into it; and these rivers abound in fish. In this *bay*
bay is a cove 2 1/2 sazhen deep which could serve as a
harbor for ships. The timber growing here includes alders,
mountain ash, willow and small birch, while in the
mountain ranges there are good-sized poplars from which
boats [boty] similar to the Kamchadal ones are made and
in which five people can sit. There is also a good supply
of sweet grass. The berries are shiksha, raspberry,
partridge berry, cloudberry, blackberry, blueberry, and
there are also roots. There is a plentitude of all kinds
of fish. The animals are black and cross and red foxes,
ground squirrels, [land] otter, ermine, and sable; the
only sea animals noted are seals.

The residents of this island live in yurts placed on posts, their sides planked with wood and roofed with grass; they have many kazenki [storage spaces]. Inside they are lined with wooden tsyrelki resembling worked hides [rogozhi]. The entrance is by a window covered with a pane of intestine ends. In the winter these compartments are heated with hot stones and the toens and foremost men live in them. They have clay and wooden vessels. The number of inhabitants is unknown.

[Here the compiler of the 1793 edition turns back, word for word, to the 1781 source, pp. 365-382. The material is based on the account by the fur trader Solov'ev. This account was summarized in J. L. S., Neue Nachrichten..., Bremen, 1776.]

All the islanders live in communities of about 50 people although occasionally of up to 200 or 300, in large underground yurts or caves which are from 60 to 80 arshin long and 6 to 8 arshin wide and 4 to 5 arshin high. The roofs of these dwellings are latticed and are first covered with grass then earth. In the roof are two or three openings and in some even five or six. They clamber in and out through these using ladders. Each family has a separate compartment in the cave marked by posts. The men and women sit separately while the children lie on the ground and their feet are tied so that they can learn to sit on their haunches [gokke, from German Hocke?].

Their dewellings are much cleaner than those of the Kamchadals, and although they do not light any fire, it is so warm that the men and women usually sit naked. Should they become chilled while away from home in the winter, upon returning they set fire to dry grass which they put-in for future use in the summer, then stand over the fire and in this manner get dressed in their skin tunics. It is dark in their dwellings so they keep a light in large oil lamps, especially in winter. These lamps are made out of stone and have wicks made from stems or sitnik. This shaped [vytochennyi] stone is called chaduk.

The islanders here are of middle height, yellow in body, faces flat and hair black. The men shave their heads all round with a sharpened stone or a knife, however they leave a small circle of hair right on top which hands to all sides. Some men grow beards while others shave or pluck the hairs out by the roots. The women trim their hair level with their foreheads in front and tie the rest in the back (of the head) in a bunch.

They make patterns on their faces, backs, arms and arm pits; these are first pricked out with a needle and then rubbed with a type of black clay. They cut three

slits in their lower lips, inserting a flat bone or a
small colored stone in the middle one while in the other
two side-slits they insert long sharpened bones which
reach up to their ears. They make similar slits in the
nasal cartilage through which they thread some small bones
which causes their nostrils to be always extended upward.
They also make slits in their ears in which they wear all
types of decoration, or beads, also pieces of amber which
the residents of the various islands barter from the
inhabitants of Alaksa Island [sic] for arrows and stones.
The men wear tunics made from bird skins reaching to their
knees, putting them over their heads. These tunics
appear to cling to the body in front and back. In rainy *kamlei*
weather they wear an outer garment or kamlei made from
the bladder and other interior parts of sea lions and
whales, which they blow up and dry.

The clothing of the women is cut in the same manner
as that of the men and differs only in that it is made
from the skins of sea otters and bears. These skins are
tinted with a certain kind of red earth [ochre] and
tightly sewn with gut. In addition they decorate their
clothing with an edging of sea otter and leather fringe;
[they] wear beads around their necks. They sew with
bone needles using sinew thread.

Caps

Some wear caps made of bright bird skins with parts
of the tails and wings left intact. The ordinary caps which
they wear when going fishing or hunting have a small flat
piece of wood sticking up decorated with sea lion root
teeth [i.e., molars] or strings of beads, which they have
obtained by barter from the Russians. During their
festivals they wear even better caps.

[The compiler of the 1793 edition continues to borrow from
the 1781 account. From this point the compiler of the
latter account takes only occasional bits from Solov'ev,
skipping ahead in J. L. S. (Coxe, 1787:141) to borrow
from the accounts of the fur traders Ocheredin and Popov.]

Among themselves they barter sea otters, clothing
made from bird skins, tunics made from intestines, large
sea lion skins which are used for covering the baidaras,
wooden hats, arrows and thread made from sinew and from
deer [caribou] hair which they obtain from the Aliaska
Peninsula. Their household goods consist of square-shaped
buckets and large tubs made from wood cast up from the
sea. Instead of axes they use curved knives made of stone
or bone. However, they also have metal knives which
doubtless they received from the Russians.

Sometimes they obtain flame by striking two flints
together over sea otter underfur [down-pukh] mixed with
sulphur or over dried leaves. However, their usual method

78

of obtaining flame is like that of the Kamchadals, namely
they make a hole in a board through which they thread a
stick and rotate it at great speed until the wood beings
to catch fire then catch the spark on trut (a twist of
tinder).

They have two types of **watercraft**, large and small
ones. To the first type belong the baidaras, sheathed
in skins and having oars on both sides they can accommodate
30 to 40 people. The small ones are similar to the
Greenland boats [boty], they are made from very thin
lathes and are generally sheathed with leater which covers
the vessel on the top as well as the sides and tightly
fits around the body of the person rowing it. Some of
these vessels carry two men, one rows and the other
fishes. However, this type of vessel appears to be used
principally by the toions; they are guided by a double-
bladed paddle, they are never over 30 pounds in weight.
In these vessels they travel from one island to
another and in calm weather go far out to sea to catch
cod and flounder with bone rods whose lines are made from
sinew or seaweed.

In the streams they kill fish with darts. Sometimes
whales and other sea animals are cast ashore which they
also use for food. They never hunt or fish in sufficient
quantity for their requirements and thus mainly eat snails,
seaweed and all else that is thrown up by the sea. They
like sarana and other roots best, as well as various
berries. They generally eat their food raw but should they
decide to have something cooked, they place the fish or
meat into a hollowed stone, cover it with another one and
then coat them with clay and light a fire underneath.
They preserve food by drying it out in the air without
salt.

They like Russian vegetable oil and butter but do
not like bread. When they were first shown sugar they
did not dare taste it until they saw the Russians eating
it themselves. Having found out that it was sweet they
hid it away as a treat for their wives.

They now, with great gusto, use snuff which they
first received from the Russians. They feed even the
youngest children on rough food, usually raw meat. When
a child cries the mother takes it to the shore and immerses
him into the water be it summer or winter and keeps him
there until he stops crying. However, this causes no
harm to the children but on the contrary strengthens them
and prepares them to withstand cold so that they can walk
barefoot all winter without suffering pain (discomfort).
They are also forced to bathe often as the islanders in
general think that this makes them braver, more enter-
prising and much more successful in catching fish.

Their weapons are bows, arrows, spears [Rugatina], and darts; these they throw from a small board like the Greenlanders to a distance of about 50 arshin. The darts are bout 1 1/2 arshin long and the shaft, which they finish rather well, quite often consists of two pieces. Formerly the blades of their spears were the same as for arrows and both were made of stone or bone but now they are usually of iron, which they get from the Russians. They work the iron between two stones, frequently wetting it with sea water; they also use it for knives and axes with which they build their baidaras.

According to the stories of aged people on Umnak and Unalashka Islands, the inhabitants never fought among themselves or against their neighbors except on one occasion when they fought with the inhabitants of Alashka. The cause of the fight was as follows: The son of the Unalashka toion had a dislocated arm. Residents of Alashka who had come for a visit to Unalashka decided to tie a tamborine to it and made him dance, ridiculing him. The relatives of the boy, feeling themselves insulted, quarrelled with them and since that time the inhabitants of these islands have lived in enmity, attacking and trying to ruin each other.

[The following from Krenitsyn and Levashov, see Coxe, 1787:216.] The inhabitants of Unalashka are less harsh in manners than the other island inhabitants and are much more polite and kind to strangers; nevertheless they carry on continued wars in which they try to gain victory through cunning. The inhabitants of Unimak are considered the strongest of all and in great numbers attack other islanders, kidnapping women, which is the main reason for wars. They especially disturb by their attacks the island of Alaksa, the reason naturally being that it is larger than the others and the most populated. They hate all Russians, considering them the enemies of all, and therefore attack and kill them wherever they can.

[The compiler of the 1793 edition here skips a page in the 1781 source from p. 375 to p. 376, and then continues to the end, p. 392. The following passage is extracted from the journal of the voyage of Krenitsyn and Levashov, in 1768-1770. See also Coxe, 1787:218-219.]

Each settlement has a leader whom they call tuku (toion), who cannot be distinguished from the others either by his dignity or by any special honors. He settles quarrels with the mutual agreement of neighbors and should he go out to sea in a vessel he has a servant called khate who rows in his stead. This is all the advantage he has over the others. [Otherwise] he works like the rest. This title is not hereditary but is given to one who either has outstanding qualities or a great number of friends. For this reason it is the one who has

80

the largest family that is often chosen as toion.

[The following is from J. L. S. See Coxe, 1787:201.]
When they are wounded they apply a certain yellow root to
the wound and fast for a period. Should they have a
headache they use a stone lancet to let blood out of one
of the blood vessels in the head. When they fit blades
onto the arrow [dart] shaft they hit themselves on the
nose until it starts to bleed and use this blood to glue
the points on.

They have no punishment for murder because they have
no judges. [Here the compiler of the 1781 work refers to
the account of Solov'ev, not mentioned in the 1793 volume.]
Should the islanders run out of their own stores during a
journey they go from one settlement to another begging
for charity or else demand assistance from their friends
and relatives.

They have no marriage rituals, each man taking as
many wives as he is able to support. However, no one has
more than four. Others satisfy their lusts in a manner
contrary to nature, like the Kamchadals, and these men
wear feminine clothing. The wives do not live together
but in separate yurts, as with the Kamchadals. Husbands
often exchange their wives for some necessity or other
and in times of famine even given them away in exchange
for a bladder full of oil. Some of these men try to get
their wives back; should they be unable to accomplish
this, especially those they were particularly fond of, not
infrequently they commit suicide. Should foreigners come
to one of their settlements it is customary for the women
to come out to meet them while the men remain at home,
this is considered a friendly sign and a proof that the
new arrivals can consider themselves to be safe. If the
host has many wives he supplies his guest with one of
them, if he has but one then he provides him with a servant
girl.

Should a husband die in his wife's yurta, she moves
into a dark cave where she lives for forty days. The
husband does the same upon the death of his favorite wife.
When a father and mother die, the children have to forage
for themselves. The Russians found many children in this
sad situation and some were brought to them for sale.

[The following, still from the 1781 work, is from Ocheredin
and Popov accounts, in J. L. S. See Coxe 1787:199.]

The islanders hold festivals quite often, especially
when the residents of one island come to visit those of
another. The men come forward to meet the guests beating
small drums [or tambourines], they are preceded by their
wives who come singing and dancing. At the end of the

dance the host asks the guests to take part in the
festivities, he then returns to their dwelling, sets out
a large number of rogozhi [worked skins] and places his
best food before the guests. The guests sit down, and
having eaten their fill, begin to enjoy themselves.

dancing

The children dance first, jumping and beating their
small tambourines, while the older people of both sexes
sing. Then the men dance almost naked with only their
front covered. They follow each other making small steps,
beating large tambourines. When they tire they are
replaced by the women, who dance fully dressed, sometimes
alone and sometimes in pairs they always carry blown up
bladders which they swing while dancing. When the dancing
ends they extinguish the fire which has been specially
lit in the yurta for the festivities. Should there be a
sorcerer present among them, he starts to perform,
conjure in the dark. If there is no [sorcerer present]
then the guests go to their hut, generally made from a
badiara and skins.

hunting

They hunt animals mainly from the last days of
October to the beginning of December during which period
they kill many young fur seals or sea bears whose pelts
are used for clothing. During the whole of December
they hold celebrations and these amusements differ from
the ones described above only in that the men dance in
wooden masks representing the heads of various animals
which are painted in red, green and black earth which
they find on the islands. During these festivities the
inhabitants not only visit other settlements but also
neighboring islands. At the end of the games they either
break the masks and tambourines or put them into mountain
caves and never remove them again. In the spring they
hunt old sea otters, sea lions and whales, while in the
summer they catch fish at sea.

Some Russian sailors maintain that the islanders
have no conception of God whatsoever, but this opinion is
unfair because one can clearly see traces of the worship
of a deity among them, though unsystematic, but as much
as one can expect from an unenlightened people.

It has already been mentioned above that during their
festivals they use sorcerers who announce they are inspired
by the Kugans or demons. If they prophecy anything they
put on wooden masks representing these same Kugan, who
according to their tales had appeared to them, after this
they dance, grimacing excessively and beat drums covered
with fish skin. The islanders wear effigies on their
hats and in addition place effigies in front of their yurta
to repulse devils and evil spiritis, all of which shows
that they too have a form of belief.

When a poor person dies they wrap the body in his
clothing or a skin mat, place it in a coffin and cover it

with earth. When a rich person dies they place the clothed
body in a small baidara together with his weapons. These
baidaras are made from driftwood and are hung on posts
which have been placed in the shape of a cross, after
which the body decomposes in the open air.

The manners and customs of the Aleutian Islanders
are quite similar to the manners and customs of the
inhabitants of the Fox Islands. At present the Aleuts
pay iasak* and are completely subject to Russia. Some
of them have already learned some Russian from the Russian
hunters. In general, the residents of the islands of
the Eastern Ocean are notably eager to learn, and come to
understand the Russian language quite quickly. [End of
selection from 1781 work, p. 382.]

---

* Iasak had ceased to be exacted in the Aleutians by
  official decree in 1788.

3.

Descriptions
of
land –

THE VOYAGE OF IZMAILOV AND BOCHAROV

Concerning the galiot <u>Three Saints</u>, dispatched in 1788
under the command of the two navigators, Izmailov and
Bocharov.

In accordance with instructions received from
Lieutenant-General and Cavalier Iakobi, the Governor-
General of Irkutsk, the Chief Agent of the American
Company, the Greek Delarov, who had been appointed by
Shelikhov, issued on April 28th, 1788, upon his arrival on
Kad'iak Island from Okhotsk where the company is based,
the following instructions to the two navigators Izmailov
and Bocharov. They were to put out to sea from the said
island on the galiot <u>Three Saints</u>, follow the shores of
the American mainland to discover new islands and bring   *new*
the islanders under the power of the Russian Empire, and   *islands*
affirm the acquisition of all the newly acquired part of
America, marking the land with signs appropriate and
natural to the Might and Name of Russia.

The two navigators, following orders, took 40 Russian
company workers, two interpreters who were natives of the
Fox Islands, and four Koniags, equipped the galiot with
stores and rigging necessary for the voyage, furnished it
with trading goods, and on instruction by the Greek   *Imperial*
Delarov, took five copper plates from Navigator Samoilov,   *Chests*
stationed here by the Company, and five copper crests which *+*
had been entrusted to Delarov by the above named Lieutenant- *plates*
General Iakobi. On April 30th, they set sail from the so-
called harbor of the "Tri Sviatitelia" [Three Saints Bay].

Using this harbor as the first meridian in our
calculations,[1] we rounded the south   side of the island
called Shelidak [Sitkalidak], then neared the eastern
promontory of Kiktak from which the little island of Ugak
is visible. On May 2nd at 2 o'clock in the afternoon, we
took a bearing of it and sailed on course, as winds
permitted, for Chiugatsk Bay. From May 3rd to 4th we
endured a violent storm from the east.

On May 5th we sighted Suklia [Montague] Island, one
of those in Chugatsk Bay which extends in a southerly
direction, the one which Bering's expedition called Cape
St. Ilia [St. Elias].[2] Due to a contrary north east
wind, we remained in sight of this island and the mainland
until the 8th, tacking, and when the wind dropped to dead
calm, approached the shore at about 9 o'clock after
midnight of the 8th.

At that time two Chiugach neared the galiot in a two-hatch baidarka and invited us to come and trade, but first questioning them about a suitable place to anchor, we lowered our two baidaras into the water and entered under tow a small strait which lies north and south by the compass. To the right of the strait is Khlikakh-Lik [Latouche] Island, and to the left the mainland. Because of a strong contrary current the galiot was unable to reach the desired spot and was forced to drop a grapnel [drek: 4 prongs] anchor in the mouth of the strait at a depth of fifteen sazhen, and tied to the shore with a hawser [perlin].

On the 9th at the end of the 2d hour in the afternoon, Navigator Izmailov, accompanied by 15 Russian workmen, set out in a baidara along the strait to survey the locality and make necessary observations, and the two Chiugach who had come by baidarka to the galiot returned to their settlement. During his trip, Navigator Izmailov visited with the Chiugach inhabitants and without going ashore conducted a conversation with them on the baidara through his interpreter.

At 5 o'clock in the afternoon the current changed its direction from south to north and with its assistance, we weighed anchor and using the topsail because of light winds, the galiot was towed by one baidara through the channel into a little cove visible to the right of the strait near Khlikakh-Lik, toward a low place. At 7 o'clock we reached the said place, sheltered from the waves by several reefs [potainiki] at the entrance. We anchored here at a depth of 8 sazhen off a sandy shore and at the same time Izmailov and his baidara returned safely also. The Chiugach came here to trade and we purchased 12 sea otters and pups, paying 8 and 9 strings of blue glass beads [bisera] for the otters plus three or four korol'ki. For otter tails and land otters [vydry] we paid 5 korol'ki each.

On May 10th we went along the strait in baidaras looking for a suitable anchorage and having spotted another small cove [Montgomery Bay?] about three versts from the first of the islands in the strait, where the water was absolutely calm, beside a sandy shore, on the right side, we towed the vessel here, anchoring at a depth of 4 sazhen on sandy bottom. Another two Chiugach visited us here. In addition to doing a small amount of trading, we learned from them that a foreign three-masted vessel [the Princesa, Martinez?][3] had recently arrived and was anchored at Tkhalkha [Hinchinbrook] Island in Nuchek Bay.

On the same day we buried one of the previously mentioned copper plates with a cross and an inscription reading "Russian territory", marked No. 7, on the south side of the strait to Chugatsk Bay, at a distance of 8 1/2 versts, on the first islet lying in the middle of

the strait, on the northwest tip of the said islet on a
bluff rising 1 1/2 sazhen, between two larches [hemlock?] (4)
of medium height. The top of the tree nearest the water
has dried up and is slightly broken. On a specially
prepared map of this voyage this spot is marked with a
dot designated "A". This plate was placed between
specially made bricks and because of the hardness of the
soil the top brick is buried about 5 vershok under the
turf. From this very spot, by compass bearing past the
strait and over a tree covered promontory, lies a bare
peak NW 34.00; on the left side of the end of the strait
leading into Chugatsk Bay is a promontory lying NE 14.00;
on the right side is a tree covered point N 18.00. There
are two rocks in the water the first N 11.00, fifteen
sazhen away, the second a lower one is on the left NE
60.00, 40 sazhen from the first rock, while the one on the
right is 4 sazhen from a rocky shallow [laida] which is
completely under water when the tide is in. To the west
is a small lake beside which the sea shore lies SW 75.00
and immediately another small islet is further along the
strait NW 19.00.(5)

On May 11th, we weighed anchor, and passed under sail
the above mentioned islet. Due to contrary light winds,
we anchored in a small cove [Wilson Bay?] also on the
right side of yet another small island [Chicken Island]
which is opposite the second one. At this spot on the
other side of the strait to the east is a bay [Sawmill
Bay?] which all types of vessels and ships could enter
without any danger and find secure anchorage from the seas.
The galiot remained here to two days due to a lack of
wind and because we were waiting for fish in the streams.
At noon on the 13th observation was taken by quadrant and
latitude determined at 59° 47 14'.(6) The lunitidal
interval was 00.24, the tide 2 1/2 sazhens.(7)

On the 14th at 2 o'clock in the afternoon, we weighed
anchor, and left the strait with a southerly wind,
proceeding farther into the gulf towards some small islets
we saw ahead, and after covering 23 versts anchored in the
bay at Nikakhta Khluk Island [Knight Island?] at a depth
of 5 sazhen. We remained here until the 17th, trading
with the Chiugach who came here. On the 17th at 10 o'clock
after midnight we raised anchor and sailed through the
strait to the northern promontory of Sukli [Montague]
Island which we neared at 7:30 in the morning of the 18th.
Due to contrary winds we anchored in a small bay. Toward
ten, a Chiugach who had been hunting seal came up to the
galiot in a one-hatch baidarka. He said he was a native
of Tkhalkha [Hinchinbrook] Island, confirmed that it had
an anchorage which had been used by vessels from other
countries, and promised to show it to us. He also said
that fish were plentiful there and that the people who came
by ship took red salmon and halibut by nets in Nuchek Bay.
Wishing to see Russian people and learn about their way
of life he asked us to take him on board the galiot.

Because of what he had said we decided to go to the island
he talked about to fish and at 5 o'clock after midnight,
we weighed anchor, rounded the northern promontory of
Sukli and with a southeast wind sailed through the strait
to Tkhalkha Island. Having reached it at 3 o'clock in the
afternoon of the 19th we entered Nuchek Bay [Port Etches],
then continued into a smallish cove, one which lies on the
right side [Garden Cove], in which, according to the
local inhabitants, a three-masted foreign vessel [Prince
of Wales, Colnett?] had lain. They said it had arrived in
the spring of 1788 and had set sail again two days before
the arrival of the galiot. We anchored here at a depth of
3 1/2 sazhen on sandy bottom; the latitude was by
observation 60° 08' 50. On the 19th and 20th the workmen
dispersed to fish the small streams in baidaras also
catching fish in likely places and in the sea. We then
proceeded further but ran into difficulties as it proved
dangerous to leave the bay even with following winds. It
was decided to cross to the other side of the bay where
the northwesterly wind would be of assistance in continuing
the journey.

On the 20th the Chiugach previously mentioned as having
asked to be taken on board, returned again, this time
accompanied by two relatives. The first, who had desired
to accompany us to Russia, left the galiot and returned to
his settlement, leaving his relatives on board. The latter
informed us that though they regretted the separation from
the first Chiugach, they would not go against his wishes.
However, they demanded that a shore of the trading goods
they had seen on board the galiot be given to his wife and
children. Upon the return of the first Chiugach from the
settlement their request was acceded to. Ten strings of
blue, five of dark yellow and 1/3 sazhen of green glass
beads [bisera], together with 27 blue korol'ki satisfied
their demands. These goods, together with his parka
which he had taken off the Chiugach who was setting out on
the voyage gave his relatives and let them return to his
settlement. As a replacement for the parka the Chiugach
received from the vessel's stores a bird skin parka and
a dimity kamleia [shirt] which he continued wearing.

On the 21st at 3:30 p.m. in the afternoon we hove
anchor and stood over to an inlet [Constantine Harbor] on
the other side of the aforementioned bay, which we reached
about the 9th hour. We anchored on the left side, near
the shore, in a small cove, at a depth of 4 sazhen with
sandy bottom, where the entrance to the mouth is on the
south. On the right side of the mouth we discerned high
rocks, there are apparently no shallows around them and
the passage is safe for vessels because even at the lowest
tide the depth of water is one and a half sazhen seven
feet [sic], the water rises 2 1/2 sazhen, the [lumitidal
interval] being 11 hours 48 minutes.[8] As the local Chiugach
did not tell the name of this bay, we named it St. Konstantin
and St. Elena.

On the north side of the bay is a creek which,
according to the local inhabitants, is the first one in
the district which a variety of red fish enter. From the
entrance, calculating from the end of the woods on the
right side of the shore to the windward northeast 60.00
at a small wooded islet from which extends straight to the
southeast 77.00 a gravel shoal [laida] seen at full tide
beside a shore slightly indented towards the mountain.
The inscribed copper plate marked No. 8 was placed between
two clay bricks under black top soil in dry yellow soil.
The top brick is about 1/2 an arshin in the ground. It is
shown on the special plan by a dot under the letter "B".
Coming from the shoal side which the plate faces, the plate
stands between three fallen trees [lesina] on the right.
The first from the shoal, a larch, is thick at the bottom.
The compass bearing to it is southeast 23.00. The second
three on the left side is thinner than the first. It has
[some holes in the trunk] and at about 3/4 sazhen slants
toward the shoal. It then straightens up again and points
[?] straight with dried branch stumps northeast 67.00. All
three [logs] are two long paces away from the plate and
are surrounded, except from the shoal side, by a stand of
rather large trees.(9)

23rd. Having completed this task and as there were
no fish to be caught, it was decided to continue along the
American coast in the galiot, particularly as the natives
said they had already exchanged all their trading goods with
the vessel of another nation which had come in the spring.
Leaving the bay at about 1 p.m. we attempted to continue
the voyage, but due to contrary southwest winds it was
inconvenient to leave Nuchek Bay; we merely crossed to the
east side, where we anchored near the exit in a small
inlet at a depth of 12 sazhen, remaining until the 26th.

On the 27th at 10 after midnight, we were visited by
the brother of the toion from the so-called Chikiik settlement on Sukli [Montague] Island. His name was Nekshulk
Atasha; he was about 50 years old and came with 5 other
 Chiugach do a little trading. Judging the trustworthiness
of the former, the commanders of the galiot decided to
hand one of the copper Russian crests into his safe keeping,
particularly as it seemed very doubtful that the instructions
of Lieutenant-General Iakobi to place the crest in a
suitable location could be carried out, as the people who
hunt and fish here, though they consider themselves as
subjects of the best amongst them, are prone to thievery,
so that it would have been dangerous to leave the crest
especially as, in addition to the above characteristics,
the islanders are so greedy for articles containing iron
that their greed would have overcome any precautions we
might take. These islanders would have dared to remove
the crest from the spot where it was placed and, as is their
custom, would have made meaningless articles from the metal
or used it for arrow heads. This was obvious because when
some of the islanders came to the galiot they, in spite

of all precautions by the workmen aboard, managed to remove the nails from the leather coverings of the scupper holes or else tore them off complete with lattice work[?]. As the faithfulness of the toion's brother gave hope that the crest would be kept in safety, the commanders of the galiot gave it to him, impressing on him that he was to give it to his brother, Toion Shenuga, who, according to the brother, lives on Tytym-Lak Island in the settlement called Cheniu. The islanders said that the toion was unable, because of illness, to visit the galiot with his other relatives and this was confirmed by his brother Atasha. Among the other instructions it was stressed to Atasha very strongly that the crest given him was the [symbol] of the Russian Empire which, caring for the well-being of the islanders living so far away, solemnly promises to maintain it; for this reason, Toion Shenuga should not only strive to keep the crest in safety but should wear it on his chest over his clothing as a sign of his faithful obedience to the Russian Sovereignty and that he should show it both to the other islanders and to the crews of foreign vessels which came occasionally. This would ensure that neither he--the toion--nor his kinsmen would be insulted by them because they would know and fully recognise that he was under the protection of Russia. It was obvious that the receiver of the crest listened to these instructions attentively, accepted it with pleasure and promised in his own way to see that the instructions were carried out. After staying on board for about 2 hours he returned to the settlement with his relatives.

Chiugatsk Bay, where the incident described above took place, is quite commodious in itself. According to the islanders, and as we could see for ourselves, there are many islands and bays within it--that is the reason many were noted on the chart with sailing directions, as accurately as possible from visual observation and verbal descriptions, and others by bearings. All these islands and shores are covered with a forest of spruce, hemlock, alder, birch and poplar. The berries here are raspberry, chernika, shiksha, currants and kislitsa. Land birds are gray geese, ducks, eagles, cranes, loons, magpies and crows. The animals include two types of bear--black, and dark yellow which are here called nuni; they have prickly, bone-like bristles and claws.(10) There are 3 types of foxes, black, cross and red; marten, land otter, wolverine, mink and beaver. The natives assured us that inland there are wild sheep--those on the galiot had seen the skins and long white wool; rabbits, deer [caribou?], squirrels, ermine and dogs. Marine animals are also hunted here, that is sea otter, whale, sea lion, [hair] seal and fur seal. They are hunted with arrows made from wood, darts and throwing boards, and bows, in the same manner as by the Kenai and other tribes. The following fish can be found in the rivers: chavycha [king salmon], siumga and many other sea fish.

The islanders here have no law and do not worship
anything, however, when giving assurances under oath they
point to the sun and use it as a witness, from which one
deduces that they worship it. Their language is the same
as that of the Koniag; they exchange hostages or have ties
with the Kenai to the west of them and the Ugalakhmut to
the east. It has been noted that this people [narod]
is cunning and crafty, prone to cheat and steal, but
firm in assurances of faithfulness, talkative but impatient
about listening to strangers' discourse.

28th. At four o'clock in the afternoon when the wind
abated we hove anchor and were towed out of the small bay
through the strait into the open sea. At five o'clock
we took on board the baidaras which had been used for
towing, made them secure and then hoisted sail. It was
seen that the Chiugach we had on board was looking for a
way to leave the vessel, however, as this was no longer
possible, when we had put out to sea, he told the commander
that he knew of a small island where there were many sea
otters and where the inhabitants of Sukli had recently
hunted. This assurance encouraged us to alter course
towards where the island lay according to the Chiugach.
For this purpose we left the island of Tkhalkha and with
favorable wind set our course West South West. Having
gone seven miles past Skuch'ev Rock[11] at 1:30 in the
afternoon of the 29th we saw the island called Achak
[Middleton] and with favorable wind moved within a mile
of it, where we stopped on grapnel. As by eight o'clock
the wind began to strengthen, and wishing to safeguard
the cable, the grapnel was raised, however two of its
arms were broken, after which we tacked near the island.

On the 30th at 4 o'clock in the afternoon we neared
the island and dropped anchor at a depth of 30 sazhen.
Then Navigator Izmailov with 17 men left in a baidara to
go ashore, taking the aforementioned Chiugach with them.
They were met by the Chiugach people on the island with
their usual dances and shouts and when the hunters and
the navigator came ashore the Chiugach did a little trading
with them, exchanging various things for Russian goods.
When the exchange was concluded, the hunters wished to get
some goose and seagull eggs to eat. Although a group of
eight of them went after the eggs they returned to the
baidara in an hour's time, because they had seen that two
baidaras loaded with Chiugach had put out to sea from the
island on which they presently were, in addition two others
right beside the settlement were loaded with people and
their property. Having taken this as a sign of ill will
towards them on the part of the islanders, the hunters
decided to take necessary precautions. In the meantime,
the Chiugach who was travelling on board the vessel also
managed to vanish. One of the toions from the local
settlement came to the vessel and although he was questioned
about the lost Chiugach through an interpreter he gave no
information. Because of this the toion was then left

beside the baidara with several of the hunters and when
four of them went to explore the island further he seized
the opportunity, audaciously whipped a small spear from
under his clothing, and threw himself on the hunter
Chernykh guarding the baidara, trying to kill him. However,
he was prevented from doing so by the agility of
Chernykh, who then could not remain without assistance
and called another hunter, Volkov, thus protecting himself
from the ferocity of the toion. Neither fear nor power-
lessness could keep the toion quiet for long. After his
first failure he once again attacked with his spear the
hunter Volkov, who having carelessly tripped, fell to the
ground. Seizing this opportunity, the toion hit him hard
in the shoulder with his spear so that although Volkov had
risen and was resisting him, he fell once again to the
ground because of the wound caused by the blow. Volkov's
companion, the hunter Chernykh, seeing this was obliged to
hit the toion with the butt of his gun. He fell to the
ground but jumped up again quickly and once again threw
himself onto Chernykh and his companion Volkov, attacking
them both with his spear until they mortally wounded him,
causing his death. After this incident, the travelling
Chiugach did not return to the vessel and upon investigation
it became known that he left in one of the two baidaras
previously mentioned back to Sukli Island. The guards,
having awaited the return of their companions who had
been walking on the island, left to return to the vessel
accompanied by one of the islanders whom they had persuaded
to come with them. They reached the vessel safely at 4
in the afternoon on the 31st. There are no woods on this
island but there are great numbers of birds such as geese,
etc., there are quite a few [hair] seals and fur seals,
but despite the assurances of the travelling Chiugach
there were no otters at all.

On June 1st, having weighed anchor, we went out to sea
and at 2 a.m. neared the island called Koiak [Kayak] which
lies very close to the mainland. The island looks as
follows. It is a high island, has white scree [osyp']
on the seaward side. At the southern tip lies a high round
pointed rock. On the south side a whitish cliff is visible,
covered with grass. About a verst from it in the sea are
two rocks just under water to the south and south east.
The island itself lies north to south. On the south side
and no further than a half verst from the end is a saddle-
like formation. Beyond it to the northern headland lie low
hillocks, wooded, and according to the statement of our
newly acquired islander it is uninhabited. Chiugach and
Ugalakh-miut come here from time to time to hunt sea otters.
To the east, close by, lies a small island covered with
grass. We doubled the southern tip of Kaiak Island, then
continued along it close in-shore but did not reach the
northern tip which was visible, and appeared to be close
because of rocks which rose above the water and past them
toward the coast the low islet. We then turned northeast
towards the mainland, a tree-covered cape of medium

elevation which looked like two small islands. Having
passed it, we once again sailed close to a low sandy
shore which was covered by trees and appeared to have snow
on the mountain crest visible in the distance. Closer to
the sea, at a distance of about five versts the slopes
appeared to be covered with mounds of white sand, black
defiles and ice-covered wet areas of land. The straight
line of the shore ran East-North and East; there appeared
to be no places suitable for anchoring vessels, and
although the savage islander did point out a small stream
from the ship where he claimed there was a settlement of
Ugalakh-miut, because the entrance was not sheltered from
the sea in any way and the southerly wind was of no
assistance we left on the 2nd, going in a southeasterly
direction from the shore. Five hours later, because the
wind shifted, we once again took a northeasterly course;
at seven o'clock after midnight, the wind dropped to calm,
and toward the eleventh hour, the weather being partly
clear, partly overcast, hiding the ranges lying ahead of
the vessel, we saw something which resembled smoke in two
places on the lowlying shore not very far away from the
vessel. At times this smoke appeared like a column, then
would suddenly stop.

On the 3rd at 1 o'clock in the afternoon we stood with
a southwest wind towards the shore straight for the place
where we had seen the smoke, however, when the vessel
drew near we saw that what we had taken for smoke was sand
blown by very strong winds. At 3 o'clock the galiot was
two versts from the shore. According to soundings the
depth here was 35 sazhen and one verst away it was 22
sazhen. We now sent four Koniags in two baidarkas towards
the mouth of a stream visible ahead while the galiot
proceeded close to shore. The baidarkas passed by the
first stream because it was too shallow, but saw another
further on which appeared to be larger than the first. At
5:30 the vessel then stood towards the mouth of the second
stream. Half a verst from the second stream at five sazhens
depth, with a top-gallant wind [a light wind], we dropped
a stream anchor [verp] with hawser attached.

Navigator Izmailov, with several men, lowered a baidara
and sailed in it to measure the depth of the river mouth,
which proved at low tide to be only half a sazhen. This
stream runs from between high rocky ranges, and divides
into two branches. The current is moderate along low lying
sandy areas, the water is muddied and sandy. The mouth is
about 50 sazhen wide and at flood tide even wider. Judging
from the marks which it left on trees, the height of the
tide was estimated to be one sazhen, judging from the
visible trees. They followed the stream inland for about
two versts, where the depth was only half a sazhen. On
the shore here they saw fresh tracks of man and with it
others similar to a dog's. There is flounder and red fish
here, seal was also seen. Between the two estuaries on
both sides lie sandy hillocks, and standing wood is

visible. Judging by the trees lying about at the estuary and along the seashore it must consist of larch [hemlock] and spruce. The baidara returned to the vessel at 9 o'clock, and because the estuary was so shallow we raised the drag anchor, set the sails and proceeded ahead.

About 10 1/2 miles from this spot at 8 o'clock after midnight on June 4th we neared a bay [Icy Bay][12] and having sent some Koniag and one Russian ashore in four baidarkas to explore, we began to tack with the wind. At 3:30 in the afternoon of the 5th the baidarkas returned to the ship with the information that they had found an inner bay and had seen human tracks on the shore. At 6 o'clock in the afternoon of the same day we neared the shore by tacking, reached a depth of 12 sazhen over sandy bottom and dropped the best bower anchor [plekht]. At 10 o'clock the next morning, the east wind blowing strongly, we hove anchor, set the sails and began tacking again. When the wind weakened at 9 o'clock in the afternoon of the 7th, we drew close to the shore and dropped the drag anchor [verp] with hawser [perlin] attached at a depth of 15 sazhen. Navigator Izmailov, accompanied by 11 hunters and three baidarkas of Koniag, explored the bay here, sailing near a low-lying sandy shore along which is a stand of spruce, larch [hemlock], poplar, willow, alder and thin birch. Here they found a creek whose estuary is about 200 sazhen wide, on the stream's right to southeast the entrance is clear, the right shore is low with small stands of trees which look like small islands. To the left a fairly large rocky promontory reaches right up to the river mouth, past it both sides of the river are low, sandy and wooded. Even at that date the river was covered with ice which was just beginning to break up. The baidaras stopped on the shore here, nearly all the hunters walked about three versts inland along the river. They saw a bark-covered hut [shalash] and signs of human habitation but found no people.

Near the bay mentioned above are the dwellings of the so-called Ugalakh-miut who continuously quarrel and fight with the neighboring Koliuzh peoples. Judging from the animal tracks seen there must be bears, wolves and foxes here. The river flows from the northeast, the current is moderate, on the right are high ridges. Here a number of [hair] seals were seen, while close to the river mouth there were sea otters which also often were seen close to the ship. At 4 o'clock in the morning, the party left this shore and returned to the vessel. The Koniags brought with them two sea otter cubs they had killed with their arrows.

As [we] could not enter the river because of floating ice, at 10 o'clock we raised the drag anchor [verp] and continued parallel to the shore which from the mouth of the river lies southeast by the compass, and upon leaving the bay sailed east by south and east by east. Along the shore is a low-lying slope [otval] and beyond it a range

with extremely high peaks.(13)   As in this part of the sea
a current flowed which was always predominantly from the
north and northeast, we stood off from the shore somewhat
and on the 8th and 9th proceeded south by east.   Due to
overcast weather the coast was visible only intermittently,
although no more than 17 versts away.

After sailing 14 miles, at 8 o'clock in the evening of
the 10th we saw a bay [Yakutat Bay] between ranges to the
north.   We made towards it, but as within half an hour we
saw a low shore which appeared like a group of islands, we
took into consideration the coming of night and altered
course to the east and northeast.   At daylight due to
contrary winds we sailed close hauled [beidevint] on the
right tack where we saw the above-mentioned tree-covered
shore.   At 9 o'clock after midnight, as the wind died
away, we sent two Russians and 4 Koniags in 4 baidarkas to
explore the bay and search for a stream to enable us to
take on a supply of food and water; the galiot followed on
light winds.

At 11 o'clock the baidarkas returned to the vessel
followed by two large wooden baidaras from the island.
These had very high pointed prows, the sterns were much
lower with the additional difference that the prows had
large round slits and three smaller holes.   Each baidara
had an upright pole in the center with otters [i.e., pelts]
tied to the top.   There were up to 15 people in each
baidara.   They wore clothing made of otter, sable, marten,
wolverine and marmot.   They also wore European clothing
apparently bartered from foreign vessels, made from thin
green serge and bright printed linen [naboika].   Having
neared the vessel they pointed with their arms to a bay
close to the above-mentioned islands.   As no one on board
knew their language we guessed that the islanders were
advising us to go into the bay.   When we threw lines down
to them they accepted them willingly and tried to tow the
vessel into the convenient anchorage.   To assist them in
the labor they took upon themselves, we lowered a baidara
from the ship with several workmen, which was supplied
with the necessities for self defence should some unfore-
seen incident occur.   An hour later two more baidaras
came from the shore and assisted in rapidly towing the ship.

At 3 o'clock in the afternoon on the 11th, we first
entered the bay and then a small inlet lying to the right
of the mainland [east side of Point Carrew].   Here,
right opposite the settlement of the islanders we dropped
anchor close to shore at a depth of 10 sazhen with sandy
bottom.   As from previous experience this did not appear
to be a very good place to anchor, Navigator Izmailov with
11 workmen set out in a baidara to find a more convenient
spot, in which he was very successful, because close to
the above-mentioned inlet he found a bay [Ankau Creek]
which was small but so convenient that it induced us to
later move into it.   From the most careful enquiries we

found that the natives call this bay Yakutat. In the
meantime, the men remaining on board the galiot traded with
the islanders and having spent the following night there,
at four o'clock in the morning were towed into the aforementioned bay and anchored in 12 sazhen on a muddy bottom.

The scattered dwellings of the islanders are square,
the outside of earch and overlapping uprights boards one or
two arshin in height which rest against crosspieces lying
on 4 posts. Above are other long boards, also overlapping
one on the other and on all sides the ends are made secure
in the form of a square, the so-called tvoril or komyn.
This komyn serves as a chimney through which the smoke
escapes. Entrances to these residences are from the side
and instead of doors are covered with straw mats or
carpets, and covered on the outside with spruce roots.

The islanders living here, as we found out, had left
their winter quarters temporarily in boats [v lodkakh i
botakh] similar to those used in Kamchatka, to obtain
supplies of food. The people here are the Koliuzh, and
their settlements are along various streams running on the
mainland. In addition to lesser toions they have one head
toion whose name is Ilkhak, whom everyone obeys without
exception. The Koliuzh assured us that this toion had come
with his subjects from his real settlement in baidaras,
and that the group consisted of 170 people of both sexes
excluding the children. He has two sons called Nek-khut
and Khink; his real residence is on the shore to the
southeast, far past Ltua Bay on the large Chichkhat
[Chilkat] River. His land borders that of the people
called Chichkhan [Chilkats].

These people, like the Koliuzh, have disagreements
and attack each other. The above named toion has under his
control all the Koliuzh who live along the shore as far
as Yakutat Bay. This bay is the farthest point under his
control and though he does not live here permanently, he
comes here every spring in baidarkas to trade and check on
his subjects. This bay is ice-covered not only up to July
26th but even later. The islanders assure us that two
fairly large rivers run into it and when the ice breaks
a great variety of fish enter. Beside this bay, as on the
Koliuzh islands, there are numerous stands of trees
similar to those described above near the ice-covered
river. The time the vessel spent in Yakutat Bay showed
that bears, wolves, wolverine, land otters, foxes, marten,
sable, squirrel, ermine, sheep, and raccoon are all found
here; there are also various sea animals, and shore and
land birds of all kinds in great numbers.

The greatest drawback noted is the lack of water
suitable for use; although we were obliged to travel a
distance of 4 versts from the bay to a river at the head
of the bay, we were unable to satisfy our need except to
catch red fish and golets, so having filled only one

barrel we travelled north and north east along the strait
between small islands to the mainland for water where
there is a special small stream containing fresh water
which is harmless and suitable for human consumption. In
every part of Yakutat Bay the air, in fine weather, is
quite warm, and it is sheltered from the winds by the
surrounding forests.

The Koliuzh living here are quite tall and dark
complexioned like the Koniag, however among them are some
blond and white. The men do not trim the hair on their
heads, but tie it in a particular spot in a bunch on top.
They paint this red with a specially made paintbrush of
sheep wool, then they decorate it with bird down. They
cut their beards and mustaches, and paint their faces in
various colors; they pierce their ears but do not cut
their lips as some of the others. Instead of wearing hats,
some of them wind around their heads and necks strips made
from thin roots which resemble hemp thread and stick eagle
feathers in the back; a few have hats which they have
apparently received from Europeans, like grenadier caps
with copper emblems. They wear clothing made with the
fur side out, like a cloak and then over one shoulder only.

Under their cloaks they always have spears [kop'ë][14]
slung over the shoulders by a leather thong [nagalishche -
probably the blade cover] with a case [blade sheath]. These
spears have a convex protrusion on one side and on the
other a piece of wood set as in a groove. They are about
two quarters of an arshin in length, in the middle they
are about 3 vershok wide, at the end and on the sides
they are sharp, they hammer these themselves on rocks.[15]
Many of them wear such spears from the belt down to their
knees, aothers like among the Tungus. In addition, they
have zapany with ties on the back, hung with geegaws on
the bottom made from bird beaks and other things. They
hunt otters and [hair] seal with the same type of blades
[nosok],[16] mainly when the animals are sleeping or on
the ice. They have special bows and arrows, but catch
fish with the same blades, weapons, stone weirs placed in
the water, and small nets.

The women wear the same type of clothing as the men,
they comb their hair with wooden combs, part it and tie
it in a bunch. They slit their lower lips the full length
of the mouth, filling the gash with a piece of wood made
like a spoon about two inches long and 1 1/2 inches wide.
They pierce from five to six holes in their ears and some
tattoo [vyshyvaiut - literally, embroider] their chins.

These people have no laws and do not worship anything,
however, they rather honor a bird, the raven, and say that
they were born from it. During shaman rites which they
hold they call on this raven when in need of assistance
and say he gives it to them. In recognition of his charity
they make an object in the shape of a raven's beak from

iron with brass eyebrows, which they carry not only during
their campaigns and games but always, and it has been
noticed that they imagine they get great assistance from
it and a strengthening of their health. These people are
coarse by nature and tend to steal; the dead are not buried
but burnt and the ashes and remaining bones are placed in
a specially made box, placed on a carved [structure] called
a lazabakh.(17) In peacetime they trade with the Chich'khants
to the east and the Ugalakhmiut and Chiugach to the west;
since 1786 they have also traded with Europeans who come
there. They greedily trade for various clothing, iron,
kettles and kuby [casks]; they are not as willing to accept
odekui [? - possibly misprint for odezhdy, clothing] and
glass beads. Right from the time the galiot arrived and
until [we] left they came daily in large and small
baidarkas with their wives and children trading sea otter
and beaver, various beaver scraps and tails, land otter,
wolverine, sable, beaver, also sable, marten and wolverine
cloaks, sheep wool, and woolen items they weave themselves,
and multicolored root and grass satchels. From the vessel
they received for their sea otters and capes different kinds
of cotton cloths, lidded [kubiki] pots, linen and other
shirts, while for the other animal skins and articles blue
and red korol'ki for earrings and blue glass beads [biser].
Because of their strong but irregular trading they are
greedy in trying to obtain as many Russian goods as
possible so that they always demand a bit extra for each
article. They have been seen to have European axes the
butts of which are narrow and the blade high. They must
have got them in trade from foreign vessels because the
local islanders said that in the current spring of 1788 a
three-masted vessel called on them and anchored close to
the bay among the islands, then, after shooting one of
island men from a pistol, went out to sea. Among the
other trade goods which this people brought for exchange
with the galiot were two boys about twelve years old, one
of them a Koniag captured by the Kenais before Kyktak
Island was occupied by the company; he was sold to the
Chiugach, then to the Ugalakhmiuts and finally became the
property of the Koliuzh; his name is Noiak-Koin. Because
this boy knows the Koliuzh and Koniag languages well, he
was bought from the trader for 4 1/4 lbs. of iron, one
large korolëk and three sazhen of glass beads [biser]. As
soon as he came on board he was used as interpreter with
the local islanders. The other boy of the Chich'khan gens,
his name is Nakhuseinatsk; he knows the Chich'khan and
Koliuzh languages and although he was not bought, the
islanders gave him to the ship of their own free will,
taking instead of him the Chiugach who had come on board
the ship, and who, not having been used to sailing on board
a ship, was obviously desirous to remain with the islanders.
He gave as a reason for going that he had previously lived
close to Koliuzh and Ugalakhmiut islanders. As will be
told of him later, when this Chiuchkhan sailed on the ship
he showed us many small rivers and Ltua Bay.

When on June 15th the chief of the local Koliuzh
people, Toion Ilkhaku, came on board the vessel and
entered the cabin accompanied by an artist who had painted
various little things on wooden boards and other articles
with natural dyes, and who had previously been on board
without the toion on a number of times, he insisted upon
seeing the portraits in the cabin and that we explain to
him in detail about them. Although no opportunity had
been lost to impress on the toion and his subjects whom
the portraits represented, we satisifed his wishes and said
that the portraits represented Her Imperial Majesty the
sovereign and most benevolent Russian ruler, the others
were portraits of the Imperial Russian Heirs, the Great Lord
and his spouse, the Grand Duchess, and still others
represented in turn their heirs, the Grand Dukes and
princes, and that many peoples are their subjects living
in the vast Russian Empire. When the toion had heard this
explanation it was noted that he was both surprised and
had taken note of what was said. After this it was
impressed on him that the Russian Empress and Her Great Heir
are most gracious. Out of their great generosity they pour
countless blessings on their faithful subjects which
increase their peace and well-being, and have constant
care for all people living close to the vast Russian borders
which are as yet unprotected with the end in view of giving
them an opportunity of seeing the benefits which can be
dervied, the ability to live in absolute security and
plenty, and that Russian protection and patronage are so
strong and unshakable that no foreigner would dare to cause
any harm to a country under such protection. As the toion
was assured that all the American land the and islands have
been under Russian protection for a long time, and in
order to impress him all the more, this was a suitable
opportunity to present him with a copper Russian crest, and
after speeches suitable to the occasion, he was given the
crest on the condition that he wear it on his chest over
his clothing, thus safeguarding both himself and his
Koliuzh subjects from foreign vessels which occasionally
visit them. During the galiot's stay in this locality we
noted that the islanders here are not as strictly controlled
by their toions as elsewhere; that is why it seemed
hazardous to leave the crest somewhere near the anchorage
harbor. It was stressed to the toion that he should carefully guard the crest and be sure to show it to any visiting
foreigners that this was demanded by his duty to the Russian
state. The toion, having listened to all the above,
accepted the crest very happily and then left for his
settlement.

On the 16th the same toion came back on board the
vessel with two elders and the crest was already sewn onto
his beaver cloak with red wool [staméd] which he had
received in trade earlier. After some remarks of greeting
he earnestly asked that he be given one of the portraits
he had seen in the cabin to perpetuate the memory of the
Grand Russian Heir. As there were two copies of the

portrait aboard the vessel, it was possible to fulfil his
desire without much difficulty. Upon the direction of the
commanders of the vessel a copy the size of a folio [sheet]
was prepared, glued on to white linen. Before giving it
to the toion, the following was written on it in Russian
and German: "The Lord the Tsarevich and Grand Duke Pavel
Petrovich, Heir to the Russian Throne, and Owner of the
Duchy of Schleswig-Holstein". Above that the following
inscription was added:

> 1788, in June in the bay called Yakutat by
> the natives, the seafarers Navigators Gerasim
> Izmailov and Dmitrii Bocharov of the Golikov
> and Shelikhov Company called here together
> with 40 men on board the galiot Three
> Saints. Thanks to the kindness and
> friendliness of toion Ilkhaku and his Koliuzh
> subjects they traded here and before leaving
> persuaded them to come under the protection
> and patronage of the Imperial Russian Throne,
> as a token they left the above mentioned toion
> a copper Russian crest and this portrait of
> the Heir to the Russian Crown, His Imperial
> Highness. It is affirmed that everyone coming
> here on Russian or foreign vessels should
> treat this toion kindly and with good will,
> taking only the essential precautions for
> safety. The above mentioned navigators stayed
> here with their galiot from June 11th to 21st,
> did not note any bad actions on the part of
> the toion or his people and safely went out
> to sea.

Having completed these inscriptions the portrait was
given the toion, who accepted it with great joy expressing
it through his usual enthusiasm and shouting. In token
of his subjection to Russia he presented us with one of
those iron things in the shape of a raven's beak which
they deem to be a deity, a bag plaited of varicolored
grass, six sea otter parkas and two painted slabs, one
of leather and one of wood which had small stones set into
it. He remained on the vessel for some time and then
returned to his settlement with the elders in baidaras.
As mentioned above, the galiot remained in the bay up to
June 21st, both to bring about the agreement entered into
with the Koliuzh and trading, and also, because the islanders
assured us that large numbers of various fish enter the
bay, to collect fresh stocks of food for the workers. We
now give the following description:

June 18th. At the mouth of the Bay, directly at the
entry on the left side there is a stony base [outcrop]
about one arshin high, and near by are four not inconsider-
able rocks. A hill, flanked by two ravines, rises directly
above these rocks. On the seaward slope of this hill,
under the roots of a large spruce tree, which hang down

the slope, the copper plate No. 9 was placed between two bricks. To the SE 47.00 of this tree, stands a second one, which leans toward the left hand valley. In front of these trees, toward the sea is a small alder thicket, while farther up the mountain spruce and larch woods are visible. The latter join [farther up the mountain] with bush growth of various small-sized and prickly woody plants.[18]

On the 21st we fired a gun as a signal of departure, weighed anchor and were towed into the large bay or strait and from thence, because of little wind, out to sea still under tow. One baidara of Koliuzh assisted us in the tow. About 6 o'clock in the afternoon, the wind blowing fresh from the east and northeast under lowering skies which lasted until the 27th, and those on board the galiot bade farewell to the Koliuzh who had been assisting them. The latter insisted that the galiot return to trade there again, in expectation of which they would prepare a greater number of furs. We successfully stood out to sea but after tacking [for a time] were obliged to go down west a certain distance. At 7 o'clock that evening we decided to sail toward and anchor in the previously mentioned icy river [strait?] in the expectation that after 18 days the ice had been carried out to sea and it would be a convenient place to get a stock of fish to replace the fish which had been taken from the home port and which was now completely spoilt due to the warm weather. Besides, the salted food was becoming onerous and unhealthy for the men.

At 8 o'clock after midnight, sailing northwest by north, we drew near the river's mouth, but because of contrary winds had to anchor at a depth of 10 sazhen on a sandy bottom. Here, when the fog lifted we saw numerous great slabs of ice being carried out of the whole estuary. At about 4 o'clock on the 26th the anchor began to drift, and as it was dangerous to remain, we hoisted anchor, set the sails, and though the wind was contrary, sailed closehauled, intending to go forward in the open sea so long as the season permitted

On the 27th we sailed with a light breeze, under fair wind, along the coast, which was continually in sight to the east. At 2 o'clock in the afternoon of the 28th we drew level with Yakutat Bay where we had been previously anchored at one mile's distance. Two hours later the Koliuzh mentioned earlier came out to the vessel in three baidaras. One of them turned back into the bay while the first two came closer to the vessel. When those in the baidara were questioned, they replied that they had come just for a visit out of friendship. However, it was obvious that the islanders had thought the galiot was not the one they had previously seen, so after staying close for a while, they turned back after the first baidara into the bay while the vessel, under full sails, moved parallel

along the shore, which was no more than 4 versts away.
This shore is low, sandy and tree covered. At 6:30 the
vessel was directly before the estuary of the Antlin
River[19] which flows through a wide valley, which cuts
the mountain range, toward the sea from the north-west,
along a lowland. On one side of this river a treeless
sandspit extends into the sea, forming a bay. Its mouth
is wide, and on both sides of the spit [the bay] is,
as we were assured by the Koliuzh boy aboard, who has
been mentioned previously, so deep that the galiot could
enter it freely and safely. The shore was low and sandy,
but inland extended three snow-covered mountain ranges.
After 2 1/2 miles the vessel drew level with the mouth of
the Kalkho River; which we sailed by at first, but were
compelled by contrary winds to return there and cast anchor.

On June 29th, Navigator Izmailov with twelve men went
to explore this river in a baidara. It flowed from the
north between mountain ranges out of two valleys full of
snow and reaches the sea along the lowest lying land.
To the east, at some distance, a forest was visible.
Towards the west there were no trees at all. The depth
of the mouth at low tide is 1 1/4 sazhen. We saw no fish
there nor were there any people there at the time although
we saw some of their tracks which were not yet covered
over. When the baidara returned to the vessel we once
again hoisted anchor and sailed on with a light following,
top-gallant, topsail [bramsel] wind, keeping in sight the
absolutely straight, but entirely low wooded shoreline.
At a distance of about five miles from the previously
mentioned river mouth, the woods along the shore ended.
Toward the end of the eighth hour we drew level with
another river, the Altsekh. There was a small islet on
the east side, and past a sandbar their was a commodious
estuary. It appeared that there was probably a large
number of Koliuzh there, but as the wind blew directly on
the shore, it seemed dangerous to go in closer. We,
therefore, passed by and close on 11 o'clock saw another
river called the Kakan-in [Muddy Creek] which flows under
a cape promontory [mys] stretching from out to sea on the
northeastern side. It is inhabited by the same Koliuzh.
Past this river the shore became uneven but sandy with low
forest clad cliffs. What appeared to be flows [uval] of
snow [glaciers] emerged from the valleys.

On July 1st at 8 o'clock in the afternoon, the Koliuzh
boy we had on board pointed out a bay past a snow flow
[snezhnyi uval - i.e., a glacier] lying ahead and assured
us that in addition to there being a plentiful supply of
fish, a large vessel had recently anchored there. We
therefore altered course, sailing directly for the bay,
and at 5 o'clock after midnight drew near the shore of the
snow flow. However, there proved to be no bay there, but
instead a sandy, tree covered shore.

On the 2nd at 4 o'clock after midnight, once again

following the assurances of the same Koliuzh, the vessel
sailed towards a cape along the shore to the southeast
which was marked by two small islands. We did not reach
it due to lack of wind, but sent Koniags in two-hatch
baidarkas to investigate. They returned after 1 o'clock
in the afternoon saying that they not only found the bay
but that there appeared to be a fair number of people
there. However, we did not dare to enter with the
vessel because of possible unknown dangers.

On the 3rd at 4 o'clock in the afternoon, we left the
Kakan-in River and seventeen miles later neared the mouth
of the previously mentioned Ltua Bay. As this place also
presented possible dangers because of our lack of
knowledge, Navigator Izmailov with 15 men was sent ahead
in a baidara both to explore and above all to measure the
depth right at the entrance of the bay. The vessel
proceeded without any sails utilizing only the current.
Approaching the bay, we set sail and sailing close-hauled
moved out to sea. Half an hour later we turned back to
the shore where we were met by the baidara and without
stopping, accompanied by the baidara, proceeded into the
estuary with northeast and northeast-east winds. After
7 o'clock we came from the side to a free-way 7 or 8
sazhen deep which runs northwest and southeast. We
continued between a rock and a birch-covered point, the
wind being north and northeast. Having passed the rock
we turned close-hauled into the bay north-northwest, but
due to contrary current we kept to the right side of the
estuary and anchored in a bay off a sandy shore at a
depth of 4 sazhen with rocky bottom. Some savage islanders
in three baidaras came to us here, but due to the late
hour we did not trade with them and put it off for another
day.

We passed the night there, but at 4 o'clock in the
morning we began to search for a more convenient anchorage,
as the one we were in seemed dangerous being so near to the
entrance, because of the rough seas coming in over the
reef at full tide, and besides the rocky bottom made it
impossible for the vessel to hold. We then fixed the tows
and towed the vessel into the interior of the bay towards
a small islet [Cenotaph Island] where, as we found out
later from the local inhabitants, a foreign vessel had
anchored a couple of years earlier.[20] Although the cove
here was small, we found a rather convenient anchorage and
so at 8 o'clock after midnight we dropped anchor and made
fast here. At first there were no islanders here, but
shortly after noon three baidaras came into view together
with several small boats [boty] coming towards the vessel.
When they drew up it became clear that this bay is inhabited
by Koliuzh. Among the comers was a toion called Taik-nukh-
Takhtuiakh who came on board with two elders and was
allowed into the cabin. After suitable greetings he asked
through the interpreter where we had come from. This
unexpected question is worth noting because when he was

answered with a statement "that he was seeing people of
the Great Russian State and that this state and the numerous
peoples [thereof] is entirely under the sovereign government
of Her Imperial Majesty, the most wise Sovereign", he
listened with obvious attention and appeared pleased. He
also looked at the portraits of Her Imperial Majesty and
Their Imperial Highnesses. Here we reiterated the might
and power of the Ruler of All Russia and finally the
toion was convinced. Aside from their usual manners,
which is natural to them, [this toion] truly deserved [our]
full confidence. His inquisitiveness promised that he would
remain steadfast. Therefore, he was shown one of the copper
Russian Crests, which was on hand, and this satisfied his
feelings [notion] about the [Imperial] powers. Consequently,
it [the crest] was offered him in the same manner as it
has been [offered] to the first Koliuzh toion Ilkhak. He
accepted it [the crest] with respect and wishing to
demonstrate his appreciation, ordered his subordinates to
bring up from [his] baidara one new [newly caught sea]
otter and six sea otter rugs. Taking them in his own hands,
he presented them on board the vessel in token of his
zeal toward the Imperial Court and insisted that his gift
be forwarded on without fail, for which purpose this sea
otter and rugs were accepted from him. Following this
incident the voyagers traded with the Koliuzh exchanging
[sea] otter, land otter, wolverine and sable for iron,
kettles, a variety of clothing, glass beads and korol'ki,
which, as with the first Koliuzh, were not too welcome
here either. With the coming of evening the islanders
returned to their baidaras and boats [boty] going back to
their settlement, which was about 1 1/2 versts from the
vessel towards the mouth of the estuary.

Upon enquiry we found out that these were not
permanent settlements but only summer ones where they
prepare for future use fish caught at sea and along the bay,
drying it as iukola. They use halibut flesh for iukola
and [fish with] rods. They have other, winter dwellings
to the west, about 3 1/2 versts distant, across the cape
from this estuary. [The settlement] is located on a stream
which flows out of a lake. We sent there two hunters and
Koniags in two-hatch baidarkas to survey the land and
obtain fish. Upon their return they said that on the river
there are quite large dwellings. At this river's mouth
there are partially submerged rocks and shallows so that
it is difficult to enter even with a baidara, and
the only fish there is weak, evidently from the natural
formation of the bottom, however, the islanders fish for
it with previously mentioned noski [spears, fish spears,
blades]. They even brought some for sale on board ship,
where it was bought in small quantity for food.

On July 5th, the Chiuchkhansk boy we had on board said
that three summers earlier a large vessel had been here
and that they had left an iron anchor behind. The local
inhabitants got it when the tide was out and had dragged

it into the forest, he even pointed out the place where
the anchor was supposed to be. On the basis of this
information and having obtained permission from the
earlier mentioned toion Taik-nukh, we sent a baidara to
the location and indeed found an anchor which they brought
back on board. It weighs about 780 lbs. and although
the top ring and the sheet iron on the arms is broken off,
the toion exchanged it for glass beads and korol'ki.

On the same date another copper plate, No. 19, was
buried between two bricks on one side of the mouth of the
above mentioned little bay, on a rocky bar extending
toward a small low point, while to the left, off the island
opposite the southern point, is a large whitish rock which
is the last and closest to the sea. [It was placed] inshore
northwest 25.00, at a distance of 8 or 5 feet to a stand
of small alder, and along [this alder thicket] in the
same direction, to a small rock, for a distance of 5 sazhen
and 6 feet, a total distance of 14 sazhen 4 feet. The top
brick was set at a depth of about 2 feet, while the stone
placed on top of them is about half way dug into the ground.
Two paces from the plate seaward to the southeast 4300
lies the other rock, larger than the first, from which the
northeast-south end of the islet in the bay is southeast
73.00. The bearings [taken] from the elevation of the
end of the large whitish rock toward the estuary are: the
tip of the tree covered cape on the left within the bay
SW 300; the bar on the right, toward the mouth [of the bay]
the tip of a wooded cape, SW 2500; the above mentioned
islet within the bay, south-southeast 7500, north 7400.
The low wooded cape inside the bay on the left-hand side
northeast 5000. The galiot stood at anchor in the cove at
southwest 7900 and it [the galiot] could not be seen across
the woody thicket beyond the cape.(21)

The bay called Ltua is of medium size; it is marked on
special maps in detail and is deep. In the deep part the
bottom is silty while close inshore along the whole bay the
bottom is rocky with shells. The shore itself is covered
with pebbles and shingle . Surrounding the bay, particularly
inland, are high, snow-covered ranges topped by stony peaks;
half way down, in the valleys and in the lowlands are woods
and other vegetation similar to that in Yakutat Bay; only
one small stream runs into the bay, and it has no fish.
We saw multitudes of black ducks [turpan] which apparently
moult here in July.

Although the inhabitants here have their own headman,
he, together with his men, is subject to the aforementioned
head toion Ilkhaku. They subsist on fish and the flesh of
sea animals, which they hunt close to the entrance to the
sea, as there are numerous sea otters, sea lions and seal.
As regards the manners and customs of the people, they
are exactly the same as the Koliuzh described earlier.

Having made provisions of water and firewood we decided
to go to the earlier spot near the estuary to hunt furs

and catch halibut. We reached it at 6 o'clock on the 6th
safely and made fast. At the mouth the [lunitidal
interval] is 1 hour 13 minutes. Here, while the halibut
was being prepared, which was easy to catch going out to
sea in baidaras, the hunters went ashore to gather malina
[raspberries or salmonberries] which could be seen nearby.
In addition, they set up a wooden cross on the spit on
the east side right at the entrance. A strong east-southeast
wind was rising and to ensure safety for the night, at
about 8 o'clock, two grapnel [drek] were dropped. In the
meantime very heavy rain began to fall. Right at midnight,
the local inhabitants cut the cable from a four pud grapnel
and took it away even though men from the ship went after
them in a baidara. Because of the dark they did not go
ashore then but at dawn tried unsuccessfully to find it
searching along the shore and in the woods. They saw the
smoke from the toion's habitation but did not approach it
in order not to offend either him or his subjects, and so
the grapnel was left behind [its disposition] unknown.

The dangers of this place, and the unsuitability of
the bottom for an anchorage moved us to go on, particularly
as the unchanging diet was causing scurvy among the hunters.
We therefore decided to discontinue our search for other
islands and return to our harbor at Kyktak, especially as
the steady southwest and west winds which were now beginning
to blow made sailing onerous and difficult.

On the 9th at 2 o'clock in the afternoon, at full tide,
we raised anchor, set the sails, and went out to sea, setting
course 58-59 degrees southwest from our anchorage strait
for Kyktak Island. However, as the strong winds and rough
seas often caused a deviation in our course toward south, we
made a slight error in our calculations. Despite this, having
sailed 135 miles from Ltua Bay, at 1:30 in the morning of
the 13th we sighted Shelik [evident misprint for Shelidak or
Sitkalidak] Island five Russian versts from the vessel.
Because of the dark night we went out to sea but at dawn
once again turned towards the shore. At 7:30, having rounded
the southern tip of this island we sailed close-hauled
toward the harbor. Due to contrary winds we did not reach
it but anchored in the shelter of the point in another bay
on the 14th. After the wind dropped, at 12 hours after
midnight of the 15th we entered Kyktak harbor safely,
under tow.

The Chief Agent of the Company, the Greek Delarov, took
charge of the aforementioned galiot once again, settled with
the men on board and stopped the further dispatch to Okhotsk
harbor. Later, when the spring of 1789 drew near, he manned
another vessel with a crew and all supplies necessary for
the voyage, provisions, tackle and a load of goods of the
American company. On April 28th the vessel set sail under
the command of Navigator Bocharov, with a crew of 28.
Sailing between 48 and 55 degrees latitude, without making
landfall anywhere because of most severe winds and storms,

the vessel successfully reached the port of Okhotsk on August 6th, where he delivered the journal, and the above mentioned maps and items previously mentioned to the local authorities and to the owner of the company, the Eminent Citizen of Ryl'sk, Shelekhov, who was in Okhotsk at the time.

Notes to Part 3

1. To facilitate reading, and avoid ambiguity, the third person plural in the published original has been changed here to first person plural.

2. Coxe (1803:304) says this misnomer was an error of "some of the Russians." The true Cape St. Elias is the south end of Kayak Island.

3. Several vessels, of different countries, cruised in Prince William Sound that summer, making identification difficult.

4. L.S. Berg (1948:216-217) points out that the Russians in North America commonly misnamed the trees Tsuga heterophylla and Tsuga mertensiana or hemlock as listvianichnyi or larch. See Polevoi (1971:158)

5. See R.A. Pierce and A. Dolgopolov, "Alaska treasure: Our search for the Russian plates," Alaska Journal, v. 1, Winter, 1971, pp. 2-7, recounting an unsuccessful attempt to find the several plates left by this expedition. Changes in elevation, disappearance of trees used as landmarks, and vagueness of the original directions have insured that most of the plates will remain where they were deposited.

6. Corrected from lat. 50°47'14", an obvious misprint. First noted by Coxe (1803:307).

7. The lunitidal interval (prikladnyi chas): the average time between the moment of lunar passage across the meridian and the next following lunar high tide, specific for each locality.

8. Sic. This figure for the lunitidal interval at that point seems excessive. Belcher gives it as 1 h. 15 m.

9. See Note 5.

10. Sic.

11. Skuch'ev Rock, probably a misprint for Sivuchii (Sea Lion) Rock.

12. Icy Bay, 16 miles long, at the terminus of Guyot and Malaspina Glaciers, 66 miles NW of Yakutat, on the Malaspina coastal plain. As stated in Orth, Dictionary of Alaska Place Names (Washington, D.C., 1967), p. 442, the bay, as seen and described in the 18th and 19th centuries, seems to have been an indentation of the Malaspina Glacier front located near where the mouth of the Yahtse River is now. The present Icy Bay was uncovered in the retreat of the glacier since 1899. The bay was explored by Joseph

Whidbey on June 4, 1794, and named by Vancouver (1798,
v. 3, pp. 204, 210, 225). However, as seen here, Bocharov
and Izmailov noted it in 1788. Purtov, in a report to
Baranov in 1794, mentions killing 500 sea otters there,
and uses the native name of Nachik (P.A. Tikhmenev, v. 2,
1979, p. 49).

13. Mt. St. Elias and adjacent ranges and peaks.

14. Kop'e, spear, is often used to describe the form
and construction of a blade.

15. This sentence refers to a stemmed spear blade.

16. Nosok, an 18th century technical term to designate
a blade, point, or arrowhead.

17. Corrected from misprint in 1793 edition, p. 57.

18. See note 5.

19. Polevoi (1971: 159) errs in identifying the
Antlin River with the Mednoi (Copper) River. However, as
he states, the Antlin River is shown on the extreme right
of the Izmailov-Talin map in the Efimov Atlas (1964, Map
183). This depicts the Antlak (Antlin), the Kalkho (?),
Alshchek (Alsek) and Kankana (Muddy Creek) rivers.

20. See J. F. La-Perouse, A voyage round the world,
performed in the years 1785...1788 by the Boussole and
Astrolabe, London, 1799, 2 v. See v. 1, pp. 364-411.
LaPerouse discovered Lituya Bay on July 2, 1786 and entered
it at great risk ("During the thirty years that I have
followed the sea I never saw two vessels so near being
lost...") the following day. He called the bay Port de
Français, hoping that a French trading post could be established there. On July 13, twenty-one of his men were lost
at the mouth of the bay. Cenotaph Island in the bay is
named for a monument erected in their memory.

21. See note 5. The Lituya Bay possession plate,
No. 19, is said to have been found in the late 1950's, and
to be in private hands. Only one other plate, No. 12, has
been found. It came to light during the excavation of
the first Russian settlement at Sitka, destroyed by the
Tlingit in 1802, and is now displayed at the Sitka National
Historic Park, though without the specially made bricks
which enclosed it.
Of the Imperial crests, which were usually placed
somewhere in the vicinity of the plates, or given to a local
chief, one is in the Alaska Historical Museum in Juneau.
Another turned up during   "archeological salvage work at
The Dalles dam site on the Columbia River. It was found on
Memaloose Island, Wasco County, Oregon. Like the one at
Juneau, it is of bronze, and it measures nine inches long
by seven and five-eighths inches wide. It is now in the
Smithsonian Institution in Washington, D.C." (Alaska Journal,
Summer 1971, v. 1:3, p. 51). It was evidently left at some
point on the coast by the Russians, and passed from hand to
hand until it ended up in a burial mound in the interior.

GLOSSARY

Flora and Fauna

Russian	English
el'	dwarf spruce, fir
elnik	spruce
ol'kha	alder
ol'khóvnik	alder grove
kedr	cedar
listviak, listviag, listvennitsa	larch (hemlock)
berézina	birch tree
bereznik	birch grove
tal'nik	willow
slanets kedrovago	creeping cedar
riabínnik, riabína	mountain ash
cheremukha	bird cherry
malina	raspberry
golubitsa, golubika	bilberry, blueberry
chernitsa, chernika	bilberry, blackberry
maroshka, moróshka	salmonberry, cloudberry
brusníka, brusnitsa	red bilberry, cranberry, partridge berry
kalína	snowdrop tree
kliukva	cranberry, bogberry
knezhenika, kniazhenika	nagoon berry, Rubus arcticus, kniagenika, brambleberry
shiksha	crowberry
smorodina	currant
zhímolost'	honeysuckle, woodbine
vodianitsa	bear whortleberry
travá sladkaia	sweetgrass
kupren' (kipréi?)	willow-herb or rose-bay
kutagarnik	dog cabbage
morkovnik	carrot root
krapíva	nettle
kislitsa	woodsorrel
shalamainik	meadow sweet
liútik	buttercup, ranunculus
shchabél', shchabel'naia	dock
sarana	martagon lily
makarsha	pink plume ?
upiava	
usut	
kutash	
mitu	
cheremsha	wild onion
paporotnoe zholtoe	yellow fern
zverobói	St. John's wort
shipishnik	(shipóvnik - wild rose?)

Russian	English
morskoi bobr	sea otter ("sea beaver")
rechnoi bobr	land otter ("river beaver")
sivuch, siuch, morskoi lev	Steller's sea-lion, northern sea-lion
kit	whale
nerpa	any small seal
tiulén	harbor seal, earless seal
kot, kotik	fur seal, sea bear
lisitsa	fox
chernoburaia lisitsa	silver black fox
belaia lisitsa	white fox
buraia lisitsa	brown fox
sivodushka	cross fox
krasnaia lisitsa	red fox
peséts	arctic fox
volk	wolf
med'ved	bear
chernyi med'ved	black bear
temno-zheltyi med'ved (nuni)	("dark yellow bear")
gornostai	ermine
olén'	deer, caribou
dikii baran	wild sheep
kunitsa	marten
norka	mink
sobol	sable
záiats	hare
rossomakh	wolverine
rys	lynx
tarbagan	marmot
evrashka	ground squirrel
belka	squirrel
ɵzh	hedgehog
mysh	mouse
gus	goose
seryi gus	gray goose
utka	duck
lébed'	swan
uril	cormorant, shag
chaika	seagull
ará, arún, arú	murre
kuropatka	partridge
vóron	raven
galka	jackdaw
soroka	magpie (jay?)
zhurávl'	crane
tsaplia	heron
kulik	snipe, wader
glupýsh	fulmar
topórok, topórik	tufted puffin
gagára	loon, diver
kipareika (napoika)	black canary (?)

Russian	English
treska (and treon?)	cod
kambala	flounder, plaice
paltus	halibut
sel'd, seledka	herring
chavycha	king salmon, chinook
belaia ryba, kizhuch	silver or coho salmon
keta, kaiko, khaiko	dog or chum salmon
krasnaia ryba, nerka, niarka	red, sockeye, or bluebacked salmon
gorbusha	pink, or humpback salmon
losos', semga	Atlantic salmon
terputi	mackerel
kundzha, kunzha, kumzha, malma, golets (pl. gol'tsy)	Dolly Varden trout, Arctic char, salmon trout
rak	crayfish, crab
karakatitsa	cuttlefish

artel - a permanent work crew with a specified internal structure, headed by a foreman or leader. In Russian America, usually a hunting group stationed permanently in an outlying area.
baidarshchik - head of an artel and the territory in which it operated.
promyshlennik - Russian fur hunter or trapper.
peredovshchik - foreman.
prikashchik - agent of the chief manager; supercargo.

toion, toen - Kamchadal word for chieftain, used in Russian America.
amanat - Arabic word, adopted in Russian, for a hostage.
iasak - a Turkish word, adopted in Russian, for fur tribute or tax paid by Siberian tribesmen and, until 1788, in the Aleutian Islands.

kopek, kopeck - 1/100 ruble, approx. U.S. ½ cent.
ruble - 100 kopeks, or U.S.$0.50.
pud, pood - 36.11 pounds avoirdupois.
arshin - 2.37 feet or 28 inches.
sazhen - 7 feet or 1.16 fathom.
verst - 0.6629 mile, or 1.067 kilometers.

baidara - originally a Russian term for a river boat. In NE Siberia and in Alaska, applied to a native skin boat, as an Eskimo umiak, holding 20-25 persons.
baidarka - an Eskimo or Aleut kayak. In the Aleutians, single-hatch, two-hatch, and three-hatch baidarkas were in use.
kamleia, kamleika - Chukchi term for outer garment worn in bad weather or when hunting at sea, or worn by itself as a summer garment. Originally fashioned from sea mammal intestines or fish skins.
barabora, barabara - Kamchadal word for a hut erected for summer camping. In Alaska, applied to permanent dwellings or other buildings, including kazarma (Russ.) or barracks.

kazhim - Eskimo or Aleut communal dwelling.
shalash - (Russ.) hut of branches or straw.
zemlianka - (Russ.) a dugout dwelling.
yurta - term of Siberian origin. May refer to any type of
    Siberian or Alaska native construction, from a tent
    to a subterranean dwelling.

kekur - old Siberian term for a large single rock formation
    overlooking the sea or just offshore.
laida - a gravel shoal.

verp - stream or drag anchor.
plekht - best bower anchor.
perlin - hawser.
beidevint - sailing by the wind; close-hauled.
top-gallant, topsail, etc. wind - early measure of wind
    force by the amount of sail which could be carried.

Koliuzhi, Koloshi - Russian term for Tlingit Indians of
    SE Alaska.

bisera i korol'ki - trade beads, of various colors. Bisera
    (singular biser) were small beads, bestowed in strings
    of a sazhen or more; korol'ki (sing. korolёk) were
    larger, used individually as ear ornaments, etc.

APPENDIX

1.

Petition, Petr Kutyshkin to His Imperial Majesty, the
Emperor Paul I, Peterhof, June 29, 1800. The Procurator-
General of the Senate, Petr Obolianinov, had written to
the Governor-General of Irkutsk, Boris Letstsano, regarding
Kutyshkin's complaints about Golikov and Shelikhov,
enclosing a copy of the petition. He requested Latstsano
to investigate the matter and report to him for decision
in the Senate. This copy was enclosed in a letter from
Latstsano to the Board of Directors of the Russian-American
Company, at Irkutsk, August 27, 1800.

"The attached copies of the contract and the project
presented by me to Procurator-General Prince Viazemsky,
prove my interest in the welfare of the state. The Russian
American Company (organized in 1799), under the wise
protection of Your Imperial Majesty, to date has gained
about five million roubles for private persons and over
20,000 souls [subjects] for Your Imperial Majesty. Yet,
I, your loyal subject, the first founder of these trading
operations, not only do not profit from this fur trade but
remain entirely forgotten. I take the liberty to report
briefly to Your Imperial Majesty how I was deprived of my
share in the Company.

"In 1775, being at Irkutsk, I had occasion to talk
with the sea hunters and to learn that the hunting
regulations by which they guided themselves were not only
unprofitable and inefficient but calamitous to the subjects
of Your Imperial Majesty because of the heavy losses of
men and property. In order to improve the conditions and
preserve the state interests unmolested, I undertook an
extensive study of various ways and means, not in books
but in the actual situation. I exhausted all my funds in
this undertaking for my own pleasure and for the public
weal. Having gathered the [necessary] data, I planned a
project which I showed to Golikov in 1779. He took it
from me and invited me to join the Company as the holder
of 100 shares at 500 roubles each.[1]

"As I have stated, the same project was presented by
me to Procurator-General Prince Viazemsky, who for some
unknown reasons kept it for nine months without any further
move. Meanwhile, I had to make a trip to Siberia on some

---

[1] It is impossible to determine whether Kutyshkin received
these shares in payment for his project or had to pay
cash for them. The first is more probable because, as
he states, he spent all his funds in gathering data for
this project.

pressing business and could not wait for the [Senate's] decision on my project. Upon my arrival to Tobolsk, I found that Golikov was getting ready to go to St. Petersburg in 1781. I informed him that my project had not yet been approved, requested him to intercede for me at St. Petersburg, and to that end I intrusted to him the copy of the project and other documents pertaining to it. Having received all of these, he did not care, as the circumstances show, to do anything about it [the project]; but, instead, he, his nephew Captain Golikov, and the merchant of Rylsk, Shelikhov, privately formed a company the same year, 1781, and bound each other with a contract without letting me know about it.

"I did not find out about this [treacherous] act of Golikov until 1787, when Captain Golikov published a map of the lands discovered by Shelikhov's company. When the said Golikov and Shelikhov came on business to St. Petersburg, in 1788, I requested them to place me in the company, but Golikov objected. Under such conditions I was forced to present a petition to His Majesty through Count Bezhorodko, but he left my petition without any action until his death, and thus it remained unknown.

"Because the said Company is under the special protection of Your Imperial Majesty, I take the liberty to lay at your feet my loyal petition: Most Merciful Sire, issue an order to find the project presented by me in 1780 and to ascertain by it the justice of my claims. [My project will prove that] Golikov and Shelikhov organized their company in every detail according to my project. The name is proved also by Golikov's own subscription, a copy of which is attached. [Deign to] issue an order to deduct, in compliance with this subscription, ten shares from Golikov's funds and transfer them to me in settlement of my claim. If you will find it unadvisable to do so, All Merciful Sire, grant, then, an interest on my fund of at least five kopeks on a rouble from the profits received by the Company from fur trade; it should not be too burdensome for the Company, if your treasury, Sire, will receive a tenth of their gain. Owing to my labor, privations and loss of all my possessions, the said Company enjoyed a tremendous profit for many years and my claim for some kind of settlement, for which I now loyally petition, should not inconvenience it; they reap unjustly the seeds which I planted.

"All these I lay before your sacred throne, O Sire, and surrender to the will of Your Imperial Majesty.

"All Merciful Sire, there will be [found] many who take a deep interest in the welfare of the state, as I do, if my labors will be adequately rewarded through the good will of Your Imperial Majesty.

Yudin Collection, Box 3, Folder 15.

"With deep reverence I throw myself at your feet, Enlightened Emperor, All Merciful Monarch, most loyal subject of Your Imperial Majesty

Peter Kutyshkin

Common citizen of Suzdal.

"Witnessed by [unreadable]

"The copy collated by Registrar ..."

[Copy of Golikov's subscription, made by Matvei Petrov.]

"August ..., 1779, we, the undersigned, merchants of various cities, desirous of establishing a company for hunting and trading from Okhotsk Port to Kamchatka and the Pacific Sea [Ocean], in case the exclusive privilege will be granted to us according to the project presented by one of us, merchant of Suzdal, Peter Kutyshkin, which provides for a capital made up of 400 shares equal to 200,000 roubles; and because of the evident usefulness of such an undertaking, we subscribe hereby to form a company and to buy as many shares as each one is able. Signed, Ivan Larionov Golikov, merchant of the first guild, together with the merchants of various cities who authorized me to act as their proxy, I take part in this company and subscribe to 100 shares. Peter Grigoriev Kutyshkin, merchant of Suzdal: I take part in this company and subscribe to 10 shares. Stepan Fyodorov Shumilov, merchant of Tomsk: I take part in this company and subscribe to 5 shares. Ivan Grigoriev Skuliabin, merchant of Vologda: I take part in this company and subscribe to 5 shares.

"On the copy it is written: I keep the original subscription, Kutyshkin.

Assessor Ivan Koriukov.

Matvei Petrov."

Yudin Collection, Box 3, Folder 15; from translation in DRAH, v. 2, pp. 293-295.

2.

The "Personnel Book" of the <u>Three</u> <u>Saints</u>

This book, "B", is made of heavy white paper, size 13 by 16¼ inches, 70 sheets folded once, sewn and corded, the ends of the cord fastened with a wax seal; watermarks: lines, characters and date 1781. Two pages are assigned to each employee: Left, Page 1. Balance sheet of finances, containing two columns: a. Overcharge of the employee's account during the voyage for goods taken in excess of the contractual allowance. These goods consisted of alcohol, sugar, tea, food and clothing. b. Payments on the overcharge. Right, Page 2. Balance sheet of character, also containing two columns: a. Praiseworthy actions for the benefit of the Company. b. Immoral and harmful actions against the Company or others. Each sheet is signed partially by Shelikhov, "Ryl'sk merchant companion Grigorii Shelikhov", so that consecutive sheets contain the full name and title, evidently to authenticate each sheet and prevent forgery. Most of the items, especially financial, are recorded in Shelikhov's hand, but there are entries in other hands as well. The literate employees Petr Golikov, Aleksandr Molev, Ivan Mershenin, Vasilii Shelikhov, Petr Merkul'ev (or Merkusev), Ivan Palamoshnoi, Konstantin Samoilov, Miron Britekov, Sidor Shelikhov and others sign for those who were illiterate.

"B"   No._____

November 10, 1783.

"BOOK

of the Company of the merchant of Ryl'sk, Grigorii Shelekhov, and his companions on the vessel <u>Tri Sviatitelia</u>, which contains the record of personnel of the ship from the navigator and peredovshchik to the last workman, with zealous acts for the good of the Company worthy of praise and reward, as well as corrupt acts harmful to the Company, negligence, impertinence, obscenity, neglect of duty, punished with a fine, collected by the master for the benefit of the orphanage at the Okhotsk Port, and with removal from the intrusted position. All these records are to be made by Second Sergeant Miron Britekov and witnessed by the master.

This book contains also records of the indebtedness of the employees to the master and of their debt payments during the voyage.

[The following names are recorded in the book. Because of the unusually difficult script, many comments are given only in brief form, and financial entries are omitted.

The enumeration is altered from item 27, with addition of
another number, given here in parentheses.I

Contract   Name and Comment
   1   Ivan Ivanov Kholshevnikov. Caught in thievery...
          harmful...
   2   Danilo Osimov Mirochnikov. Died of scurvy on
          Kad'iak Island, January 7, 1785. Aleksei
          Belianinov was employed in his place, May 20,
          1786.
   3   Nestor Osipov Bakurinskoi. Showed excellent
          courage during the attack on the kekur and was
          the fourth man to enter it. Rewarded with
          20 rubles.
   4   Mikhailo Stepanov Tarutin. At his request Petr
          ... signed for him.
   5   Aleksei Semen Chernykh. At his request Petr
          Golikov signed for him.
   6   Afanasei Semenov Lisenkov. Showed valor during
          the attack on the kekur on Kad'iak Island,
          August 13, 1784.
   7   Filip Fedorov Reviakin. Caught in thievery...on
          Bering Island, September 25, 1783.
   8   Ivan Afanas'ev Kraev. At his request Konstantin
          Samoilov signed for him.
   9   Ivan Grigor'ev Palamoshnoi. Trustworthy man, took
          good care of the Company's property during the
          absence of Shelikhov. Rewarded with 100 rubles.
  10   Nikolai Ivanov Maltsov.
  11   Vasilei Ivanov Davydov.
  12   Timofei Levon't'ev Chumovitskoi.
  13   Mikhailo Anan'in Sabinin. Died of scurvy, April 9,
          1785, on Kad'iak Island.
  14   Ivan Stepanov Belonogov.
  15   Nikolai Ivanov Vlasov. Petr Merkusev signed for him.
  16   Egor Sergeev Bronnikov.
  17   Kipriian Titov Sukhanov. Aleksei Mezentsev signed
          for him.
  18   Dmitrei Andreev Basov.
  19   Filip Fedorov Osetrov. Vasilii Shelikhov signed
          for him.
  20   Grigorei Matveev Konovalov. Useful man...
  21   Egor Mikhail Baranov. Vasilii Shelikhov signed
          for him. On August 13, 1784, during the attack
          on the kekur on Kad'iak Island, he was the
          first man to enter it boldly; for this he was
          promised a reward of 50 rubles. The others
          entered this stronghold after him. Thus God
          helped us to conquer a large band of Aleuts,
          which consisted of 2,000 men and women. We
          captured more than 1,000 people. 71 Russians
          took part. Died February 3, 1787 in the
          Okhotsk region. ...boisterous and once broke
          an interpreter's arm.
  22   Fedor Nikitin Sapozhnikov. Petr Merkus'ev signed
          for him.

Contract	Name and Comment
23	Ivan Vasil'ev Mershenin.
24	Semen Farafontov Kuznetsov. Caught in thievery.
25	Iakov Ivanov Shangin.
26	Ivan Vasil'ev Shtinnikov.
27	Pavel Ivanov Simachev. Died February 25, 1785, after three months' illness.
28(29)	Kuzma Dmitriev Glotov.
29(30)	Grigorei Antropov Kolodeshnikov. Died on Kad'iak, January 27, 1785. In his place was hired May 20, 1786 the Velikii Ustiug townsman Ivan Ptitsyn.
30(31)	Prokopy Timofei Frolov. Petr Golikov signed for him.
31(32)	Iakut Tarkhan Itykei(Polevoi). Iakov Shangin signed for him.
32(33)	Vasilei Grigor'ev Igushev (Died of scurvy on Kad'iak Island, April 6, 1785, after five months illness. The Irkutsk iasashnyi Dmitrii Tatarinov was employed in his place, May 20, 1786.
33(34)	Ivan Terent'ev. Iakov Shangin signed for him.
34(35)	Aleksei Sergeev Novoselov. Caught in thievery.
36(37)	Boris Ivanov Komornikov. Iakov Shangin signed for him.
37(38)	Mikhailo Grigor'ev Kopeikin. Petr Merkusev signed for him.
38(39)	Grigorei Andreev Kotonaev. Died June 1, 1784 on Komandorskie Islands. Aleksandr Vasil'ev Gvakin (?) was employed in his place, May 20, 1786.
39(40)	Epifan Maksimov Shchepin. Died in 1784 on Komandorskie Islands (?). Radion Shabalin, a newly baptised Iakut who took Shchepin's place, died of scurvy March 25, 1785 on Kyktak Island. The Velikii Ustiug peasant Fedor Kartaman was employed in Shabalin's place, May 20, 1786.
40(41)	Fedor Andreev Bydanov. Petr Merkusev signed for him.
41(42)	Ivan Fedorov Chianiavin. A good man, very zealous for the Company.
42(43)	Ivan Arkhipov Repin. Scoundrel.
43(44)	Aleksei Ivanov Parnoi. Died of scurvy on Kyktak Island in 1784. The Irkutsk artisan Grigorei Semenov was employed in his place, May 20, 1786.
44(45)	Terentei Maksimov Krasil'nikov. Died February 15, 1785.
45(46)	Il'ia Alekseev Kazantsov. Petr Golikov signed for him.
46(47)	Iakov Aleksei Skobasov. Petr Merkusov signed for him.
47(48)	Koz'ma Mikhailov Semushin.
48(49)	Stepan Kozmin Sekerin. Many times caught stealing from his master. At the beginning of December, 1785, Sekerin, Labanov, and interpreter Efrem

Contract   Name and Comment
                    Shelikhov, together with the toion of Shuiakh
                    who was held as hostage, were sent to trade
                    with the Kenaitsy. On March 27, 1786, Shelikhov
                    was informed that the toion of Shuiakh and his
                    relatives had murdered the Russians and
                    divided the Company's goods with the Afognak
                    and Chiniak toions. Mikhailo Balushin was
                    employed to replace Sekerin, May 20, 1786.
49(50) Andrei Danilov Strizhnev. Died February 26, 1785.
        A good man. In his place was employed the
        Kursk peasant Osip Mikhalin, May 20, 1786.
50(51) Emelian Iakov Nekipelov. Demid Konovalov signed
        for him.
51(52) Petr Timofeev Popov. Petr Golikov signed for him.
52(53) Petr Ivanov Kalmyk. Petr Golikov signed for him.
53(54) Maksim Ivan Rukavishnikov. Scoundrel. Petr
        Medkusov signed for him.
54(55) Dmitri Vasili Korobkov. Died of scurvy April 24,
        1785. The Krasnoiarsk peasant Egor Tatin was
        employed in his place, May 20, 1786.
55(56) Vasilei Gerasim Gorin. Scoundrel.
56(57) Vasilei Mikhailov Evsev'ev. Died on Komandorskie
        Islands in February, 1784. Gavrila Protasov
        was employed in his place.
57(58) Fedor Andreev Kochnev. Corrupt person. Gorin
        signed for him.
58(59) Demid Il'in Kulikalov. Good and industrious man.
59(60) Nikifor Vasil'ev Koz'min. Died on March 21, 1785,
        at 11 o'clock in the morning, by the will of
        God, of scurvy. Efim Berezin was employed in
        his place, May 20, 1786.
60(61) The Iakut Dmitri Pinegin. Died on Kad'iak Island
        at the beginning of January, 1785 of French
        disease which he contracted at Okhotsk. The
        Krasnoiarsk peasant Dmitri Kovrigin was employed
        in his place, May 20, 1786.
61(62) Navigator Gerasim Grigor'ev Izmailov. Took 1,008
  (63)   rubles worth of vodka, clothing, foodstuffs
        and utensils; stole 600 rubles worth of spirits.
62(64) Aleksei Afanas'ev Karmalin. Petr Medkusov signed
        for him.
63(65) Aleksandr Fedorov Molev.
64(66) Demid Dmitriev Konovalov. Died of scurvy, March 10,
        1785. The Iarensk peasant Nikita Zelenin was
        employed in his place, May 20, 1786.
65(67) Sergeant Miron Stepanov Britekov. On May 20, 1786
        the Sol'vychegodsk townsman Grigorei Kantsyn
        was employed to replace him.
66(68) Sidor Andreev Shelikhov.
67(69) Mikhailo Petrov Novikov.
68(70) Vasilei Potapov Shelikhov.

Yudin Collection, Box 1, Folder 3.

3.

Notes, by Grigorii I. Shelikhov, on Conversations with
John Ledyard, Irkutsk, August 18/29, 1787.

1st

He asked me with ardent curiosity which places I had
visited, how far Russian trade and commerce extended into
the northeastern ocean and on the American continent, in
what localities and at what degrees north latitude our
estab lishments were, where state markers were placed, and
in what years and by whom they had been set up. My reply
to him was that our trade and commerce had been started a
long time ago in the northeastern, southeastern, and
eastern oceans (and state markers had also been placed in
many places in those days), but I could not recall exactly
when and where. On the American continent, from Cape St.
Hermogen, well-known to him, our trade had been started
earlier by the expeditions of Bering and others, but now
our company has put them in perfect order, and the settlements extend to Cape St. Elias and further along the coast
to California, and inland. This is why these people were
made Russian subjects. In the area between California,
Unalaska, and Cape St. Hermogen, which is Kodiak, in the
triangle bordering on 65 degrees north latitude south to
40 degrees, two vessels of our company have now been
cruising for three summers to patrol the new islands.

2nd

He also tried to find out from me how many Russian
vessels were engaged at the present time in the trade with
these islands in the abovementioned sea, and how many Russians
they had on board. He further inquired about the people I
had left on the American continent and how many there were.
He then said that north of California there were more than
ten thousand people from European countries, and that the
coast north of California from 50 degrees north latitude to
Cape St. Elias had been occupied by them for a long time.
And he uttered these words as a threat, which I countered
by saying that people from other states had no right to
exercise power over these areas without permission from the
Russian Monarch.

3rd

He also claimed that he had been with Cook off Cape
Chukotsk at 73 degrees north latitude and that they took
sea otter pelts from the Chukchi as tribute, and that
allegedly some of these peoples had been made subjects of
the English Crown. This is where he revealed himself as

incorrect, because the peoples living at Cape Chukotsk,
known as the Chukchi, and all the more so at 73 degrees
north latitude, never hunt sea otters. Instead they acquire
sea otters, brought from many places at very high prices,
by exchanging marten pelts for them. All this shows that
he incorrectly regards as subjects of the English Crown
peoples who for a long time have been subjects of the
Russian Scepter.

4th

He claimed that he had participated in Mr. Cook's last
trip and therefore had been in Kamchatka. But after a
further analysis of his words and reports on Mr. Cook's
visit to Kamchatka from people I know who live there, I am
convinced that he has never been there, and that he relates
things he either has learned from someone else or has read
about. He claimed, for example, that some Aleuts and
Russians from the Aleutian Islands came aboard their vessel
and left a note. But when I enquired further, namely from
which island did these people come, were they old or young,
he immediately said that he himself had not been present,
because he had been on another ship. And he evaded many
such questions of mine by similar obscure and confusing
replies.

5th

He said that he urgently needed to see Mr. Billings in
order to get to the American continent with his help,
whereupon he intends to walk inland and cross North America.
But when I told him that the peoples of the northern part
of America, from the Alaskan peninsula whence he intended
to start out for Xanada, and especially in the interior,
were bellicose and always engaged in merciless warfare with
one another, and that, so far as I was concerned, it was
impossible for a European to travel alone there, he appeared
to change his mind; he said he intended to go to California
and to travel across the continent from the 49th-40th degree
north latitude perpendicular to the peninsula.

6th

The conversation then dwelt on less important aspects
from his point of view: we talked about the Kurile Islands
--whether there were any Russians on the Kurile Islands at
the present time, whether there were any Russian settlements
there, how large they were and when they were established,
on which island the main Russian settlement was located,
and whether they communicated with the Japanese. I briefly
answered him on the Kurile Islands, stating that many
Russians have always lived there near the Japanese boundary,
and I noted that he was considerably interested in this
matter, too.

LCM, Yudin Collection, Box 2, Folder 29, copy, Russian

language; TsGADA, f. 796, op. 1, d. 298, 1. 1-2, nineteenth
century typewritten copy, Russian language. Translation
from The United States and Russia. The beginning of relations,
1765-1815, Washington, 1980, pp. 232-235.

Ledyard's note on the same interview:

Wednesday   August 18th ... Went this morning to see a
Merchant owner of a Vessel that had passed from Kamschatka
to different parts of the Coast of America. Shewed some
Charts rudely discriptive of his voyages. He says there are
on different parts of the Coast of America 2000 Russians:
and that as near as he can judge the number of skins
produced by them in that Country amount to 12,000: has a
Vessel of his own at Ohotsk, which leaves that Country for
America next Summer, and offers me a passage in her.

From Stephen D. Watrous, editor, John Ledyard's Journey
through Russia and Siberia 1787-1788. The Journal and
Selected Letters. University of Wisconsin Press, Madison,
1966, pp. 158-159.

4.

Petition, Shelikhov and Golikov, to the Empress Catherine II,
St. Petersburg, February 13, 1788.

Most Gracious Sovereign!

The Governor-General of Irkutsk and Kolyvan, Mr.
Lieutenant-General and Cavalier Iakobii, has already
reported in detail to Your Imperial Majesty about the
discoveries made in the Northeastern Ocean by vessels sent
out by our company, and therefore this report by your
subjects about our deeds relative to that will be brief.

From 1781, at our own expense and risk, we built
three galiots in the port of Okhotsk. In 1783, one of the
partners in our company, Grigorii Shelekhov, set forth.
After many difficulties and dangers, he reached according
to plan the island of Kyktak, the first objective of his
voyage, built a small fort on it in a good location, and
made the people there subjects of your Imperial Majesty.
Then, making yet another voyage, he acquired a nearby
island, called Afognak, where he also erected a fortifica-
tion, and brought the inhabitants into subjection. He did
likewise with many other small islands as far as the
American mainland itself, surveyed their environs and the

mainland, and brought into subjection the people on the
islands and along the coast, up to 50,000 in all, took
from the best people up to 50 children as hostages, and
placed on the map the true location, based on practical
observations. Meanwhile, living on the main island almost
two years, he endeavored to get the people to obey him,
not by fear and need, but by love and their own benefit.
The means he used, corresponding with the rules of humanity
and their rights, crowned his labors with complete success:
he stilled former hostilities and discord which from time
immemorial had caused them to annihilate each other. He
showed them means for getting nourishment unknown to them
until then, and for lack of which they had often been
victims of famine, and furnished them with necessary tools.
By such means, and with his kindly treatment, he inclined
them to him in love, aroused their trust and convinced them
that the arrival of the Russians in their land had brought
them innumerable advantages, security and prosperity. Now
many of them voluntarily serve us and join our people in
their labors; they live together with them and are kept at
our expense.

Doing all this, subjecting ourselves to innumerable
labors and dangers, we have had no object in view except
love for our country and zeal for the public good; these
have been the main motives in our enterprises and have
encouraged us in difficulties; our success now will benefit
our own future enterprises.

We have therefore ordered the following, for the
common good: 1st, our aforementioned comrade has dispatched
two vessels for further discoveries: one between California
and the Kurile Islands from 40° to 55°, and the other
between Asia and America from the Aleutian Island chain
from 55° to 68°. 2nd, we regard it as necessary, to prevent
attacks by other powers, to build a fort and harbor on the
21st or 22nd of the Kurile Islands for carrying on trade
with China and Japan and to facilitate discoveries and
to put under your Imperial Majesty's rule neighboring
islands, which we know are not now dependant on any power.
3rd, we intend soon to move southward as far as possible
along the American coast, and to establish there a
settlement in a suitable locality, in order to prevent
attack by foreigners on this region, and to make the
peoples there subject to Russia. 4th, to furnish the
government with reports about the success of our activities,
we wish to establish a post [route] by land from the
American mainland across the strait along the Chukotka
Peninsula via Aklansk and Zhiginsk and Okhotsk oblast,
and another by sea, by means of a transport vessel. During
his journey from there to Russia, [Shelikhov] made all
necessary preparations and issued orders, entrusting
matters to our agent until his return and furnished
necessary orders. The vessel on which he went to Okhotsk
last summer has returned to America with supplies for the
people and for equipping a packetboat under construction

there. In completion of all this, putting our hope in
God, and aided by good intentions, no obstacles are foreseen.
However, we consider it necessary this summer for Shelikhov
to set out there again, for which purpose a fourth galiot
has been prepared for us in Okhotsk.

On the above enterprises we have spent more than
250,000 rubles, not receiving a kopek in return. Moreover,
about the same amount will be needed to complete the
projects initiated, and to maintain operations. But our
resources do not correspond to our need. The stopping
of the Kiakhta trade makes it impossible for us to obtain
money needed to continue our enterprise. Therefore we
most humbly beg your Supreme Imperial Majesty's mercy and
ask that we be supplied 200,000 rubles from the Loan Bank,
on the basis of your most gracious manifest, published in
1786. We humbly beg that in order to defend our property
from others, who would want to profit from our discoveries
and from our expenditures and labor, so as not to put what
we have now built or will build henceforth in danger of
destruction and annihilation.

We also take the liberty to petition Your Monarchial
Grace to bestow upon us distinctions according to our
calling [rank] and to honor our achievements with a public
ukaz, by virtue of which we may receive in that remote
region, in pressed circumstances, protection and assistance
from the government against intruders, and to secure at
least 100 soldiers, including at least four artillerymen
and two gunsmiths for service in the forts now or to be
established. These soldiers are not so much needed for
the said Kyktak and Afognak Islands as for the forts which
we plan to build on the American coast and on the Kurile
Islands, especially during the initial stages of our
settlement there, until the aborigines have been brought
up to have a friendly disposition toward the Russians.
To assist the soldiers we can use with advantage several
thousands of the people inhabiting the islands, who are
brave, strong, accustomed to bearing hardships, enter-
prising and intrepid, whose obedience to the Russian
commanders and devotion to Your Imperial Majesty has been
tested and proven on many occasions. As to their loyalty
to Russia, we take the liberty to guarantee to Your
Imperial Majesty that the islands of Kyktak, Afognak and
others populated by them are not only safe from internal
rebellions but secure in regard to possible unfriendly
acts of foreign powers, as we can unconditionally rely
upon their [the islanders] support in repelling them
[foreigners]. Besides, the said tribes can be useful for
our navigation there; we shall not need many Russian
sailors, because the islanders, by their nature, are
daring navigators, willingly enter this service, and learn
naval theory and practice faster than the Russians.

All Merciful Empress! Reverently kissing the dust of

the most sacred feet of Your Imperial Majesty, we most
devotedly submit this petition.

The most devoted subjects of Your Imperial Majesty,
The Merchant of Kursk, Ivan Golikov
The Merchant of Ryl'sk, Grigorei Shelekhov

February 13, 1788
St. Petersburg.

LCM, Golder Collection (photostat). Manuscript copy in
LOII, Vorontsov Collection, File 476, 416-419 ob. Full
text in A. I. Andreev, ed., Russkie otkrytiia v Tikhom
Okeane i Severnoi Amerike v XVIII veke, Moscow, 1948, pp.
265-269. Partial translation in DRAH, v. 2, pp. 330-331.

5.

Confidential report of Acting Governor-General of Irkutsk
and Kolyvan, Ivan Peel, to the Ruling Senate, #1210,
Irkutsk, September 19, 1789.

This report incorporates three documents: (1) report
of the Admiralty Collegium to the Ruling Senate of August
8, 1789, #11; (2) copy of the report of Under Surgeon Miron
Britukov to Captain Billings of November 2, 1788 and (3)
copy of the report of Acting Governor-General Peel to the
Admiralty Collegium of September 19, 1789.

1. The report of the Admiralty Collegium to the Ruling
Senate merely forwards the copy of Britukov's letter and
informs the Senate that it has referred the matter for
investigation to the local authorities at Irkutsk.

2. "Copy of the report of Under Surgeon Miron
Britukov presented to Navy Captain of the Second Rank
Billings, at Yakutsk, November 2, 1788.

"In 1783, I was transferred by the government from the
Okhotsk Office (which is now a commandant's office) to the
Merchant of Rylsk, Grigory Shelekhov, a head of the company
then departing to the expedition on a hunting vessel, to
take care of him and his fellow travellers. We departed on
August 15 of that year, and from that time I was entirely
under his orders. Having wintered on one of the Commander
Islands, we proceeded directly to America. Upon our arrival
at the first island, Kodiak, the following events took place:
Companion Shelekhov, as master of the ship and of all the
people thereon, proclaimed himself a person of such great
authority as to be empowered to punish and to hang not only
the islanders, but us, the loyal subjects of our Most Merciful Empress. Being frightened, we acknowledged him as
indeed a man vested by the highest authorities with full
power and intrusted with important secrets, which he was
not allowed to disclose, and we obeyed all his orders.

"When the boat pulled into the harbor on this island, the employees were sent on five bidarkas to seek the inhabitants of the island. Seeing them [come], the islanders left their village and ran away. Our men pursued them and found that the islanders from other villages also run away discarding all their property; they succeeded in catching two natives who led them to the place where a large crowd had gathered. Having found a great multitude gathered on an island [detached cliff], the name of which I cannot now recall, near the coast--this island is surrounded by rocks and cannot be approached by water from any side; it is impossible to reach it only at low tide by the strip of dry land connecting it with the beach [of Kodiak]-- our men spent five days in their bidarkas near that island: to protect us from being attacked and to secure friendly relations with the natives they asked the natives for hostages, but were refused; they informed the said chief, Mr. Shelekhov, who remained in the harbor, about the results [of their mission]. Meanwhile, one night our sentinels noticed the islanders approaching them in the dark; they shot several times but did not kill any of them and, having met no response from the enemy, disregarded this disturbance. Yet, the said Shelekhov loaded two bidaras with his people the same night, and at daybreak, at low tide, crossed with them by the land to the island, and with the armed band murdered about 500 of these speechless people; if we also count those who ran in fear to their bidarkas and, trying to escape, stampeded and drowned each other, the number will exceed 500. Many men and women were taken as prisoners of war. By order of Mr. Shelekhov, the men were led to the tundra and speared, the remaining women and children, about 600 altogether, he took with him to the harbor and kept them for three weeks. The husbands who succeeded in escaping the murder began to come. Shelekhov returned their wives to them, but he retained one child from each family as a hostage. Finally he permitted the [women and children who remained] unclaimed to go free. At the same time, the employees were sent from the harbor in five bidaras to the eastern side of the island to seek the inhabitants; they were away a whole month; I do not know about their treatment of the islanders; upon their return they reported that the islanders attacked them and wounded six of them with spears, but I do not know what loss was suffered by the islanders. Returning to the harbor, they caught two men, whom they recognized as the conspirators in the attack, and brought them to the harbor to their chief, the said Shelekhov. He had them tortured with whalebone and gunsticks, trying to get their confession of a plot, but they (perhaps not knowing what it was all about) did not make any acknowledgment. Finally, Shelekhov shot one of them with his pistol and ordered the other to be speared and their bodies taken to the tundra.

"At that time when the Russians made trips to the various islands to the east, as was stated before, two

reports on [?] treatment of natives?

native men came in a bidarka from the west and reported
that they were sent by their chiefs to have a friendly visit
and to trade with the Russians and that the Russians should
not be afraid of the arrival of a large number of natives
and should not use arms against them. Mr. Shelekhov
received them [messengers] with kindness, recorded their
names and expressed his consent to their wishes. After
they had gone, we waited all winter for the islanders,
but nobody came. In the spring of 1785, the Russians were
sent in bidaras to the west side of the island to explore
and to secure hostages from the inhabitants. They returned
with children, taken from the native chiefs, as hostages.
The fathers, then, had to come to see their children. Mr.
Shelekhov inquired of them whether they sent two messengers
last summer to tell him about their desire to establish
communication and trade. To this the chiefs replied that
they had not sent anybody. Shelekhov then told them the
names of those two men, as he recorded them, and ordered
the chiefs to find these men and bring them to him. This
was done. Mr. Shelekhov questioned them regarding the
authenticity of their message and ordered Pilot Izmailov
to shoot them both with one shot from a rifle; and so it
was done.

"This was not all. Among the many chiefs visiting
their children who were kept as hostages came some from
Shuiakh Island. When they were ready to return home, two
Russians with various small wares, used in the local trade,
were sent to accompany them. These two Russians were
killed by the inhabitants [of Shuiakh], either because of
their greed for the [Russian] wares or because of hatred.
We did not know about this until one native from Afognak
learned about this murder. This native, being afraid to
report to the Russians about the murder of the two Russians,
told the Kodiak natives who accompanied the Russian
expedition to Afognak and Shuiakh about it; he assured
them of the accuracy of his information and said that he
had not the courage to report about it to the Russians.
Being informed by the Kodiak people, the Russians sent
the Afognak reporter to their chief, Shelekhov. Shelekhov
questioned him, with partiality, whether or not he took
part in the murder, but the native replied that he did not
participate in it but merely wanted to inform the Russians
after he found out about it. He was then questioned
whether anybody else knew about it and [he] replied that
another native of his island also heard about it. Mr.
Shelekhov immediately sent for the native, but the latter
testified also that neither he nor his friend took part
in the occasions, but merely heard about it. They were
accused, then, of not reporting the matter sooner, and he
[Shelekhov] ordered them put together so that he could
shoot them both with one shot from a gun. He then shot,
killed one of them, but the other was only wounded; he
ordered his head cut off. Three bidaras with Russians
were dispatched to Afognak and Shuiakh to exterminate the
people and to find the chief with whom the two Russian traders

were sent. Later we heard that according to his [Shelekhov's] orders, one village was entirely eradicated and the people from other villages had run away. What is going on there after our departure, I do not know.

"Such acts terrified me; though I have heard from Mr. Shelekhov that he was granted the authority to execute and to hang not only the aborigines but the Russians as well, I do not have any proof that such power was given to him indeed. Being afraid of his power I did not dare to inform any government office against him immediately upon my return. My oath, however, forbids me to pass up this matter silently. I heard that you, Sir, according to the authority invested in you by our Empress, enter into particulars of all the oppressed in this remote region and mercifully treat those who have recourse to your protection. I beg you, Sir, to investigate the important matter which I described herein, and see if it is worthy of reporting to the higher authorities and if it is identical with the records in Shelekhov's journal; I have no doubt though that he [Shelekhov] made a perfect report to our Empress. I do not know whether he had indeed been granted such power by the Supreme Authority as he told us, but I do not wish to be punished for leaving his terrible acts unreported; as I am obliged by my oath to do so though I am but a mute [unimportant] man. Therefore, I petition you, Sir, to accept this paper and either forward it where it should go or keep it in your file, so that in case of the prosecution for further concealment of information I may refer to it for my justification.

Secretary Sergii Zolotov."

3. "Copy   Secret

"To the Admiralty Collegium from Lieutenant-General Acting Governor-General of Irkutsk and Kolyvan   and Knight, [Ivan Peel], September 19, 1789."

In the first six paragraphs, Peel denounced the meddling of Billings into matters pertaining entirely to the local authorities. He states that Baranov and Krechevtsov were granted permission by former Governor Yacobi to trade with the Chuckchees and Koriaks in 1788 and that these traders treated the aborigines justly. If there were any disturbances among the natives, they were the result of savagery. The trade with the aborigines must be encouraged as, under the supervision of the government officials, it is the means for the improvement of native character. Besides, the traders serve the government in in extending the sphere of its influence. As an example of the latter, Peel mentions the acquisition of several islands in the Arctic Ocean by Mr. Banner.

"7. Having, thus, explained the conditions among the Chuckchees, I now turn to the description of the denounce- ment presented to Mr. Billings by Under Surgeon Britukov.

As it had been already stated, there can be no comparison
between the traders with the Chuckchees and the sea hunters.
The latter use their own ships to navigate the newly dis-
covered northeastern ocean. I must state here that Mr.
Billings sent my the copy of the denouncement by the said
Britukov of the eminent Rylsk merchant, Shelekhov. After
diligent study of it, I compared it with the ukase of Her
Imperial Majesty of August 13, 1787 to my predecessor,
Lieutenant General and Knight Yacobi, and I have found
that it was nothing but the product of hatred and deception;
moreover that all acts of Merchant Shelekhov with the
American aborigines were described accurately and in
detail and presented to Her Majesty's consideration. If
such were found daring and impudent, he could not have
enjoyed the special monarchial consideration. Yet this
is not the case, as may be seen from his letter to Mr.
Drozman, acting commandant of Yakutsk and aulic counsellor,
in which he describes how the All Merciful Empress, esteeming
his, Shelekhov's, deeds, condescended to reward him with an
open laudatory charter, sword and gold medal.

"8. The Admiralty Collegium may learn about the acts
of this sea hunter from his travel journal, which I
presented to it last July 25. In it Shelekhov frankly
describes all attempts of the Americans against his party
and his own against them. It shows clearly that the
explanation of the said under surgeon, who, according to
Shelekhov, was but a burden on the ship, does not deserve
even the semblance of truth ..."

Peel informs the Collegium that he advised Billings
to attend to his direct duties and to leave the investigation of complaints to the local authorities.

LCM, Golder Collection, photostats, Box 3; from Russian
Archives of the State, Petrograd, 1789, VII, #2742, Russian;
also in Pamiatniki novoi russkoi istorii. Sbornik
istoricheskikh statei i materialov, St. Petersburg, 1873,
vol. 3, pp. 373-383; as translated in DRAH, vol. 2, pp. 332-
336.

6.

Complaints made by natives of Unalaska district to Government inspectors in 1789-1790. The document contains five reports copied in chronological order in the same handwriting, evidently made for the Golikov-Shelikhov company at the time. No heading, date or signature.

1. June 7, 1789, the Aleuts of Unalaska Island-- Chief Algamalinag, in Russian "Michael;" interpreter "Saguiakh, formerly called by the Russians <u>monkey</u>, but after baptism Ivan Chuloshnikov" and the Aleut woman, Anshiges--being questioned about the conduct of the Company's hunters, testified that during the wintering of navigators Ocheredin and Orekhov with their assistants, Izmailov, Gogolev and Lukanin, a quarrel arose over the division of hunting places. Ocheredin and Polutov, as the strongest, took most of the Aleut workers and forced them to hunt even during the worst winter storms, which resulted in the drowning of three Aleuts.

Leaving Unalaska for Alaska, Ocheredin and Polutov carried with them over a hundred Aleut men and women; from those who were left on the islands they took all bidarkas, arrows, parkas and foodstuffs. Only a few of the hundred remained alive after four years' privation of food and clothing.

Among the worst oppressors at Unalaska was named baidarshchik [work crew leader] Pshenichnoy, who "treated the islanders tyrannically, kept several Aleut girls and women as mistresses, mercilessly whipped the Aleuts with ropes and sticks." Six Aleuts were whipped to death and sixteen were starved to death; more than three hundred Aleuts died of starvation during two winter months because their foodstuffs were taken away by the hunters.

The Aleuts suffered similar treatment from Polutov, Panin and Popov. The last one murdered ["speared"] all the Aleut girls and two men in the Bobrovoy settlement.

"After that Unalaska was visited by the hunting ships of Greek Delarov, Cherepanov and Nagaev; there were Shishaev and Pilot Potap Zaikov of Orekhov's company; Shelekhov also stopped for a brief time and left the same summer. Delarov spent the winter, took the best Aleut men from Krgalgan and Unimak and went to Kodiak. Shishaev and Zaikov of Orekhov's company carried away about thirty men and twenty women; these people have not returned. Cherepanov and Nagaev remained on the islands.

"Now Cherepanov's and Nagaev's companies do not in- dulge in such cruel tyranny and murder (as described above), yet they send us to hunt against our will, to provide food and to do domestic work without pay. From Cherepanov's company we get for each sea otter either a kettle or a shirt or a knife or a kerchief or a plane for making arrows

or ten strings of corals or five, six to ten leaves of
tobacco with the addition of a handful of beads to each of
these things paid for a sea otter. ...

"The difference between these two companies is that
... the other [Nagaev's] company pays less for a sea otter
and does not supply any clothing, either to domestic
servants or to hunters, who are often sent naked to hunt
and to fish. From such poor keeping and treatment many
run away to Cherepanov's company, seeking protection from
these unbearable conditions.

"Not a little do we suffer from the seizure of our
girls, wives, daughters and sisters, practised in general
by all companies (except Panov's which acted in an orderly
manner in comparison with the companies which were here
before and after it). [Though] seeing our women kept as
mistresses and cruelly treated and knowing the beastly
temperament of the hunters, we can not oppose, can not even
raise our vocies against it. We have to suffer it, being
afraid of the recurrence of the event which happened in
the time of peredovschik Solovey, who plundered the
islands of Unalaska, Sannak, Akun, Akutan, Asutan and
Igilga and shot the entire male population on them. Even
more so, as a final outrage, he lined up the men and
tested his rifles on them to find how many men could be
killed with one bullet. The cruel treatment of us by
their hunters is known to all the companies. Sergeant
Builov, who was here to collect the taxes, said that such
treatment is forbidden by the Government and he promised
us that upon his return to Russia he would [take steps to]
stop the cruelties of the hunters. Yet, even now we do
not see any relief.

"We learned that your ship is not a company ship but
one sent by the Russian Empress, and that its commanders
are higher than the navigators of the company ships, whom
we considered the greatest masters because of severity in
actions and because they themselves proclaimed that there
are no masters over them. Seeing the obedience shown to
you by the hunters and their chiefs, we do not hesitate
to report to you about the oppression by the hunters and
traders and to request your protection from them. Collated
with the original draft of the inquest, Acting Secretary
and Collegiate Registrar, Gavrilo Ermilov."

2. June 25, 1790, Hunter Egor Purtov, citizen of
Irkutsk, from the ship of merchant of Kursk, Golikov, and
merchant of Rylsk, Shelikhov, being questioned, testified
on Nagai Island:

That he did not take part in the acquisition of Kodiak
Island and came to Kodiak during the time of Greek Delarov,
after Shelikhov had gone. He could not report anything
about the conditions of that company, except that the
natives of the island are sent by the company's agents to

hunt for animals and are paid for the skins with shirts, parkas, Kamleias or some other things. "According to rumors, Shelikhov reported to the Government that he found almost 20,000 people on the islands and that 500 of them are paying taxes and that the Russians desire to settle on these islands permanently. All these reports are not true: the total number of natives on all the islands near-by is not more than 3,000 people, and the taxpayers not more than 50. As to the desire of the Russians to settle here permanently, perhaps those men who married native women of these islands and have children from them will consent to it. The truth of my statement about the number of the islanders can be proved by, first, navigator and under pilot Gavrilo Pribylov from the ship of Lebedev-Lastochkin Company, who had an opportunity to see them, recorded it in his journal and reported it to [the authorities at] Okhotsk; second, all the hunters of the company of the said Shelikhov, who, as I, being employed by him, buy everything at prices four times higher than Okhotsk prices ...[Few words not clear.], that is the reason why we involve ourselves in insolvable debts and have no means to return home before the company's terms [are satisfied]. Foreseeing this, Shelikhov said that we shall all remain on this island. ... Original signed, citizen of Irkutsk, Egor Purtov. Collated with the original, Collegiate Registrar, Gavrilo Ermilov."

3. July 1, 1790, at Kodiak, pilot of under officer's rank, Gerasim Grigoriev Izmailov, was questioned regarding the report of Under Surgeon Bratikov and testified:

That upon his arrival to these islands, Shelikhov never proclaimed that he had power and authority to punish and to hang the islanders and the Russian subjects.

That he, Izmailov, never heard and does not know that from 150 and 200 native men and women and Russians were killed during the attack on Kodiak when the islanders refused to send hostages. He surmised that many of them [natives] in fear jumped from cliffs into the water and into bidaras and were drowned. "We found out about it when the sea cast their bodies on the beach. Six Russians were wounded in that fight. From 200 to 300 natives were taken as prisoners of war. From this number Shelikhov ordered the selection of six to ten, I cannot recall the exact number, old men; they were taken to the tundra and speared. The remaining natives were kept in the harbor for one and a half months, many of them were given presents; Shelikhov chose from among them the most gifted man to be the chief, to his care he intrusted all the women and children. When husbands came to visit their wives, and fathers and relatives [came to see] their children, Shelikhov returned each [wives and children] to whom he belonged; finally, he let all of them go. ..."

Izmailov denies the shooting of a man by Shelikhov and the spearing of another by Shelikhov's order, and as proof he points out that one of these men who were supposed to be murdered lives at Kodiak and his son goes to the Russian school. Izmailov does not deny that he himself shot two native conspirators upon Shelikhov's order, and that Konstantin Samoilov and Vasili Malakhov executed the leaders of the mutiny against the Russian party on Afognak and Shuiak islands. Izmailov mentions that he presented his report on the matters of this inquest to the Okhotsk Government Office in 1787.

"Original signed, Pilot Gerasim Izmailov. This testimony, signed by Pilot Gerasim Izmailov, was recorded from his words by the acting secretary and gubernatorial registrar, Vasili Diakonov; witness, Priest Vasili Sivtsov. This inquest was written in my presence, Navy Captain of the Second Rank, Robert Gall [Hall?]. Collated with the original, Collegiate Registrar, Gavrilo Ermilov."

4. "July 4, 1790, Kodiak Island, the agent of Golikov and Shelikhov Company, citizen of Tomsk, Vasili Petrov Merkuriev, being questioned by the order of the chief of the expedition, Captain of the Second Rank, Iosif Iosifovich Billings ..., testified that:

"He does not know anything about the affairs of the Company, that he did not and does not take part in anything, and that only the local Administrator-General, Greek Evstrat Delarov, can report about everything clearly and in detail. ..."

5. "July 5, 1790, Kodiak Island, Pilot Gerasim Izmailov, employed by the Golikov and Shelikhov Company, was again questioned by Navy Captain of the Second Rank, Gavrilo Sarychev ..., and testified:

"That, according to the information furnished by Delarov's peredovschik , Purtov was sent to hunt various animals not in 200 but in 20 bidarkas, and that Delarov used to send up to 600 bidarkas to hunt sea otters in the so-called Gros Fles Bay. ... The hunter chosen to make settlement with the islanders is supplied by the Company with beads, corals and iron hatchets about four inches long. I was not present at the hunt and do not know about the number [of animals killed]. An order is [usually] issued to have the new bidarkas finished and the old repaired and ready by April 15; on this date they go [to hunt]. Original signed, Pilot Gerasim Izmailov. Collated with the original, Collegiate Registrar, Gavrilo Ermilov."

LCM, Yudin Collection, Box 2, Folder 23, as translated in DRAH, vol. 2, pp. 237-240.

7.

Order, Lieutenant-General Ivan Peel to G. I. Shelikhov, #991, Irkutsk, May 12, 1794.

"ORDER

to Mr. Shelekhov, eminent citizen of Rylsk and companion of the North American Company.

"Her Imperial Majesty, all-merciful Empress, condescending to your petition presented with my most devoted report, September 28, 1793, for Her Majesty's august decision, by her personal ukase issued to me December 31 of the same year, deigned to order that you be given twenty workers from the exiles and ten families of farmers (these men have already been transferred [to you] in accordance with my ordinance), whom you requested for the construction of a wharf near Cape St. Elias and for the introduction of agriculture at proper places on the American mainland and on the Kuril Islands, at your own expense; because Her Imperial Majesty considers your said undertakings very useful for the state and wishes to see them progressing successfully. Besides that, [she] deigned to order me to report to Her Imperial Majesty about the progress of the said undertakings and about all that happens in the colonies. ..." Having thus informed Shelikhov about the Imperial will, Peel proceeds to instruct him to double his efforts in the exploration of the North Sea and of the American coasts; to use peaceful means for encouraging the settlers in their activities but to counteract promptly all insubordination and violence. He incorporated his instructions into ten paragraphs as follows:

1. Upon his arrival to the colonies the Administrator-General must immediately build a fortress as a defense against the natives and for protection of the Company's property.

2. To build a small town. "The houses with all additional buildings must be comfortable and attractive, properly removed from each other for fire safety. The streets must be straight, wide and divided into blocks with vacant plazas left in convenient places for future public buildings. In a word, knowing the local conditions, order this first settlement in America to be built as a standard city. Any disfiguring of it with crooked, narrow, impassable lanes and bypaths must not be permitted, so that in the future this first settlement may become the beautiful abode of a multitude of people, and the glory and renown of Russian art and taste may not be impared!" Recommends that the church and houses for the missionaries be built at the same time as the homes for the settlers.

Yudin Collection, Box 1, Folder 4.

3. To develop agriculture, to raise grains and vegetables for your own consumption and for export to Okhotsk
and Kamchatka. To build a reserve store for grain and
vegetables for emergencies. To encourage agriculture by
payment to the settlers for products sold to the Company
and to encourage the use of local foodstuffs; such as fish,
game and roots. To raise cattle and poultry.

4. To encourage industry; "to use all means for
finding out about the mineral resources of the country ...
no doubt there should be ore, especially iron"; to instruct
the settlers in tanning, soap making and other crafts;
to make the settlement self-supporting, independent of
Russia for supplies. To raise hemp and flax and to work
them into canvas, sailcloth and rope. "If the iron ore
is found and worked into iron, which must be the property
of the settlers, then you will have no need to import
anchors, bolts and all kinds of ship's nails that are
produced here. The discovery of other ores will enrich
your settlement there even more. In a word, you must
order that everything acquired by the settlers through
their labor must be their property, except the [products
of the] fur trade with the Americans, which does not per-
tain to their position as it may distract them from
agriculture and other profitable occupations, and which
must belong exclusively to your Company." For better
order and safety, to divide the settlers into large groups
according to family relationship, to encourage the natives
to live with the settlers, treating them with kindness
and teaching them the Russian way of living and various
arts and crafts "so that in time these Americans may become
not only citizens of this first town in America, but can
be hired to serve on the sea vessels." After agriculture
is firmly established, the settlers may be divided into
smaller groups so that each Russian and native can have
his own property. "The unmarried settlers should marry
'American' girls and train them in the various household
duties by the Russian women who were sent with their
families. Equally, the 'American' men should be encouraged
to marry the Russian girls or widows in order to establish
mutual relationship."

5. To keep order; to promote welfare; to punish the
disorderly and the criminals, yet to do it with discretion,
seeking the counsel of Archimandrite Ioasaph, who is a
learned man of peaceful disposition and high morals, in
difficult cases. To respect the clergymen, to assist them
in their spiritual and scholarly pursuits, especially in
the study of ores and other natural resources. "Your
Administrator-General will act wisely if he will strictly
supervise the conduct of each of the settlers of this new
town and will try to eradicate even the use of obscene
language by the settlers."

6. To civilize and to Christianize the Americans.
"Their children learn not only to speak Russian but to

134

read and to write; some of them have even studied mathe-
matics, two of whom were sent by you in 1792 to Japan to
practice navigation and seven were used for the same
purpose in America. To promote learning it is necessary
for your Administrator-General and his subordinates to
exert united effort, watchful earnestness, kind and just
treatment and relief in need as means to attract them
[natives] to the Russian settlements, where they can live
with the Russians, become acquainted with the Russian
mode of life and be trained in various arts and crafts,
whichever they can learn, as well as agriculture and
cattle breeding; the more so that the Americans have
naturally keen minds and good memories, and are strong,
agile and, consequently, able to profit by such training."
To take as hostages young and gifted people who have better
ability for learning. To keep spies among the Americans
to insure the safety of the settlers.

7. To build a dock and small boats for the use of the
settlers.

8. To avoid dealings with foreign vessels, except
through loyal Americans; not to enter their ships, but to
be hospitable; not to show them the fortifications or the
property. "Seek the advice of Archimandrite [Ioasaph],
who, in these cases, will decide how to receive the
visiting foreigners." To watch especially for English,
Swedish and French vessels, the last-mentioned to be
treated as belonging to a Russian enemy, until legitimate
authority is re-established in France.

9. To instruct the manager of Urup Island to show
all possible courtesy toward the Japanese and to study the
conditions of Japan--population, resources, commerce,
fortifications, customs, law, opinion about Russians,
etc.--through the hairy Kuril Islanders, who are not
attached to the Japanese. To be on guard against an
unexpected attack by the Kuril Islanders.

10. To report on the condition of the Kuril Islands
and navigation there, and to furnish maps, logbooks and
descriptions of the country, as well as all sorts of
unusual objects--for reporting to Her Imperial Majesty.

Original signed by

Lieutenant-General and Knight, Ivan Peel.

LCM, Yudin Collection, Box 1, Folder 4, Russian; as
translated in DRAH, vol. 2, pp. 161-163.

8.

[Draft of the inscription to be written on the monument erected in memory of Shelikhov in the city of Rylsk. There is no indication of who made this draft.]

"Instead of Rest with the saints,[1] it is better to write the Scriptures' text: 'Blessed are the dying in the Lord,' and on the opposite side:

"'He was sincere to his own, was kind to the strange,
His dust is here, but [his] spirit in the holy
lights [abides].'

"As it will be impossible to put this on one line, write it as follows:

"'He was sincere to his own,
Was kind to the strange,
His dust is here, but [his] spirit
In the holy lights [abides].'

"Make indentations in the lines exactly as here."

[Three variations of the four inscriptions on Shelikhov's mausoleum. They are written on three sheets of paper in different handwriting. Shelikhov's name is spelled with i in one and e in two of them. One of these drafts is evidently final. The most complete version is translated here, and the parts omitted in the final version are indicated in footnotes.]

"I

"Here
In expectation of the Coming of Christ
Is buried a body [of one]
By name Shelikhov,
By acts Invaluable,
By occupation Citizen,[2]
By designs Honorable Man,
Of broad and strong mind;

"As
During the reign
of Catherine the Second
Empress and Autocrat of All Russia,
Glorious and great ruler,
Who enlarged Her Empire
By victories over Her enemies
In the west and in the south,

---

[1] Church hymn, "With Thy saints, O Lord, give rest to the soul of Thy servant ..."

[2] This line is omitted in the final version.

Yudin Collection, Box 1, Folder 5.

<pre>
              "He
    By his daring sea voyages
            in the east
Discovered, subdued and added
    To Her dominion not only the islands
Kyktak [Kodiak], Afognak and many others
But the mainland of America
              extending toward the northeast;
    [He] established on them
House building, shipbuilding, agriculture,
And through the protection and intercession
              at the throne by the patron,
Count Platon Alexandrovich Zubov,[1]
Having procured Archimandrite with brethren and
              choir
    [He] Proclaimed
Among the uncivilized[2] people, by unheard of
              ignorance trampled down,
The name of God, unknown to them,
And, in the name of the Holy Life-Giving Trinity,
    Implanted [there]
The Orthodox Christian faith
              in the year 1794.
</pre>

<pre>
    Christ the Savior!
Adjoin him to the community of Saints
              who lighted Thine Light on the
              earth among men."
</pre>

<pre>
          "II

"Grigorei Ivanovich Shelikhov
    Eminent Citizen of Rylsk
              Born
              1748
            Married[3]
              1775
Began his trade in the regions of Siberia
              in 1773
          Made sea voyages
    in 1783, 1784 and 1785
    Died July 20, 1795."
</pre>

---

[1] This line is omitted in the final version.

[2] In the final draft, evidently by mistake of the copyist, deep is written in place of uncivilized.

[3] The next six lines are missing in one of the drafts.

Yudin Collection, Box 1, Folder 5.

"This mausoleum is erected[1]
In Memory
Of an esteemed and kind
Husband, friend and benefactor,
By [his] sorrowful widow
With shedding of burning tears
And contrite sighing
To the Lord,
This _____, 1796 (Date [to be in-
(serted] when
(mausoleum is
(completed."

"III[2]

"The Russian Columbus here is buried,
[Who] Crossed the seas, discovered unknown
countries,
And seeing that everything on earth is corrupt,
He set his sail
To the heavenly ocean
To seek treasures celestial, not earthly.
The Treasury of Good,
O God, rest his soul.

:Gav.: Derjh.:

"IV[3]

"As kingdoms fell to the feet of Catherine,
Russ Shelikhov, without armies, with thunderous
force,
Arrived to America, across the stormy deep,
And conquered for her and for God a new region.
Do not forget, descendant,
That Russ, thine ancestor, was famous even in
the East.
Passer-by, honor the dust in this sepulcher:
A Columbus of Russia is buried here.

--Captain of the Imperial Guard,
Iv. Dmitriev.

LCM, Yudin Collection, Box 1, Folder 5, Russian; as
translated in DRAH, vol. 2, pp. 164-166.

---

1 and 2 In the final version, the third inscription begins
"This mausoleum is erected ..." The full name of the
poet who wrote the eight lines of poetry in the third
inscription is Gavriil Derjhavin.

3 Verses by Ivan Dmitriev were added later and perhaps are
written in the poet's own hand.

138

9.

Extract, from Iurii Radchenko, "Kolumbu Rosskomu..."
(To the Russian Columbus...), Panorama Iskusstv (Panorama
of the arts), Moscow, 1979, pp. 340-351.

The Soviet writer Iurii Radchenko, author of this
recent popular article, concerns himself with the monument
over G. I. Shelikhov's grave. He sees significance in the
size and cost of the monument, unusual for that time and
place, and scrutinizes the wording of the epitaph. He
suggests that Shelikhov's progress toward wealth was aided
by his marriage in 1773 to Natal'ia Alekseevna Rezanova.
Natal'ia Shelikhova is thus supplied with a maiden name;
if she was indeed a Rezanov, this would give Shelikhov
another, earlier tie to that family before N. P. Rezanov's
marriage to his daughter Anna. But Radchenko does not cite
a source for this. He then reviews Shteingel's assertions
regarding Natal'ia (already mentioned in the introduction
to this volume) and touches briefly on Shelikhov's achievements, followed by the decline in his affairs in 1795, and
his death. He has examined in the Central State Archive of
Ancient Acts (TsGADA) in Moscow "a small but very curious
file," containing petitions sent by Shelikhov and his family
to the Empress Catherine II. Of particular interest is a
letter dated June 30, 1795, written in Irkutsk:

. . . . . .

... The ninth sheet of this file is filled on both
sides in the uncertain, not always literate hand of Shelikhov's
elder daughter. Only the signature, "Grigorii Shelikhov",
is undoubtedly in his own hand.

Most Gracious Sovereign!

Three days ago I, who from childhood have never
before been sick, came down at 47 years with a severe,
threatening illness. If death comes, then my wife and
children will be left orphaned, and all the more
afflicted because they will be troubled by relatives
eager for my estate, acquired by my labors, in which
no one has a right to share except my wife, my son and
my daughters, and enemies will make every effort to
disconcert my heirs in various ways for the sake of my
trading establishments in Siberia and on the Eastern
Sea. In consideration of this, and as my wife, who
accompanied me on the sea voyage for the acquisition
of estates, and who assisted me by raising my children
and keeping my house, deserves all my trust, it is
she, and no other, with my children, who should inherit
my property, acquired by my efforts and industry. ...
if it is my fate that death will take me in my present
illness, I devotedly and tearfully request that she and

my children be my sole heirs, and if any of my
relatives or anyone else shall attempt in any way
to hinder this division, I, being still of unwavering memory, leave this, my loyal petition, to your
Imperial Highness, so that she can overcome it, and
in this, probably my last letter, I beg this of you,
for my family has no one to protect them except God
and Your Majesty, the mother of our country.

A strange letter!

At the end is written the date: in Irkutsk, June 30,
1795. But clearly the date 30 was inserted later in a
space left after the word "June". The space is small, and
does not even leave room for quotation marks in which by
the rules of that time a letter had to be concluded. In
all other Shelikhov documents it is everywhere March "9" or
April "30".

Nevertheless, the exact date of Grigorii Ivanovich's
death on the monument is July 20th. It appears that the
request was written three weeks before his end, the inevi-
tability of which is stressed: "and in this, probably my
last letter..." Even his strong previous health is given
as proof of inescapable death, although, it would appear
that if he had never been ill, illness would not be something to fear. But no, there is another logic in the
letter: if he has not been ill it means mortal illness!

The natural solution of all difficulties would have
been for him to compile, in customary fashion, a legal will
for his wife and children. There was still time; his memory
was still unwavering...

But there is no will! Neither will nor explanation
(nor can there be!), because such an important document is
not compiled under such strained circumstances... Clearly
that letter must replace and compensate for the lack of the
main paper.

And thus are enumerated possible misfortunes, snares,
and intrigues by enemies of the Shelikhov family; beforehand,
even before their appearance, are enumerated offenses which
they, the enemies, will inflict against the widow and children.
Again is repeated the hardly ever changing formula of the
Shelikhov writings: "My wife, who accompanied me on the sea
voyage for the acquisition of estates, and who assisted me
...deserves all my trust toward her."

As if someone contests, and seeks to refute this natural
situation - contests and refutes solely the lack of a will.

Something bad took place in the Shelikhov house that
summer... There were tales that Grigorii Ivanovich was rent
by pains in his stomach, and that "in an effort to relieve
them, if only for a moment, he gulped down a whole plate
of ice". One of his contemporaries, close to the family,

maintained that he died "by his own doing"; in other words, that he poisoned himself.

But why would he have done this?

Complete bankruptcy, as we will see farther on, was not in question. There were court cases, debts, and difficulties, but there were also hopes, for a new letter requesting support had only just arrived in Petersburg! And if he had killed himself and finally, keeping secret such a violation of church laws, it would have been natural to compose a will.

A strange case!

The remarkable monument has already stood in Znamenskii Irkutsk monastery for two centuries, concealing a secret that is still barely outlined.

Meanwhile, there are only hypotheses...

Shelikhov may have been in sharp conflict with his wife, and with her relatives. It may be that a will was composed which was not what those nearest him wanted, and they hid it. Or, worse, that they, the relatives, may have helped hasten the end of the mighty voyager, in full strength and energy. The letter to the highest name in the land is backdated, not at Shelikhov's dictation but by that of his wife, who, as we will see, was illiterate...

We note that in the text of the petition it is stated that it was compiled, so to speak, for any eventuality, so that if enemies did attack, then the letter would put them to flight. But, it appears that it was compiled without Shelikhov, after Shelikhov...

Someone close to Natal'ia Shelikhova, or a relative, wrote in place of the missing will a clever document, where much, even beyond measure, was foreseen.

The date "June 30": to this, of course, the authors of the request gave thought. It would have been better to show a July date, before Shelikhov's very end. But there were probably doubts, and the space for the "exact date" was not filled in. Then they put in a safer, comparatively early date, and the reason, one must think, is the importunately expressed phrase about 'unwavering memory' - with a later date this could have been contested - they could say that Grigorii Ivanovich, in agony, had been unable to think properly!

Or, another thing - one must show a long illness, and not sudden death.

But how could they explain Shelikhov's own signature under such an astonishing missive to the Empress? If his hand was weak or uncertain, then one could suppose that they had passed off some sort of will on the dying man. But the signature is the usually "healthy" one; just like his signatures on other, earlier documents, and it is at the very bottom of the paper. It was probably a paper signed earlier, and given to some person of trust. In one way or another Shelikhov's wife or someone else could have got hold of such a paper...

It is only a hypothesis. But even without all such hypotheses it is obvious that the letter "of June 30" is strange and suspicious!

The document which follows (all in that same file, begun in Petersburg) in no way diminishes our suspicions.

Grigorii Ivanovich had already been dead for three months. The new letter to the Most Gracious Sovereign (in TsGADA, Razriad XI, No. 1117, 1. 4-5) is signed

> In Irkutsk, 1795, October "15". The true subject, Natal'ia Shelikhova, widow of the Honored Citizen of Ryl'sk, Grigorii Shelikhov. In her place has signed their dauthter, the maiden Ekaterina Shelikhova. Maiden Avdot'ia Shelikhova.

The mother, obviously, was illiterate. Half of the epistle is taken up with an enumeration of the services of the late seafarer, his voyages and economic organizational affairs. It is a strong, impressive enumeration--as if it were the draft of the inscription for the future monument.

"In the midst of such important enterprises," continues the author of the letter, "in full health and in the middle

> years of his life--last July Shelikhov took ill with cattarhal ague, lingered with perfect memory for 25 days, and finally died. On his death I was left with our children - 1 son and 5 daughters - and although without a written will compiled in accepted form, with detailed oral instructions.

Not explaining why the head of the house did not leave a will, Natal'ia Shelikhova (or, obviously, those around her) explains the appearance of the letter "of June 30" as follows, in very naive fashion: "I am left by law, with

> my children, the sole heiress of his estate and possessions. If at any time someone threatens this right, my husband entrusted me in such a case to take from his files and for my defense use his petition to Your Imperial Majesty written at the beginning of his illness by my elder daughter, as if foreseeing his death.

Judging by Natal'ia Alekseevna's letter, the hour of sending the letter left by her husband had come: she had already proclaimed to the Irkutsk authorities her right,

> guided by both the law and my blameless conduct, surrounded not only by my children but by close relatives of my husband, I am entirely able to account to the treasury for the remaining capital of the American company of half a million rubles.

However, the Irkutsk crown court, it appears, on October 6, 1795, "decided to rule on whether it can trust

> me, for not having a written will from my husband. Such enterprise of the crown court is not within

its jurisdiction, and is done at the instigation of
several powerful enemies of my husband and of myself.
Envious of his far-flung enterprises, they wish
forcibly to disrupt them under the pretense of
taking them under wardship, through which they can
plunder them, thus making me, and my children,
sacrifices to their cunning.

Both documents, Shelikhov's "last letter" of June 30,
and his widow's complaint of October 15, were sent to St.
Petersburg together, raising the strong suspicion that the
"June message" was prepared now, in the autumn, three months
after the death of its "author".

How the government reacted we do not know. The file
does not contain any sort of draft of a reply. To the
experienced jurist Troshchinskii [Catherine's secretary] all
this, of course, must have seemed very strange. However,
the main pressure of Irkutsk on the capital came through an
unofficial channel: the Rezanovs had, as we will see, good
connections in St. Petersburg...

In any case, the theme of the energetic widow, victor-
iously looking after her own after the mysterious death of
her husband, was not unfamiliar to the Empress Catherine II,
from her own experience...

Even without knowing the details of the whole intrigue,
we know that Natal'ia Shelikhova achieved what she sought:
the capital, or a large part of it, remained with her.
And there and then wheels are set in motion toward building
a memorial, of a size which astonished contemporaries.
What did this actually conceal? The natural wish of a widow
to perpetuate the memory of her husband, which was to be
illuminated as well by the Russian-American Company itself
(finally confirmed by the new emperor Paul I, four years
after the death of its initiator)? And was not a special
monument called for to redeem certain dark deeds of the
widow regarding her so early deceased spouse? The unprece-
dented memorial outlined the family succession, and easily
refuted any unfavorable rumor...

And rumors there were. As the Decembrist Vladimir
Ivanovich Shteingel', returning to the land of his birth
on service matters seven years after Shelikhov's death,
wrote later: "Many ascribed Shelikhov's sudden demise to
his wife..."

Work on the monument dragged out for five years. The
monument even gets in the Irkutsk chronicle:

In 1800 the heirs raised a magnificent monument,
enveloped in marble, in the shape of a pyramidal
obelisk with a three-stage base, 7 arshins high,
with his portrait in bronze bas-relief. This
mausoleum was made in Ekaterinburg.

From the Urals to Irkutsk, for three thousand versts
and more, they carry the many ton mausoleum. They chip out
the verses of Derzhavin (perhaps composed by order), and
the verses of Dmitriev, and decorate the north side with

the proud, very merchant-like inscription:

> The grief-stricken widow, with a flood of bitter
> tears, and sighs to the Lord, has erected this
> monument in memory of her honored and virtuous
> spouse. In all it cost 11,760 rubles.

Both the sum and the epitaph were unheard of for the
merchantry; it is no wonder the chronicler mentioned it.

Much, very much, even importunately, is the sorrowful
role of the widow stressed in the inscriptions - it all
arouses a feeling that the monument covers a dark deed.

That the mausoleum of Shelikhov actually sumbolized much
and was an element of a bitter struggle is shown by yet
another complex of documents, preserved in the Manuscript
Division of the public library in Leningrad. (Otdel
rukopisei Gos. publichnoi biblioteki SSSR, f. 859 (N.K.
Shil'der) k. 33, No. 12). It relates to the year 1800.
The bishop of Irkutsk, Veniamin, wrote the archbishop of
St. Petersburg, Amvrosii, expressing his doubts regarding
the request by the relatives of the late Shelikhov to erect
a monument in the Znamenskii monastery. Reports the bishop:

> Mrs. Shelikhov's son-in-law, Mr. Buldakov, has
> recently come to me; he declared that they intend
> to erect a monument to Shelikhov, and asked my
> consent for this. But this monument is extraordinary
> in both its size and its decoration, for according
> to Buldakov it is five arshins high, and as the
> abbot says, it is higher than the altar; the
> decorations on it represent Mr. Shelikhov as a
> subjugator of peoples...because of all this I
> decided to delay giving any assent to erection of
> this monument pending instructions from your High
> Excellency.

The scene is clear enough: the energetic son-in-law of
Mrs. Shelikhov (might it not have been he who compiled the
letter to the Empress?) chats freely with the bishop.
Veniamin, frightened at the depiction on the memorial of
the merchant-conqueror of peoples (as in Dmitriev's verses)
and by the audacious size of the monument ("there is nothing
like it in the Aleksandr Nevskii monastery") does not want
to authorize it independently. Among other things he
complains that he asked the Shelikhovs for a picture of the
monument, to enclose with his enquiry, "but they refused."

Evidently, knowing more than a little about the secret
history of the mausoleum, but cowering before his wealthiest
and most influential parishioners, the bishop assures the
higher religious personage of the capital that has "no
desire whatever to cause Mrs. Shelikhov any sort of
dissatisfaction through this..."

Metropolitan Amvrosii did not know what to decide
either. At that time one person decided everything: the
Emperor Paul, who in a rare good mood would say that in
Russia two people decided things - he himself and his first

assistant, the procurator-general. Therefore, on July 19,
1800, Amvrosii turned to the mighty procurator-general,
Petr Obol'ianinov. As we see, the seven arshin monument
at Znamenskii monastery has become a secret and important
state affair, and the highest persons are deciding its fate.

Obol'ianinov, in his function, quickly orients himself
and discovers a close relative of the Shelikhovs in the
same city with him: Nikolai Petrovich Rezanov, manager of
newly confirmed Russian-American Company, a person very
interesting to the procurator-general and other persons
because of his wealth, influence and generosity (soon to
be the first ambassador of the Russian state to Japan).

Obol'ianinov asked Rezanov for a picture of the monument. The Siberian replied with no little acerbity, and
if we recall the political climate in Paul's Petersburg,
and how frightening and mighty was Petr Khrisanfovich
Obol'ianinov at that time, then we can guess the power of
Mr. Rezanov:

> Dear Sir, Petr Khrisanfovich!
>
> In Your High Excellency's most honored communi-
> cation you request a picture of the Shelikhov
> monument. I see that the hatred of the Irkutsk
> merchants and others ill-disposed toward us, and
> of the bishop there, Veniamin, who is evidently in
> league with them, have represented this family
> exploit in altogether another light to the
> government. First, this is not a monument but a
> mausoleum, of which there are many here in the
> Nevskii monastery, but in Irkutsk, of course, this
> is the first. Second, it will not be placed in a
> square nor in the town... Third, it will beautify
> the monastery, and will be for posterity a memorial
> to Russian enterprise.

Describing the monument in detail, and not forgetting
to mention its great cost, Rezanov concludes:

> These expenditures are the sacrifice of our
> generosity. However, when in foreign states they
> raise public monuments to great men, whether writers,
> musicians or artists, then really does not this
> Russian, who made subjects of many peoples, deserve
> some sort of inscription regarding this on his tomb?

Rezanov asked Obol'ianinov not to permit "the malicious
and ignorant [to detract from] the happiness of our family.
Indeed the very monastery in which my father-in-law is
buried benefitted from us in the form a large loan, besides
repairs, made by us, at one time or another, to stone walls,
etc."

A day later, on July 23, 1800, Obol'ianinov reported
to the Emperor. Probably he presented the matter neatly
and carefully. If Paul found, as he easily could, that
almost tsar-like glory was ascribed to the Ryl'sk merchant,
and if Paul realized that the inscriptions on the monument

repeatedly praised the deeds of his hated mother Catherine,
there would be hell to pay, and - there would be no
monument! However, he got around it:

Obol'ianinov - to Veniamin of Irkutsk:

I had the good fortune to report to the Sovereign
Emperor and receive His Imperial Majesty's Highest
Order to erect the monument.

Thus, thanks to a successful confluence of circumstances,
the beautiful obelisk was preserved...

Gradually the passions died down, diminished and
disappeared, and the talk called forth by the monument's
appearance. Ten years later, on March 25, 1810, Natal'ia
Alekseevna Shelikhova ended her days in Moscow. Obviously
it was impossible for her to remain in Irkutsk. Shteingel',
whom we have already cited more than once, notes that the
widow of the first discoverer, "well-known for her debauchery,
ended her life in unfortunate fashion, brought to extremity
by one of her sycophants. Such," he concludes, "is always
the end of sin. He whom wealth and chance may screen before
people, can conceal nothing before providence."

More decades passed, and beyond the monastery enclosure
appeared the modest and simple graves of the Decembrists
and their wives.

Not far from them is the monument to Shelikhov, unusual
in its history, form, and hero. There resides the memory of
an astonishing personage. His name is recalled by a small
town not far from Irkutsk, by Shelikhov Bay in the Sea of
Okhotsk, and by Shelikhov Strait in the northeastern part
of the Pacific Ocean.

In the proud Irkutsk monument come together geography
and poetry, history and multi-faceted human passions, "like
a dancing flame."

EDITORIAL NOTE. This selection presents some new facts
and interesting theories. The letter of June 30, 1795 states
that Shelikhov was then 47, supporting the birthdate of 1748
on his epitaph instead of the accepted one of 1747. In her
letter of October 15, 1795, Natal'ia mentions one son and
five daughters, which clarifies the question of the size of
the family. As for the hypothesis of Natal'ia's villainy,
more evidence is needed. Her letters (e.g., Tikhmenev, v. 2,
1979:85-90), show her to have been clever and businesslike.
Her signature on two documents in the Yudin Collection of
the Library of Congress refutes Radchenko's contention that
she was illiterate. After her death, on March 25, 1810, she
was interred in the Donskoi monastery cemetery in Moscow.
Her grave is not to be found. Unlike that which she provided
her husband, it must have had only a modest marker, which
has long since disappeared.--R.P.

146

BIBLIOGRAPHY

Editions of G.I. Shelikhov's 'Travels'

1. Rossiiskago kuptsa Grigor'ia Shelekhova stranstvovanie s 1783 po 1787 god iz Okhotska po Vostochnomu Okeanu
k Amerikanskim beregam... (Travels of the Russian merchant
Grigorii Shelekhov from 1783 to 1787 from Okhotsk on the
Eastern Ocean to the American shores...). St. Petersburg,
1791. Published by V.S. 74 pp. With map and "depiction
of the seafarer and the savage peoples he found." The
first edition, based upon his report of 1787. See No. 11.

2. Rossiiskago kuptsa Grigoriia Shelekhova prodol-
zhenie stranstvovaniia po Vostochnomu Okeanu k Amerikanskim
beregam v 1788 godu... (A continuation of the travels of
the Russian merchant Grigorii Shelekhov on the Eastern
Ocean to the American shores in 1788...) St. Petersburg,
1792. Published by V.S. 95 pp. A summary, in the third
person, of the voyage of Bocharov and Izmailov from Kodiak
through Prince William Sound to Lituya Bay and back, based
on the ship's journal.

3. Rossiiskago kuptsa imenitago Ryl'skago grazhdanina
Grigoriia Shelekhova pervoe stranstvovanie... St. Petersburg, 1793. Published by V.S. Pages 1-86 contain the text
of the first edition (1791), pages 87-172 the added
Istoricheskoe i Geograficheskoe opisanie Kuril'skikh,
Aleutskikh, Andreianovskikh i Lis'evskikh ostrovov,
prostiraiushchikhsia ot Kamchatki k Amerike na Vostochnom
Okeane (Historical and geographical description of the
Kurile, Aleutian, Andreianov and Fox islands, extending
from Kamchatka to America on the Eastern Ocean), compiled,
evidently at the behest of the publisher, from earlier
accounts. Sometimes bound with No. 2.

4. Grigori Schelechof Russischen Kaufmanns Erste und
Zweyte Reise von Ochotsk in Sibirien durch den ostlichen
Ocean nach den Küsten von Amerika in den jahren 1783 bis
1789... Translated from the Russian by J.Z. Logan, publisher.
St. Petersburg, 1793. Pp. 1-84. A translation of Nos. 1
and 2.

5. "Des Russischen Kaufmanns Gregor Schelechow Reise
in den Jahren 1783 bis 1787 von Ochotsk auf dem westlichen
Ocean nach den ufern von Amerika, und seine Rükkehr nach
Russland..." Journal von Russland, published by Johann
Heinrich Busse. St. Petersburg, 1793, July, pp. 11-29;
August, pp. 59-75; October, pp. 237-246. Transl. of No. 1.

6. "Schelechof's Reise von Ochotsk nach Amerika vom Jahr 1783 bis 1787," Neue Nordische Beyträge..., v. 6, publ. by Johann Zacharias Logan, 1793, pp. 165-249. Text of No. 4.

7. Grigori Schelechof Russischen Kaufmanns Erste und Zweyte Reise von Ochotsk in Sibirien durch den ostlichen Ocean nach den Küsten von Amerika in den Jahren 1783 bis 1789... St. Petersburg, 1793. Published by J.Z. Logan. 84 pp. A separate reprint of No. 6, using the same type.

8. "The Voyage of Gregory Shelekhof, a Russian Merchant, from Okhotzk on the Eastern ocean, to the coast of America in the years 1783, 1784, 1785, 1786, 1787 and his return to Russia. From his own journal," The Varieties of Literature from foreign literary journals and original manuscripts, now first published, edited by the Reverend William Tooke. London, 1795, v. 2, pp. 1-42. Translation from the German, No. 4.

9. "Narrative of Shelekof's Voyage to Kodiak from 1783 to 1787," in William Coxe, Account of the Russian discoveries between Asia and America. Fourth edition. London, 1803, pp. 269-301. Followed by "Voyage of Ismaelof and Betsharoff," pp. 302-343. Translated from the German, No. 6.

10. Puteshestvie G. Shelekhova s 1783 po 1790 god iz Okhotska... In two parts, with a picture. St. Petersburg, 1812. Frontispiece, 2, 172 pp., 1 l., 90 pp. Combines Nos. 3 and 2.

11. "Rossiiskogo kuptsa imenitogo Ryl'skogo grazhdanina Grigoriia Shelekhova pervoe stranstvovanie...," in Pamiatnaia knizhka Kurskoi gubernii na 1894 god... Kursk gubernia administration, Kursk, 1894. 41 pp. Reprint of No. 3. Followed by reprint of No. 2, 22 pp.

12. "Zapiska Shelikhova stranstvovaniiu ego v Vostochnom more," in Russkie otkrytiia v Tikhom okeane i Severnoi Amerike v XVIII veke, edited by A. I. Andreev. Moscow, 1948, pp. 226-249. Shelikhov's original report of his voyage, submitted in 1787, which was published in 1791 (No. 1).

13. Rossiiskogo kuptsa Grigoriia Shelikhova stranstvovaniia iz Okhotska po Vostochnomu Okeanu k Amerikanskim beregam. Edited, with introduction and epilogue, by B.P. Polevoi. Extensive notes and bibliography. Text of No. 10. Khabarovsk, 1971. 174 pp.

Sources and Literature

Adamov, Arkadii. Grigorii Ivanovich Shelekhov (1747-1795). SOVETSKAIA ETNOGRAFIIA. M.-L., 1948:1. p. 189-201. Portrait and bibliog.

-----. SHELEKHOV NA KAD'IAKE; POVEST'. M., 1948. 119 p. Fictional account. Biographical sketch at the end.

-----. Novye materialy o "Kolumba Rossiiskom." KURSKII ALMANAKH, 1950:1, p. 137-144. Discusses documents compiled by A. I. Andreev.

-----. G.I. SHELIKHOV: ZAMECHATEL'NYI RUSSKII MOREPLAVATEL' I ISSLEDOVATEL'. M., 1951. 31 p. incl. bibliography. Text of a public lecture, given in Moscow.

-----. G.I. SHELEKHOV. ed. by M.S. Bondarskii. M., 1952. 43 p. Same as 1951 lecture text.

-----. PRAVDA O RUSSKIKH OTKRYTIIAKH V AMERIKE. M., 1952. 31 p.

Alekseev, A.I. SYNY OTVAZHNYE ROSSII. Magadan, 1970. 368 p. (See: Russian Columbuses, p. 130-142).

-----. 'Kolumb Rosskii.' VOPROSY ISTORII, 1973:1, p. 210-213. Discusses new information found in archives, included in following book:

-----. SUD'BA RUSSKOI AMERIKI. Magadan, 1975. 328 p., illus. and maps. See: p. 100-136.

Andreev, A.I. Foreword to RUSSKIE OTKRYTIIA V TIKHOM OKEANE V XVIII V. (q.v.)

Andrews, C.L. THE STORY OF ALASKA. 1938/Caldwell, Idaho, 1953. 332 p.

ARKHIV GRAFOV MORDVINOVYKH. St. Petersburg, 1901- .

ATLAS GEOGRAFICHESKIKH OTKRYTII V SIBIRI I V SEVERO-ZAPADNOI AMERIKE. Compiled, with introduction, by A.V. Efimov. M., 1964. xvi + 137 p. Superb collection of 174 maps of early Siberia and Russian America.

B-ov, I.N. Pamiati G.I. Shelekhova, RUSSKII VESTNIK, 1895, No. 38.

Bashilov, B. IUNOST' KOLUMBA ROSSIISKOGO. München, 194-? 72 p.

Berkh, V.N. KHRONOLOGICHESKAIA ISTORIIA OTKRYTIIA ALEUTSKIKH OSTROVOV... St. P., 1823. Transl., by Dmitri Krenov, A CHRONOLOGICAL HISTORY OF THE DISCOVERY OF THE ALEUTIAN ISLANDS. Kingston, Ont., 1974. 127 p.

Bancroft, H.H. HISTORY OF ALASKA, 1730-1885. v. 38 of WORKS. San Francisco, 1886/N.Y., 1960. 775 p. Still an outstanding comprehensive account, in spite of some errors.

Bodnarskii, M.S. O knigakh G.I. Shelekhova (istoriko-bibliografo-geograficheskaia zametka), IZVESTIIA VSES. GEOGR. O-VA, 1950:5, v. 82, p. 545-548. Analysis of maps in Shelikhov's book. Shows likelihood that Capt. M.S. Golikov made them.

Bolkhovitinov, N.N. STANOVLENIE RUSSKO-AMERIKANSKIKH OTNOSHENII, 1775-18 1775-1815. M., 1966. 640 p. Bibliog. p. 601-625. Transl. by Elena Levin, THE BEGINNINGS OF RUSSIAN-AMERICAN RELATIONS, 1775-1815. Cambridge/London, 1975. 484 p. The best account. Some discussion of Shelikhov.

Chevigny, H. LOST EMPIRE. THE LIFE AND ADVENTURES OF NIKOLAI PETROVICH
REZANOV. N.Y., 1937. 356 p.

-----. LORD OF ALASKA. THE STORY OF BARANOV AND THE RUSSIAN ADVENTURE.
N.Y., 1942/Portland, 1952. 320 p.

-----. RUSSIAN AMERICA... 1741-1867. N.Y., 1965. 274 p.

Coxe, William. ACCOUNT OF THE RUSSIAN DISCOVERIES BETWEEN ASIA AND
AMERICA. London, 1780. 344 p. 2nd ed., 1780; 3rd ed., 1787;
4th ed., 1803, 500 p. The latter includes transl. (from German)
of Shelikhov's account (p. 269-301) and Bocharov and Izmailov
(p. 302-343).

Dubrovskii, K. Russkii kolumb, SIBIRSKII SBORNIK, vyp. 1, 1901.

Fedorchenko, T.P. K voprosu o kartakh plavaniia I.L. Golikova i G.I.
Shelikhova k Tikhookeanskim beregam Severnoi Ameriki v 1783-1786 gg.
VOPROSY GEOGRAFII, sb. 22, M., 1950, p. 181-185.

Fedorova, S.G. RUSSKOE NASELENIE ALIASKI I KALIFORNII, KONETS XVIII
VEKA - 1867 g. M., 1971. 276 p. Based on archival materials;
many previously unpublished maps and illustrations. Transl. by
R.A.Pierce and A.S. Donnelly, THE RUSSIAN POPULATION IN ALASKA
AND CALIFORNIA, LATE 18TH CENTURY - 1867. Kingston, Ont., 1973.
376 p.

G.I. Shelekhov, uchreditel' Rossiisko-Amerikanskoi kompanii, IRKUTSKIE
GUBERNSKIE VEDOMOSTI, 1860:18.

G.I. Shelekhov (1745-1795), osnovatel' Rossiisko-amerikanskoi kompanii,
RUSSKIE LIUDI, v. 1, publ. by M.O. Vol'f, St. P., 1866, p. 15-30.

Grigorii Ivanovich Shelikhov, MIRSKOI VESTNIK, 1873:1, p. 43-54.

Grigorii Ivanovich Shelekhov, PAMIATNAIA KNIZHKA KURSKOI GUBERNII NA
1894. Compiled by secretary of Kursk gubernia statistical
committee, T.I. Verzhbitskii. Kursk, 1894. Introduction, p. 1-5,
mentions members of Shelekhov family still residing in Ryl'sk.
Portrait and 2 maps followed by reprint of Shelikhov's book,
p. 1-41, 1-22.

Grigor'ev, V.S. GRIGORII SHELIKHOV. ISTORICHESKII ROMAN. M., 1952,
1956, 1961. 592 p. Rev.: Leon I. Twarog, Russian novelists look
at America, AMERICAN SLAVIC AND EAST EUROPEAN REVIEW, v. 19:4, Dec.
1960, p. 561-576. M.A. Sergeev, O pravde istoricheskoi i
khudozhestvennoi, DAL'NII VOSTOK, 1953:2. Although excessively
nationalistic, and sometimes careless with facts, Grigor'ev has
put out a tale of some interest, especially since there are so
few historical novels about this period.

IRKUTSKAIA LETOPIS'. Irkutsk, 1911.

Iurkevich, B. Grigorii Shelekhov, LITERATURNYI ALMANAKH, Kursk,
1940:2, p. 230-269. Largely imaginary; fiction masquerading as
history.

Khlebnikov, K.T. G.I. Shelekhov, ZHURNAL DLIA CHTENIIA VOSPITANNIKOV
VOENNO-UCHEBNYKH ZAVEDENII, 1840, no. 89.

Khlebnikov, K.T.   RUSSKAIA AMERIKA V NEOPUBLIKOVANNYKH ZAPISKAKH
    K.T. KHLEBNIKOVA. Compiled, with introd. and commentary, by
    R.G. Liapunova and S.G. Fedorova. Leningrad, 1979. 280 p.
    Four parts (Kad'iak, eastern Aleutians, western Aleutians, and
    Pribylov Islands and northern regions) of six-part manuscript.
    (Two other parts, on Sitka and Fort Ross, published previously).
    A fundamental work. Many references to Shelikhov.

-----. Zhizneopisanie dostopamiatnykh russkikh. Grigorii Ivanovich
    Shelekhov, SYN OTECHESTVA, 1838, v. 2, otd. 3, p. 66-83.
    Authoritative, but contains only standard fund of facts.

-----. Zhizneopisanie Gr. I. Shelekhova, RUSSKII INVALID, 1838, Nos.
    77-82, 84. Same as above.

K ISTORII ROSSIISKO-AMERIKANSKOI KOMPANII (SBORNIK DOKUMENTAL'NYKH
    MATERIALOV). Krasnoiarsk, 1957. Transl. by Marina Ramsay,
    DOCUMENTS ON THE HISTORY OF THE RUSSIAN-AMERICAN COMPANY, Kingston,
    Ontario, 1976. 220 p.

Koe-chto o Shelikhove, Khlebnikove i Rezanove, MORSKOI SBORNIK, 1869:7,
    neof. chast'.

KURSKIE GUBERNSKIE VEDOMOSTI, Kursk. 1894, No. 131, G.I. Shelekhov
    (by T. Verzhbitskii); 1895, No. 155, G.I. Shelekhov, with portrait,
    by T.I.V. No. 162, Prazdnovanie stoletiia konchiny G.I. Shelekhova;
    1902, No. 155, Korrespondentsiia iz g. Ryl'ska po voprosu ob
    uvekovechenoi pamiati izvestnogo moreplavatelia-urozhentsa Ryl'ska
    G.I. Shelekhova, by P. Iakovlev; 1903, No. 169, Kor-tsiia iz g.
    Ryl'ska o predstoiashchem otkrytii pamiatnika izvestnomu
    moreplavateliu Gr. Iv. Shelekhovu; No. 182, Peredovaia stat'ia po
    povodu otkrytii v Ryl'ske pamiatnika G.I.Shelekhovu.

Lada-Mocarski, Valerian. BIBLIOGRAPHY OF BOOKS ON ALASKA PUBLISHED
    BEFORE 1868. New Haven and London, 1969. 567 p. Meticulous
    bibliographic analysis of 161 basic works, but treats only
    first (1791) ed. of Shelikhov book, p. 186-189. For discussion
    of other editions, see A. Yarmolinsky.

Makarova, R.V. RUSSKIE NA TIKHOM OKEANE VO VTOROI POLOVINY XVIII VEKA,
    M., 1968, 200 p. Transl. by R.A.Pierce and A.S. Donnelly, RUSSIANS
    ON THE PACIFIC, 1743-1799. Kingston, Ont. 1975. 301 p.

Markov, S.N. Kolumby Rossiiskie, SOVETSKOE KRAEVEDENIE, 1936:6.

-----. Russkie na Tikhom okeane, SIBIRSKIE OGNI, 1941:3-4.

-----. Ob arkhive Iudina, OMSKAIA OBLAST', 1939:8.

-----. Grigorii Shelekhov - kolumb Rossiiskii, 30 DNEI, M., 1940,
    v. 16:9-10, p. 106-113.

-----. Letopisi morskoi slavy (arkhivy issledovatelei Tikhogo okeana),
    NAUKA I ZHIZN', 1944:1-2.

-----. Russkie otkrytiia v Tikhom okeane v XVIII-XIX vv., KRASNYI FLOT,
    12 Sept. 1944.

-----. O Shelekhove, NAUKA I ZHIZN, 1945: 1-2.

-----. Klady "Kolumbov Rossiiskikh," MORSKOI sbornik, 1944:8-10.

Markov, S.N. LETOPIS ALIASKI. M., 1946, and as part of IUKONSKII
VORON, M. 1970 (p. 191-366). An "Alaska chronicle" made up of
bits of information derived from a lifetime of study. Often very
interesting, but with no indication of sources.

-----. ZEMNOI KRUG. M., 1971. 560 p. Popular work on explorations,
including a section on Shelikhov.

-----. VECHNYE SLEDY. M., 1973. 496 p. Content is similar to that
of ZEMNOI KRUG, but is arranged differently. In the late 1930's
Markov discovered various rare documents on early Alaska. A
popularizer, he introduced hundreds of thousands of readers to
his field.

Okun', S.B. ROSSIISKO-AMERIKANSKAIA KOMPANIIA. M.-L., 1939. 260 p.
Transl. by Carl Ginsburg, THE RUSSIAN-AMERICAN COMPANY. Cambridge,
1951. 311 p. An essential work, based on unpublished material.

Pallas, P.S. Perechen' puteshestviia shturmana Zaikova k ostrovam
mezhdu Azieiu i Amerikoiu, nakhodiashchimsia na bote Sv. Vladimira,
MESIATSOSLOV ISTORICHESKII I GEOGRAFICHESKII NA 1782 GOD. St.P.,
1782.

-----. O rossiiskikh otkrytiiakh na moriakh mezhdu Azieiu i Amerikoiu,
SOBR. SOCHINENII VYBRANNYKH IZ MESIATSOSLOVOV, v. 4, St. P., 1790.

(Derzhavin, G.P.) Nadgrobie Ryl'skomu imianitomu grazhdaninu Shelekhovu,
MUZA, 1796, Feb., p. 100.

Pamiatnik G.I. Shelekhova, ZHURNAL DLIA CHETENIIA VOSPITANNIKOV
VOENNO-UCHEBNYKH ZAVEDENII, 1839, v. 18, no. 70, p. 206-208.
Inscription text.

Pamiatnik G.I. Shelekhova i ego biografiia, SYN OTECHESTVA, 1839,
v. 7, p. 20-21. Descrip. of obelisk purchased by his heirs.
Same in RUSSKII INVALID, 1839:4, p. 135, 136.

Paramuzin, Iu. P. Grigorii Ivanovich Shelikhov (147-1795), OTECHESTVENNYE
FIZIKO-GEOGRAFY I PUTESHESTVENNIKI, M., 1959.

Petrov, Viktor. KOLUMBY ROSSIISKIE. Washington, 1971. 197 p.

Polevoi, B.P. GRIGORII SHELIKHOV - "KOLUMB ROSSKII". Magadan, 1960.

-----. Introduction, after word and notes to G.I. Shelikhov,
ROSSIISKOGO KUPTSA... (q.v.)

Preobrazhenskii, A.A. O sostave aktsionerov Rossiisko-Amerikanskoi
kompanii v nachale XIX v. ISTORICHESKIE ZAPISKI, v. 67, 1960.

Prosetskii, V.A. G.I. Shelikhov kak prosvetitel' narodov "Russkoi
Ameriki," UCHEN. ZAPISKI ELETSKII PED. IN-T, Lipetsk, 1957, v. 2,
p. 15-42. Bibliog.

Pypin, A.N. ISTORIIA RUSSKOI ETNOGRAFII. St. P., 1890-1892. 4 v.
(See v. 4, p. 251-254 re Shelikhov).

Pierce, R.A. Seward's 18th century beginnings, ALASKA SPORTSMAN,
August 1969, p. 18-19, 49.

-----. (and A.F. Dolgopolov). Alaska treasure: Our search for the
Russian plates, ALASKA JOURNAL, v. 1:1, Winter, 1971, p. 2-7.

152

Radchenko, Iurii. "Kolumbu Rosskomu..." PANORAMA ISKUSSTV, M., 1979, p. 340-351.

Raikhenberg, M. Grigorii Shelekhov, NASHA STRANA, 1940:2, p. 28-32.

Rikhter, G.D. G.I. Shelekhov, GEOGRAFIIA V SHKOLE, 1941:2, p. 35-50.

RUSSKIE OTKRYTIIA V TIKHOM OKEANE I V SEVERNOI AMERIKE V XVIII-XIX VEKAKH. SBORNIK MATERIALOV. Compiled by A.I. Andreev. M.-L., 1944. Transl., Carl Ginsburg, RUSSIAN DISCOVERIES IN THE PACIFIC AND IN NORTH AMERICA IN THE EIGHTEENTH AND NINETEENTH CENTURIES. A COLLECTION OF MATERIALS. Ann Arbor, 1952. 214 p.

RUSSKIE OTKRYTIIA V TIKHOM OKEANE I SEVERNOI AMERIKE V XVIII-XIX VEKAKH. SBORNIK DOKUMENTOV. Compiled by A.I. Andreev. M., 1948. 383 p., illus., maps. Dedicated to the memory of G.I. Shelikhov, for the two hundredth anniversary of his birth (1747-1947). Contains some of the documents from the 1944 edition, but has many additional ones, mainly on Shelikhov.

Rodionoff, N.R. Shelekhov, Grigorii Ivanovich, DICTIONARY OF AMERICAN BIOGRAPHY, v. 17, 1935, p. 67-68.

Shelekhov, BROCKHAUS-EFRON ENTSIKLOPEDICHESKII SLOVAR'. St. P., 1903, v. 77, p. 405.

Shelekhov - Stoletie so dnia ego konchiny, ISTORICHESKII VESTNIK, 1895:9, p. 807. Same, 1897:4, p. 88-89.

Shelekhov (Shelikhov), Grigorii Ivanovich, RUSSKII BIOGRAFICHESKII SLOVAR', v. "Shebanov-Shiuts", St.P., 1911, p. 70-71.

Shirokii, V.F. Iz istorii khoziaistvennoi deiatel'nosti Rossiisko-amerikanskoi kompanii, ISTORICHESKIE ZAPISKI, M., 1942, vyp. 13.

Shteingel', V.I. Zapiski..., in Semevskii, OBSHCHESTVENNYI DVIZHENIIA V ROSSII V PERVUIU POLOVINU XIX VEKA, St. P., 1905, v. 1.

Smert' Shelikhova (v dramaticheskoi forme), VESTNIK EVROPY, soch. 3, 1802, ch. 1, no. 3, p. 52-61. A bad play, done in Greek style, with a chorus, expressing despair of the native "Afognaks" when a Russian ship arrives with news of Shelikhov's death.

Tikhmenev, P.A. ISTORICHESKOE OBOZRENIE OBRAZOVANIIA ROSSIISKO-AMERIKANSKOI KOMPANII I DEISTVIIA EE DO NASTOIASHCHEGO VREMENI, v. 1-2, St. P., 1861, 1863. Translation of text, R.A.Pierce and A.S. Donnelly, HISTORY OF THE RUSSIAN-AMERICAN COMPANY. Seattle and London, 1978. 522 p. Documents, in appendices of the original Russian work, were published as HISTORY OF THE RUSSIAN-AMERICAN COMPANY, v. 2, Kingston, Ont., 1979. 257 p.

THE UNITED STATES AND RUSSIA. THE BEGINNING OF RELATIONS, 1765-1815. Compiled and edited by a joint American and Soviet team. Washington, D.C., 1980. 1184 p. An identical volume, in Russian, was published in Moscow. Includes documents and notes regarding G.I. and Natal'ia Shelikhov. A mine of information.

Yarmolinsky, A. Shelekhov's voyage to Alaska. A bibliographical note, BULLETIN OF THE N.Y. PUBLIC LIBRARY, March 1932, p. 141-148.

INDEX

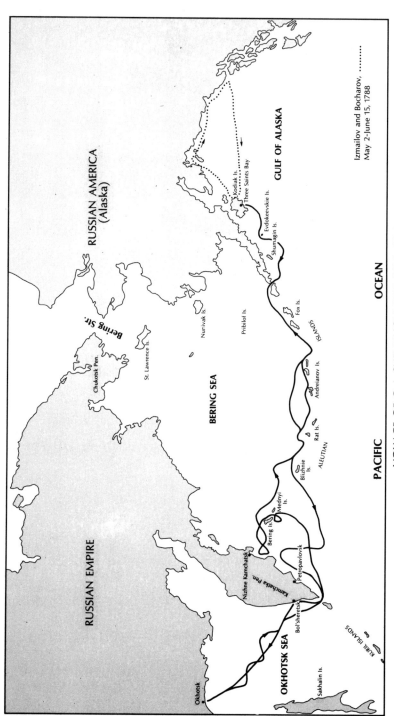

RUSSIAN EMPIRE

RUSSIAN AMERICA
(Alaska)

OKHOTSK SEA

BERING SEA

GULF OF ALASKA

PACIFIC   OCEAN

Bering Str.

Okhotsk

Sakhalin Is.

KURIL ISLANDS

Bol'sheretsk

Petropavlovsk

Kamchatka Pen.

Nizhne Kamchatsk

Bering Is.

Mednyi Is.

Blizhnie Is.

ALEUTIAN

Rat Is.

Andreianov Is.

ISLANDS

Fox Is.

Pribilof Is.

Nunivak Is.

St. Lawrence Is.

Chukotsk Pen.

Shumagin Is.

Evdokeevskie Is.

Three Saints Bay

Kodiak Is.

Izmailov and Bocharov, ...
May 2–June 15, 1788

VOYAGE OF G. I. SHELIKHOV 1783–1784, 1786

ALASKA HISTORY

(Nos. 1-17: Materials for the Study of Alaska History.)

1. R.A. Pierce. ALASKAN SHIPPING, 1867-1878. ARRIVALS AND DEPARTURES AT THE PORT OF SITKA. 1972. 72 pp.

2. F.W. Howay. A LIST OF TRADING VESSELS IN THE MARITIME FUR TRADE, 1785-1825. 1973. 209 pp., bibliog., index. Ships and fur traders on the Northwest Coast.

3. K.T. Khlebnikov. BARANOV, CHIEF MANAGER OF THE RUSSIAN COLONIES IN AMERICA. 1973. 140 pp. Transl. from the Russian edition of 1835. (OUT OF PRINT)

4. S.G. Fedorova. THE RUSSIAN POPULATION IN ALASKA AND CALIFORNIA (LATE 18TH CENTURY TO 1867). 1973. 367 pp. Transl. from the Russian edition of 1972. (OUT OF PRINT)

5. V.N. Berkh. A CHRONOLOGICAL HISTORY OF THE DISCOVERY OF THE ALEUTIAN ISLANDS. 1974. 121 pp. Transl. from the Russian edition of 1823.

6. R.V. Makarova. RUSSIANS ON THE PACIFIC, 1743-1799. 1975. 301 pp. Transl. from the Russian edition of 1968.

7. DOCUMENTS ON THE HISTORY OF THE RUSSIAN-AMERICAN COMPANY. 1976. 220 pp. Trade practices, way of life, and leading figures of early Alaska. Transl. from the Russian edition of 1957.

8. R.A. Pierce. RUSSIA'S HAWAIIAN ADVENTURE, 1815-1817. 1976. 245 pp. Documents concerning the Alaska-based attempt to take over the Hawaiian Islands for Russia. Reprint of the 1965 edition, with maps and illustrations.

9. H.W. Elliott. THE SEAL ISLANDS OF ALASKA. 1976. 176 pp., with many of Elliott's sketches. Reprint of the 1881 edition, prepared for the Tenth Census of the United States. A fundamental work on the Pribilof Islands and the sealing industry soon after the Alaska purchase.

10. G.I. Davydov. TWO VOYAGES TO RUSSIAN AMERICA, 1802-1807. 1977. 257 pp. Transl. from the Russian edition of 1810-1812. Travel, history and ethnography in Siberia and Alaska.

11. THE RUSSIAN ORTHODOX RELIGIOUS MISSION IN AMERICA, 1794-1837. 1978. 186 pp. Transl. from the Russian edition of 1894. On the life and works of the monk German (St. Herman) and ethnographic notes by the hieromonk Gedeon.

12. H.M.S. SULPHUR ON THE NORTHWEST AND CALIFORNIA COASTS, 1837 and 1839. THE ACCOUNTS OF CAPTAIN EDWARD BELCHER AND MIDSHIPMAN FRANCIS GUILLEMARD SIMPKINSON. 1979. 144 pp.

13. P.A. Tikhmenev. A HISTORY OF THE RUSSIAN-AMERICAN COMPANY. Vol. 2: DOCUMENTS. 1979. 257 pp. Transl. from the Russian edition of 1861-1863. Documents on the period 1783-1807.

14. N.A. Ivashintsov. RUSSIAN ROUND-THE-WORLD VOYAGES, 1803-1849, WITH A SUMMARY OF LATER VOYAGES TO 1867. 1980. 156 pp. Transl. from the Russian edition of 1872 by Glynn R. Barratt.

15. F.P. Wrangell. RUSSIAN AMERICA. STATISTICAL AND ETHNOGRAPHIC INFORMATION. 1980. 204 p. Transl. from the German ed. (St. P., 1839) by Mary Sadouski.

16. THE JOURNALS OF IAKOV NETSVETOV: THE ATKHA YEARS, 1828-1844. 1980. 340 p. Transl. from the Russian manuscript, with introduction and supplementary historical and ethnographical material, by Lydia Black.

17. SIBERIA AND NORTHWESTERN AMERICA, 1785-1795. THE JOURNAL OF CARL HEINRICH MERCK, NATURALIST WITH THE RUSSIAN SCIENTIFIC EXPEDITION LED BY CAPTAIN JOSEPH BILLINGS. 1980. Transl. from the German manuscript, by Fritz Jaensch.

18. D.H. Miller. THE ALASKA TREATY. 1981. 221 p. Full account, prepared for U.S. treaty series in 1944, but never published.

19. G.I. Shelikhov. A VOYAGE TO AMERICA, 1783-1786. 1981. 162 p. Transl. from the Russian edition of 1812, by Marina Ramsay.

Forthcoming:
20. KODIAK AND AFOGNAK LIFE, 1868-1870. Diaries of Lts. E.L. Huggins, J.A. Campbell, and other materials.

21. M.D. Teben'kov. ATLAS OF THE NORTHWEST COASTS OF AMERICA. Reprint of the atlas (39 maps) published in St. Petersburg in 1852, with HYDROGRAPHIC NOTES.

22. Frederick Lütke. VOYAGE TO NORTHWEST AMERICA, 1827. Transl. of vol. 1 of his VOYAGE AUTOUR DU MONDE, pertaining to the Northwest Coast and Siberia, with illus. from accompanying ATLAS. From original edition, Paris, 1835.